Quality of Decision-Making in Public Law

Europa Law Publishing, Groningen 2007

Quality of Decision-Making in Public Law

Studies in Administrative Decision-Making in the Netherlands

Edited by K.J. de Graaf, J.H. Jans, A.T. Marseille & J. de Ridder

Europa Law Publishing is a publishing company specializing in European Union law, international trade law, public international law, environmental law and comparative national law.
For further information please contact Europa Law Publishing via email: info@europalawpublishing.com or visit our website at: www.europalawpublishing.com.

Typeset in Scala and Scala Sans, Graphic design by G2K Designers, Groningen/Amsterdam

NUR 823; ISBN 978-90-76871-85-1

British Library Cataloguing-in-Publication Data
A catalogue record for this book is available from the British Library

Abbreviations

AA	Ars Aequi
AB	Administratieve Beslissingen – Rechtspraak Bestuursrecht
AC	Application Centre
Art.	Article(s)
Awb	Algemene wet bestuursrecht (General Administrative Law Act)
BR	Bouwrecht
BVerwG	Bundesverwaltungsgericht
BVerwGE	Entscheidungen des Bundesverwaltungsgericht
cf.	compare
COM	Commission of the European Communities
Diss.	Dissertation
EC	European Community
ECHR	European Court for Human Rights
ECJ	European Court of Justice of the European Communities
ECR	European Court Reports
Ed.	Edition
Ed.	Editor
Eds.	Editors
e.g.	exempli gratia
Et al.	Et alius
EUR	Euro
ff.	following
FTE	Full Time Equivalent
Gst.	Gemeentestem
i.e.	id est
ibid.	ibidem
IND	Immigratie- en Naturaliatiedienst
IPPC	Integrated Pollution Protection and Control
JABW	Jurisprudentie Algemene Bijstandswet
JB	Jurisprudentie Bestuursrecht
JBplus	Jurisprudentie Bestuursrecht plus
LIEI	Legal Issues of Economic Integration
LJN	Landelijk Jurisprudentienummer
M&R	Tijdschrift voor Milieu en Recht
MR	Milieurechtspraak
NAV	Nieuwsbrief Asiel- en Vluchtelingenrecht
NJ	Nederlandse Jurisprudentie
NJB	Nederlands Juristenblad
NJW	Neue Juristische Wochenschrift
No.	number
Nos.	numbers
NTB	Nederlands Tijdschrift voor Bestuursrecht
NTER	Nederlands Tijdschrift voor Europees Recht
p.	page

pp.	pages
para(s).	paragraph(s)
PG Awb	Parlementaire Geschiedenis Algemene wet bestuursrecht
RAwb	Rechtspraak Awb
RSV	Rechtspraak Sociale Verzekering
RV	Rechtspraak Vreemdelingenrecht
Stcrt.	Staatscourant
SVb	Sociale Verzekeringsbank
tB/S	Ten Berge/Stroink
TK	Tweede Kamerstukken (Parliamentary Proceedings of the Lower House)
US	United States of America
USZ	Uitspraken Sociale Zekerheid
UWV	Uitvoeringsinstituut werknemersverzekeringen
VAR	VAR, Vereniging voor Bestuursrecht
VROM	Volkshuisvesting, Ruimtelijke Ordening en Milieubeheer

CHAPTER I

Administrative decision-making and legal quality: an introduction

K.J. de Graaf, J.H. Jans, A.T. Marseille & J. de Ridder

1 Introduction

Administrative decisions made by government bodies are a fact of life: members of the public are confronted with them all the time. Whenever a citizen applies for a building permit, a driving licence or benefits, or is faced with an environmental enforcement measure, an administrative decision is involved; it is in administrative decisions that government bodies give legal shape to governmental regulations. Administrative decisions are juristic acts; they are as it were the legal packaging of everyday experiences such as receiving benefits, learning how to drive, building a house or paying taxes. The legal quality of administrative decisions therefore obviously matters to people. It matters in at least three ways. First of all, when issuing administrative decisions, public authorities should treat citizens according to their rights, including the right to equal treatment and the right to legal certainty. Secondly, the rights of third parties should be protected; for instance, they should not suffer from the external effects of an administrative decision without adequate compensation. Thirdly, the public is entitled to the protection of general public interests. Tax assessments should neither overcharge individual taxpayers nor reduce public revenue. Building permits should not go against the public interests as laid down in zoning laws, but at the same time they should give the applicants the building rights they are entitled to. While legal remedies (review procedures, appeal to a court of law) are usually available to citizens who feel they have been unfairly treated by a public authority, it is in the interests of both individual citizens and the general public for government bodies to make legally correct decisions the first time around. Court procedures to review incorrect decisions are cumbersome and costly, both to the individual involved and to the taxpayer. Moreover, if a public authority has a reputation for making the right decisions in the first place, this will generate public trust in the government and reinforce the legitimacy of administrative decision-making.

The legal quality of administrative decision-making is therefore of primary importance to the individual citizen and to the public at large. It is an important element in the administration of justice by public authorities and it is important in upholding the credibility and sustainability of the government as a whole. It was on these grounds that we decided to produce a volume of essays associated with this theme. This collection draws on the combined research experience of a group of Dutch scholars in administrative law and public administration, so that the topic is examined from a variety of perspectives. Before going into the way the various contributions deal with the issues at hand, let us first look at some basic questions. What is meant by this core concept of legal quality? And how can it be applied when assessing administrative decision-making?

2 Legal quality

Even though every legal scholar will agree that legal quality is recognizable when it is there, it remains an elusive concept. It is made up of two component terms that are equally intangible. It therefore seems appropriate to discuss the concept in some depth. Because this volume is about the legal quality of administrative decisions, before taking a closer look at certain components of legal quality we will start by examining administrative decision-making itself.

Administrative decision-making

Administrative decision-making can be described as the application of general rules to individual cases, often in the context of performing public tasks. The administrative decision-making process consists of both administrative activities and legal acts, acts intended to have legal consequences. A certain chronological order is inherent to this process. Activities that precede the decision can be qualified as preparatory; once the decision has been made, a second round of activities – the implementation of the decision – follows. Enforcement of the decision by the administrative body itself can also be considered part of this process. The concept of legal quality may apply both to decision-making in individual cases ('first-order legal quality') and to the decision-making process in general, abstracted from individual cases ('second-order legal quality'). Assessment of 'first-order legal quality' is primarily a subject for legal experts. For instance, legal quality of the 'going by the book' variety in mass-produced administrative decisions is routinely gauged by internal or external auditors. Some would say that the final verdict on the quality of an individual decision is given in a court of law. Nevertheless, examination of court cases and administrative decisions by legal experts can do a lot to improve our understanding of legal quality. 'Second-order legal quality' should be jointly assessed by legal scholars and empirical researchers; such an assessment might produce insights into how administrative decision-making should be organized in order to gain better first-order legal quality.

Quality

Quality is a diffuse concept. It can be applied to a variety of phenomena, such as the organization and structure of procedures and the outcomes of those procedures, including decisions. All of these phenomena can be examined and assessed as regards their quality. Essentially quality has to do with the extent to which a certain concrete phenomenon corresponds to the ideal version of that phenomenon. The more characteristics of the ideal a concrete phenomenon has, the higher its quality is. In assessing quality, the 'amount of quality' – the number of aspects which meet the criteria – is not the only issue; the quality of each aspect separately is also relevant. This can be expressed in a numerical rating or in a verbal classification ('high', 'moderate', 'poor', etc.) An additional question is whether the quality is 'sufficient or insufficient'.

For the concept of quality in itself it is not important who has defined the ideal version – with its composite characteristics – of the phenomenon. Different assessors may give different quality definitions of the same phenomenon. To put it in a different way: assessors may apply different criteria, such as lawfulness, effectiveness or acceptability. Moreover, each of these criteria may have a certain weight of its own. Assessors also establish their own quality scale and determine when there is sufficient or insufficient quality, which may also lead to differences between the assessors. Assessors may include the administrative body itself, the interested party in a particular case, the supervisory body or the court. Some assessors, such as the court and the supervisory body, have formalized positions. Their assessments are legally binding or may lead to legally binding measures.

Legal conformity

The definitive mark of legal quality in the administrative decision-making process is conformity with the legal provisions which apply to that process. This means that the decision made by the administrative body must be made by somebody who is authorized to do so. The decision itself must be consistent with national and international, written and unwritten law. During the preparation of the decision the relevant standards must be observed; the same applies to the reasoning behind the decision and to its implementation. Conformity means compliance both with substantive norms and with administrative procedure as laid down in the Dutch *Algemene wet bestuursrecht* (General Administrative Law Act).

In most cases conformity with the applicable law means that the requirement of lawfulness must be met: the primary decision-making process must take place lawfully, according to the legal standards which exist for juristic acts under public law. This is also true of juristic acts under private law and merely factual acts. Moreover, government actions must be in line with the standards of propriety developed by the National ombudsman. The standards of propriety are not as restrictive as the requirement of lawfulness. For administrative bodies, standards of propriety are standards of conduct. It is only in exceptional cases that effectiveness and efficiency are laid down as independent legal standards for administrative bodies at the level of primary decision-making. At the primary decision-making level it is not a legal requirement for decisions to be acceptable.

Often it is perfectly clear what conformity with standards implies in a particular case. Why is this? Many government decisions consist of the application of a general standard to a specific situation. This always involves assessing the applicability of the standard in question. There are plenty of examples: anyone who is 65 years old and has thus reached pensionable age may claim an old-age pension, and anyone who is unfit for work is entitled to an invalidity benefit. The administrative body must establish whether or not the person applying for the benefit meets the criteria for eligibility. In the case of the old-age pension this is not difficult. The standard is straightforward – '65 years of age' – and it is very rarely a problem to establish whether the applicant meets this criterion. There is more uncertainty if the administrative body has to decide whether an applicant is eligible for an invalidity benefit. The standard – 'unfit to work' – is not so clear-cut, and the outcome of its application is therefore uncertain. However, the situation is uncertain not only for the applicant – 'will the administrative body accept my claim?' – but also for the administrative body – 'will our interpretation of the concept of incapacity for work be approved by the court?' This is particularly applicable if new legislation has to be interpreted. Usually a court of law is the most appropriate authority to provide clarity in cases of this kind. The court can hand down a binding ruling as to whether or not the decision conforms with the standards.

Influence of judicial review on legal quality

The legal quality of administrative decision-making can be measured by judgments of the court. However, there are certain dangers involved in relying solely on the standards formulated in case law. In the first place, the court does not have exclusive rights to the assessment of the legal quality of government actions. While it is true that the court's judgment determines how much an administrative body may or must do, this does not alter the fact that it can be argued that the court has set the bar too low or too high in certain cases. In other words, court judgments of government actions taken as a whole represent only one of many possible views of the legal quality of government actions. Court judgments give an indication of the legal quality of government actions but they cannot be regarded as the only relevant benchmarks.

A second danger is that if the court exercises restraint and gives the government a considerable amount of freedom to use its discretionary powers in certain areas, the government may gear its policy to the court's custom of restraint. An example is the situation where the administrative body makes a large number of similar decisions against which only a few citizens appeal. If these citizens are successful, the court's ruling will mean that the administrative body must change the erroneous decisions which affect the people who challenged them, but not those which affect people who failed to do so. This leeway provided by the court may tempt the administrative body in question not to take any action with respect to the people who did not appeal. However, the administrative body may also choose to make its own arrangements to compensate those who sought no legal remedy against the decisions which turned out to be erroneous. In both cases the administrative body is acting within the boundaries laid down by the court, but in the second case the legal quality of the administrative body's decision-making is higher than in the first case.

Another problem arises when the rule, although correctly applied, proves to be unable to achieve a satisfactory result. In this case desirability and legal reality are at odds with each other. However, the administrative body does not have the power to change a rule or to introduce a supplementary rule, and in general the court will not be able to provide a solution either. For problems of this nature an administrative body can only turn to the legislators.

Influences on legal quality

Before suggestions can be made for improving the legal quality of the decision-making process, the problems must be pinpointed ('in which areas is there a lack of legal quality?'), and then analysed ('what factors cause the lack of quality?') Then, on the basis of the desired situation ('sufficient legal quality' or 'higher legal quality'), a solution should be thought out ('which factors will help in achieving the desired situation?'). It should be borne in mind that an improvement in the legal quality of administrative decision-making may be at odds with quality requirements which are not – or not primarily – legal in nature. For example, in terms of effectiveness increasing legal quality may be regarded as undesirable.

Insight into the factors which influence the legal quality of administrative decision-making is essential both in analysing and in solving problems. The influence of these factors may be either to raise or to reduce quality. The quality factors are legal or non-legal in nature. The legal factors consist of the regulations in the broad sense and of case law. The non-legal factors are numerous and vary widely; they include public information, the level of expertise of an administrative body's staff, supervision of implementation, cuts in implementation budgets, etc. There is no systematic overview of the non-legal factors, nor do we know very much about the way in which quality factors – separately or in conjunction – exert their influence. In this volume attempts are made to fill in some of these gaps.

3 Outline of the book

As stated above, the topic of this book is the assessment of legal quality in administrative decision-making and the factors which influence that quality. The first three papers concentrate on the concept of legal quality as applied to administrative decision-making.

Herweijer discusses the tensions between legal quality and other quality requirements which must be taken into account to arrive at an assessment of the overall quality of administrative decision-making. Examination of the lawfulness of public decisions by legal scholars is fundamentally different from empirical research into the effectiveness, efficiency and propriety of these decisions. If researchers want to pass unreserved judgment on the quality of public decisions, they should integrate the conclusions of four different types of research. We have only a modest understanding of the interactions between the four aspects of administrative quality. We should bear in mind that improvements in legal quality may be offset by reductions in efficiency, effectiveness or propriety. Successful improvements regarding one aspect of administrative quality may entail sacrifices regarding others.

Taking the relationship between bureaucracy and *Rechtsstaat* as a point of departure, De Ridder discusses the importance of administrative organization in achieving not only high legal quality in administrative bodies' decision-making but also excellence in administrative justice. Legal quality at the most basic level means administrative compliance with the law, but at the highest level it implies administrative justice. Administrative quality is more than legal quality alone. De Ridder focuses on the influence of the choices made by public servants in their day-to-day work and the factors that determine their choices.

Bröring and Tollenaar present an overview of the legal factors which have some bearing on the way administrative authorities go about making decisions. There are several legal factors which influence the quality of decision-making. These are divided into three categories. First of all there are the factors which have to do with the relationship between the government and the public as set out in administrative law. This relationship is based on the core concepts defined in the Dutch *Algemene wet bestuursrecht*. There are three elements in this relationship: an administrative decision, a public authority which has made this decision, and one or more interested parties. The first category of legal factors which may influence legal quality has to do with the implications of these three concepts. The second category of factors pertains to the regulations which govern this relationship. On the one hand the law allows public authorities a certain discretion, but on the other hand the legislator has attempted to set standards for the rules adopted by public authorities. This leads to the codification of policy rules and the existence of 'pseudo policy rules'. The last category of factors consists of those relating to systems of checking whether or not administrative authorities comply with the regulations. These systems cover both supervisory bodies and legal protection.

Three of the contributions are concerned with specific dilemmas faced by administrative authorities in their attempts to achieve legal quality. Tolsma's paper deals with a specific question in relation to the quality of administrative decision-making when a public authority is caught in the middle of conflicting interest groups. Can mediation improve the quality of decision-making? Mediation is a method of conflict resolution whereby an independent third party is brought in to supervise the parties involved in a dispute in their attempts to find a solution for that dispute. Tolsma explores possible ways of incorporating the mediation method into the current administrative decision-making process and discusses a proposal for making mediation compulsory. If administrative authorities have a legal duty to strive towards consensus, the introduction of mediation may be a pressing issue. Two questions arising from this proposal are discussed: on what legal standard might this duty be based, and in what circumstances would the duty apply? The third topic discussed is to what extent the element of mediation can be implemented in a legal system in which administrative authorities have special purpose powers.

De Graaf and Marseille focus on another dilemma which administrative authorities may have to face in their efforts to achieve legal quality. Confronted with an erroneous decision which has become legally incontestable, an administrative authority has to establish whether it can or should do anything to change the decision. The dilemma is whether the notion of legal quality is best represented by providing legal certainty – and thus by restraint as regards reconsidering unlawful decisions – or by safeguarding lawfulness, and thus by broad powers to change previously made decisions.

Jans provides some insights into the significance of European legal principles for national administrative decision-making. He focuses on the question of whether European law requires a more formal application of substantive regulations and attempts to pinpoint the obligations for public authorities which arise from Article 3:2 of the *Algemene wet bestuursrecht* (the requirement of due care) against the background of the principle of precedence and the doctrine of direct effect, in order to prevent decisions which contravene European law.

The exploration of the legal quality of administrative decision-making continues with two contributions which examine legal quality in different areas of administrative decision-making. Noordam presents an exposition, based on the available research data, of legal quality in the field of social security. The implementation of social security law does not have a good reputation in public opinion. This paper investigates how the implementation is judged by bodies such as the court, the National ombudsman, the Netherlands Court of Audit, the supervisory bodies, etc. The criteria used to assess the quality of implementation (lawfulness, effectiveness, efficiency, etc.), are examined one by one. In recent years the social security implementation bodies have to an increasing extent paid systematic attention to the quality of implementation. The paper is an impression; it does not provide a complete, representative picture of social security implementation. This impression confirms the implementation's unfavourable reputation. However, it is appropriate to put this into perspective: most of the implementation takes place without any problems. Moreover, the implementation bodies are frequently confronted with legislation of poor quality, passed down by the national government.

Winter and Bolt focus on the quality of decision-making in Dutch aliens law, especially with regard to asylum law. The goal of the Dutch *Vreemdelingenwet 2000* (Aliens Act 2000) was to improve the quality of decisions relating to applications for asylum and at the same time to speed up the administrative decision-making process. Winter and Bolt discuss factors which may influence the quality of decision-making, dividing them into legal and non-legal factors. On the basis of data from the recent evaluation of the *Vreemdelingenwet 2000*, reports by the National ombudsman, and annual reports from the *Immigratie- en Naturalisatiedienst* (IND) and the district courts, they attempt to analyse the relationship between legal and non-legal factors and the quality of decision-making in asylum cases.

To conclude this investigation of legal quality in administrative decision-making, two essays assess the legal quality of public administration on the basis of specific case studies. Damen's essay addresses the following question: When do administrative decisions and administrative decision-making have sufficient legal quality? Taking a specific case study about a burgomaster who failed to apply for a permit as a point of departure, Damen formulates criteria for sufficient legal quality. An administrative body which is at the service of the 'ordinary' citizen should provide information, ask questions, empathize and help to find solutions. Within the boundaries of legislation and case law and of the public interest, it should adopt a sympathetic attitude and consider how it can help citizens to get what they are entitled to, by a) active and adequate information provision, b) lending citizens a helping hand, c) fair play and giving citizens a voice, d) meticulous preparation, asking questions about the citizen's wishes and examining the feasibility of those wishes with appropriate administrative and technical accuracy, e) choosing the most favourable alternative and the least onerous decision, and f) punctual decision-making, at least always within the legal time limit.

Tromp presents a case study of administrative decision-making in a complex process of physical planning, involving many different stakeholders. In this case the primacy of the rule of law was severely tested. Tromp focuses on the decisions which had to be made by various administrative authorities before planning permission could be given for a pumping station with a lock in the province of Groningen in the Netherlands. The case study explores the hypothesis that the quality of decision-making determines whether or not the public at large will have faith in the authorities. Can the so-called 'gap' between the public and government be closed by structural reforms or is it something else that needs reform to ensure the legal quality of administrative decision-making?

CHAPTER 2

Inquiries into the quality of administrative decision-making

M. Herweijer

1 Introduction

Although researchers of administrative law and public administration share a common interest in the quality of administrative decisions, they differ in the emphasis they lay on the normative standards administrative authorities should meet. Researchers of administrative law focus their attention on standards set by the courts; their object is to assess legal quality.

However, legal quality – or more precisely lawfulness – is not the only standard an administrative authority has to meet. Authors of public administration textbooks state that administrative authorities should operate efficiently, effectively and legitimately as well.[1] Whether or not a decision is legitimate is a question of public opinion and successful argumentation; whether a decision is lawful is a question ultimately decided by experts in the court; whether a decision is effective depends on goals and ultimate consequences; and whether a decision is efficient depends on a comparison of costs and benefits.

The four criteria seem to interact, positively or negatively. An administrative decision which is strictly in accordance with the law but clearly counterproductive in attaining the legislators' objective will raise doubts concerning the wisdom of the law. An administrative authority operating inefficiently may fail to meet deadlines, which may harm legal quality. Poor communication and lack of public support may have an adverse effect on compliance with lawful decisions. In short, a good administrator tries to strike a balance between effectiveness, efficiency, lawfulness and legitimacy.

In unilaterally promoting legal quality administrative authorities run the risk of increasing the alienation between public opinion and legal expertise, of enlarging the administrative burden and of diminishing effectiveness. If public officials do not wish to over-emphasize the aspect of lawfulness, they should keep a keen eye on effectiveness (reaching the official goals), efficiency (economizing on public expenditure) and legitimacy (getting public support for lawful decisions).

However, the concepts and methods used to assess effectiveness, efficiency, lawfulness and legitimacy vary widely. To prevent confusion and to provide a basis for discussing the four normative aspects of good public administration, section 2 describes the methods used and the sources consulted in making statements concerning the lawfulness, legitimacy, effectiveness and efficiency of individual decisions made by administrative authorities.

What is the relationship between lawfulness, efficiency, effectiveness and legitimacy? The hypotheses contradict each other. In some situations the lawfulness of an administrative decision can help to enforce it and to make the norm effective. In that case the lawfulness of the decision constitutes an important argument in the attempt to win public support. Legal standards make it possible to standardize processes of information gathering, decision-making and implementation. But the opposite may be true as well.

---

[1] Henry (1986); Lane (1993); Stone (2002).

There are situations in which an unlawful decision may be quite efficient, effective and legitimate in the perception of the broader public.[2] The trade-off between the four normative aspects of the same decision has not been explored satisfactorily. Additional theorizing is needed. This issue is discussed in section 3.

The practical relevance of legal research establishing the lawfulness of specific decisions may be increased if it takes the research of economists concerning efficiency, of opinion polls concerning public support and of policy analysts concerning effectiveness into account. Then the advice concerning the lawfulness of administrative decisions discounts its side-effects on costs, public support and society.

2 Four aspects of decision-making: four evaluation criteria

The four different standards used to assess the quality of administrative authority decisions are derived from four perspectives on decision-making. Scholars in the legal profession tend to approach public administration primarily as the exercise of exclusive administrative or even constitutional, powers by competent authorities.[3] Their point of departure in examining the decisions of administrative authorities is what might be expected on the basis of legal statutes, established precedents and the official division of powers. A policy scientist[4] may conceive of the application of rules by administrative authorities as an intermediate step in the chain of causation which leads to an intervention in societal problems. Policy scientists stress that in dealing with collective problems governments sometimes need to enforce norms with the aid of authority and arguments, in order to overcome the inevitable resistance towards change.

Political scientists study formal decision-making from the perspective of power and influence. Who will get what, how and when? Has the public official succeeded in reconciling opposing interests and varying perspectives? When asked to decide a contested issue, public officials are faced with conflicting interests and different perspectives. In deciding a controversial issue and realizing its consequences, public officials may have to overrule some of the interests at stake and neglect some of the perspectives involved. What form of wheeling and dealing is successful (or not) in negotiating consensus?

Economists tend to see administrative decisions as a form of investment. Making and implementing administrative decisions entails allocating taxpayers' money and narrowing down the range of legally possible outcomes.[5] This investment may have societal consequences. When a decision results in alleviating

2 D. Stone's *Policy Paradox* contains many examples of situations where political logic demands decisions that are at odds with existing rules.

3 Hart (1981).

4 Dunn (2004).

5 Bickers (2001).

the problem or attaining the goal, the return on investment may be regarded as positive. When a decision has no positive effect on the problems defined or the goals stated, economists are eager to point out that the administrative decision is not cost-effective: the societal benefits gained do not offset the public administration's efforts.

2.1 The effectiveness of administrative decisions

Effectiveness is the extent to which an administrative decision based on legal powers contributes to the attainment of an official goal.[6] For example, when regulations related to environmental protection require industries to operate their plants in compliance with the conditions of valid permits, the process of granting permits and supervising compliance with their conditions constitutes the instrument while reduction in pollution is the relevant societal process. The permit with its conditions can be regarded as effective if it induces the plant management to make decisions to control emissions escaping during production, packaging and transport more tightly. But what mechanism causes plant managers to change their policies? Did the public official who deliberated with the plant management supply new information or new resources? Or did the plant manager anticipate incentives or the risk of being penalized?

In the perspective of the policy analyst, the legislator delegates powers to administrative authorities to intervene in undesirable behaviour. The formal definition of the problem precedes the attribution of powers. If fatal car accidents are the acknowledged problem and speed is one of the main causes, the legislator may grant the local municipality the power to introduce speed limits. A speed limit may prevent fatal accidents. In this example a process with unwelcome effects is directly manipulated. When central government requires car owners to have third-party insurance, their intervention helps to cure the unwanted effects – such as damages awarded in tort actions – of accidents.

A purposeful and committed government has an interest in the effects of its decisions on society. Policy analysts assist public officials in analysing their environment as a web of causes and effects. The test of a good decision is that the desired goal is reached as a result of the intervention chosen. This view may already have been espoused by the designers of the law. The law regulates how officials should act when certain facts are discovered. However, in most cases the law is limited to defining the problem, stating the formal goals and conferring decision-making powers on administrative authorities. The administrative authorities then have ample leeway to make their own analyses of the determinants of the problem and the most promising ways to intervene.

To determine whether decisions are effective we need to compare. We might, for example, compare the average speed of cars before and after the introduction of the speed limit. We might compare the emissions of plants with valid permits

6 Rossi & Freeman (1989).

and regular monitoring with similar plants without valid permits and without regular monitoring. Additional insight may be gained by interviewing those subject to regulation. What are their attitudes concerning the standard itself (the required actions) and the accompanying regulation?

2.2 The efficiency of public expenditure

The pursuit of efficiency implies that when the available amount of resources is fixed, the administrative authority allocates its resources in such a way that the highest possible welfare is attained.[7] When the goal to be reached is fixed, the principle of efficiency requires that the administrative authority attains this goal with the lowest use of resources. In a free demand and supply market, consumers reward producers who are able to produce cost-effectively. To solve collective problems it is often necessary to limit competition and to pool the available resources in the form of joint action. The task of administrative authorities is to carefully explore the needs of society and to thoroughly plan an accessible and reliable infrastructure. A free supply and demand market will not be able to produce the needed collective goods in sufficient quantities. Moreover, the satisfactory operation of the free market for private goods depends partly on the general accessibility and reliability of the public infrastructure.

There are two main approaches to the efficiency of administrative decisions. Taking the first approach, the societal benefits of the government's efforts should be of higher value than if these resources were not taxed away from the private sector and were instead used by private consumers to buy private goods or increase their private savings. To assess this first form of efficiency we must conduct a societal cost-benefit analysis.

Taking the second approach, administrative authorities should make decisions and deliver collective goods at the lowest possible production costs. To determine whether bureaucracies are performing efficiently, we have to compare the costs and quality of the services delivered. The pursuit of public sector efficiency has provided us with many benchmarks which make it possible to compare the costs and quality of comparable administrative authorities.

When economists turn their attention to questions of efficiency, they assume that the administrative authority has some leeway. Official decision-making may result in a range of alternative outcomes. In order to make a choice between these alternatives, this authority has to estimate costs and benefits. For one-off, irrevocable decisions, such as choosing the most appropriate route for a railroad or the best design for an important building, sometimes a separate cost-benefit analysis may be conducted. In the case of regular and recurrent decisions such as awarding grants, past experience is reflected in rules of thumb. If the number of decisions is on the rise, it may be worthwhile reducing the efforts made to collect the relevant facts in each individual request and to rely to an increasing extent on protocols and rules of thumb.

---

7 Wildavsky (1984).

2.3 Legitimacy of procedures and arguments

Legitimacy is a controversial concept. Some describe a legitimate decision as a decision whereby the decision-maker's arguments are accepted by the parties involved. The emphasis is on successful negotiation between the decision makers and the parties concerned. From this perspective, the reason why people accept a given decision is specific: they share the decision-maker's assumptions and evaluations.[8]

In the opposing definition the emphasis shifts to the practical consequences. A decision is legitimate if the people involved are likely to comply with the standard implied by the administrative decision. The reasons why people comply with administrative decisions may vary considerably; they may be related to convenience, duty or opportunity.

Administrative authorities have various means of mobilizing support for their decisions. Every four years citizens are invited to elect the members of the highest representative council at local, regional, national and Community levels. Constitutionalists regard these recurrent elections as important instruments to win and retain public support for administrative decisions. The public nature of council meetings, the formal decision-making procedures which encourage the participation of interested citizens, and freedom of the press create an atmosphere which fosters support for administrative decisions.

When is an administrative decision legitimate? Legal scholars would study the minutes of the board or council making the decision to answer this question. However, this formal approach is more suited to assessing the lawfulness of the decision. Political scientists would interview members of the public affected by the administrative decision in question to obtain information about their opinions and attitudes. But should we not go a step further and find out to what extent the individuals concerned comply with the decisions? Do they in fact comply with the standard? Or is their cooperation only on the surface? And should the dominant behaviour pattern be characterized as avoidance and escape?

In the first perspective on legitimacy decisions are accepted because the political debate has been convincing. In particular, those interested individuals who participated in the preparation of the decision may have been convinced of the wisdom of the decision. In the second perspective on the legitimacy of decisions, acceptance is partly based on resignation and convenience. Citizens have neither the time nor the means to reconsider the decision-making process. Without proof to the contrary, citizens will rely on the integrity and competence of the decision-makers. And when decision-makers make obvious mistakes they assume that other citizens will protest and that their protest will lead to corrections.

According to the communication model of decision-making, every administrative decision may be questioned. The clash of opinions and the shock of

8 Majone (1989).

expertise will sharpen the arguments used for or against the decision in question. Theoretically, every argument put forward can be tested against facts or general, normative principles. In the end weighing values against each other remains a question of informed, but personal choice.

In the opposing model of strategic decision-making, the decision-maker does not strive for the participation of all stakeholders concerning all issues but tries to anticipate all interests involved.[9] The decision-maker tries to make a package deal in which the important interests are recognized or compensated for. The test for a legitimate decision is that no alteration of the plan would be able to win a broader coalition of supporters.

Research into the legitimacy of decisions may take the simple descriptive form of opinion polls and monitoring consumer satisfaction. But the assessment of legitimacy may also take the form of a recapitulation of the public debate on a given policy decision. When a decision is not convincing for the smaller group of experts and stakeholders, the debate will be transferred from seminars and conferences to the more general and wider arena of the free press and public opinion.

2.4 The lawfulness of the exercise of legal powers

The acts and decisions of administrative authorities are bound by the rule of law. By enacting and amending general regulations, representative councils exert influence on the actions of administrative authorities. Subjection to the provisions of the general regulations makes the actions of administrative authorities predictable and accountable. Citizens can submit unwelcome decisions to the scrutiny of the courts. If administrative decisions are deemed unlawful, administrative authorities can neither implement nor enforce these decisions. Lawfulness implies that in the perception of the court the preparation, motivation, announcement, content and immediate consequences of the adjudicated decision are in accordance with current legal standards and are, in addition, fair and reasonable.[10]

To establish the lawfulness of a given administrative decision, a legal scholar will examine the limits of the jurisdiction of the administrative authority and interpret the statutes which confer the powers used by the administrative authority. What legal standards or bylaws apply? How do the facts of the request or observation qualify under these norms? How reliable are these facts which the administrative authority takes for granted? These questions can be answered by referring to material law, procedural law, principles of justice and administrative custom.

The model of legal reasoning is focused on doing justice in individual cases. What would the fairest decision have been if the administrative authority in question had impartially sought and applied the relevant standards, carefully

---

9 Parsons (2001).

10 Hertogh (2005).

established the relevant facts and weighed the interests at stake against each other? What is fair and reasonable depends to a large extent on what the citizen might have expected if he or she had consulted current statutes, bylaws and relevant case law.

Reformulating initial – pre-legal – doubts concerning the contested decision lies at the heart of legal research. Does the potential flaw in the disputed decision have something to do with the jurisdiction or powers of the administrative authority in question? Or should the deficiency be sought in the selection of the substantive norms applied by the administrative authority? Or have rules of due process been violated? In answering these legal questions one by one, various sources of law will be consulted: Community and national law, bylaws, and case law, but also administrative practice and principles of justice. In determining whether the administrative decision is valid or void, legal scholars must consider the relative importance of these different sources of law – to the extent that they have different implications – and of the various substantive or purely procedural legal issues involved. The test of a legal judgment concerning the lawfulness of an administrative decision is whether the argumentation is compelling and inescapable.

In legal research the focus is on the certainty of interpretation of the law in an individual case. Unlike the conclusions of legal research, as a rule statements about the effectiveness, efficiency and legitimacy of administrative decisions are general in character, imply chance, and offer certainty only if the administrative decision is repeated in a large number of cases. Statements about the lawfulness of general policy are usually cautiously formulated, with plenty of reservations. More than is the case with opinion polls, economic research or policy experiments, legal researchers must proceed impartially and open-mindedly, and must use existing and accepted standards.

2.5 Conclusion

Legal research into the lawfulness of administrative decisions is fundamentally different from empirical research into the effectiveness, efficiency and legitimacy of administrative decisions. Some of the differences are argumentation versus measurement and analysis; certainty in individual cases versus certainty in a large number of cases; and taking historical precedent and expectations versus emphasizing the desirability of possible outcomes. Nevertheless, all these four forms of analysis lead to normative statements implying recommendations for improvements. If researchers want to pass unreserved judgment on the quality of administrative decisions, they should integrate the conclusions of four quite different types of research.

3 Trade-offs between the four evaluation criteria

If an administrative authority invests in the legal quality of its decision-making, it is not clear what consequences this will have for the effectiveness, efficiency and legitimacy of its decisions. One hypothesis holds that if an administrative authority increases the lawfulness of its decision-making, this is no indication whatsoever as to whether it will then operate more efficiently, effectively or legitimately. This *agnostic* hypothesis will be discussed in section 3.1.

According to an *optimistic* hypothesis, in a normal and stable state the four quality criteria interact positively. Under normal conditions government investment in a more lawful way of operating makes a positive contribution to the efficiency, effectiveness and legitimacy of administrative administration. This second position will be discussed in section 3.2.

A third theory of public administration holds that political investment in public support differs greatly from economic investment in efficiency; and in the same line of thought, that efforts to increase the legal quality of decisions require different interventions than efforts to increase the external effectiveness of administrative decisions. If we assume that attention and resources are limited in respect to the need for improvement, the conclusion must be that administrative decision-makers should prioritize and concentrate their efforts on only one sort of reform and switch their attention to other aspects after they succeeded in solving the most urgent deficiencies. This third view – the *realistic* position – will be discussed in section 3.3.

3.1 Is the integration of the four perspectives a bridge too far?

Legal researchers are inclined to consider a particular administrative decision lawful if it is formally correct and has been prepared carefully – in other words if existing standards have been applied in a transparent way by competent officials and the circumstances of the case have been established with due care. An economist commissioned to determine the efficiency of the same decision will study the immediate and subsequent costs and benefits. The economist will focus not on the preparation of the decision but on what happens after the decision. To see if the decision has been efficient, the administrative decision-maker must wait and look ahead, through the windscreen. But to see if the decision is lawful, the public official must look in the rear-view mirror.

An administrative decision is efficient when the resulting outcomes are positive. The benefits realized should outweigh the costs incurred. What is more, the public return on the investment of taxpayers' money should exceed the private return in the hypothetical case that the citizens were to spend the same amount of money after a corresponding tax cut. The auditor will give an opinion after the completion of the fiscal year, when the latest information concerning outcomes is available.

An administrative decision is lawful if the administrative authority which made it had the power to do so, assessed the correct facts according to the relevant substantive standards, proceeded with due care and promptness, and had an open mind to the interests and comments of the parties involved. When an administrative authority's decision is evaluated by the court or a legal researcher, the steps in the decision-making process are repeated.[11]

To assess efficiency we measure results: did the estimations used to underpin the decision prove to be correct? To assess lawfulness we test the estimations themselves: were they valid and relevant, and was the argumentation correct? These two statements are therefore *incommensurable.*

Policy analysts report success when objectives are attained, even if the parties involved are not satisfied. Policy analysts assume that the realization of collective goods may imply the reduction of freedom and may imply a real change in behaviour. There are few situations where a policy has a positive effect without adversely affecting some interests. While a speed limit may save lives as intended, at the same time drivers will be unhappy because it takes them longer to reach their destinations. For this reason policy analysts aim at a form of objective evaluation.

Opinion pollsters on the other hand regard an administrative decision as legitimate so long as representatives of target groups and consumers of administrative services are contented, even if the actual outcomes fall short of the original goals. Assessments of effectiveness are based on the realization of assumptions about final outcomes and the adequacy of instruments. Assessments of legitimacy are based on an aggregation of subjective opinions. These two perspectives are therefore *incompatible.*[12]

Effective decisions bring about a real change in the conditions under which the individual citizen or the party concerned choose a certain course of action. The decision is effective if societal problems are solved because those parties choose different courses as a consequence of that change. For example, if as a result of new permit regulations a plant monitors its emissions more effectively and therefore reduces its pollution of the environment; or if fewer accidents take place as a result of a speed limit, even though more drivers complain about increased travelling time. Often the various parties profiting from the increase in road safety or from the reduction in air pollution will not notice the change in the objective conditions. In many cases, even though citizens are enjoying the benefits of a policy, they need explicit research and newspaper headlines to become aware of a reduction in air pollution or an improvement in road safety. The more effective a policy is, the more target groups forced to change their daily routines are likely to complain. The more ineffective a policy is, the more citizens who would profit from the fruits of effective policy – the people who do

[11] However, recent and salient information about what happened after the public decision was taken may affect the reconstruction the legal researcher makes of the way the public authority assessed the risks involved.

[12] Snellen (1991).

not have to change their own routines – are likely to complain that nothing has changed.

Assessments of the legitimacy of administrative decisions are based on the perceptions of members of the target group – those affected by the decision – and of people who reap the fruits of problem reduction or goal attainment. Whether the glass is half full or half empty depends on the interviewee's expectations. If the plant management had been expecting a permit with much more stringent regulations, the extension of the existing permit will come as a welcome surprise. But if politicians have promised during election time that the administrative burden of environmental protection will be drastically curbed, the same extension will be perceived as a deception. Satisfaction is the product of both real, possibly changed experiences and initial subjective expectations. Improving the satisfaction of consumers of administrative services can be pursued both by providing clearer explanations of current decision-making processes and by drastically improving decision-making processes.

For assessments of effectiveness, only sustainable change in relevant behaviour counts. For assessments of legitimacy only stakeholders' opinions count. It would be hard to reconcile these objective and subjective approaches. This intellectual problem has led to profound debate among the analytic and the more communication-oriented evaluators of decision-making.

This line of argument may lead to the conclusion that an assessment of effectiveness does not contain any information about the legitimacy of a decision; that an assessment of the efficiency of a decision does not contain any information about the lawfulness of that decision; and that communication between the four disciplines involved may easily result in a confusion of tongues.[13]

If we step back, we may conclude that there are four different normative criteria administrative decisions have to meet. Behind these four criteria four different disciplines are hidden, using different concepts, methods and data. Clearly, an assessment of the lawfulness of an administrative decision cannot be supported by opinion polls, benchmarks or experiments. To defend the position that an administrative decision is null and void the analyst's only option is to present a legal analysis.

If analysts want to pass unreserved judgments on the quality of administrative decisions, they should work in an interdisciplinary setting. This is difficult, but not impossible. An example of the success of such an interdisciplinary approach is the tradition of preparing new legislation. In this area legal research is successfully combined with policy analysis into effectiveness and opinion polls concerning client satisfaction.[14]

---

[13] Guba & Lincoln (1994).

[14] Herweijer & Winter (1995).

3.2 Trade-off or win-win?

In addition to the agnostic position referred to above, there are theories which claim the existence of positive or negative relationships between the four normative aspects of decision-making.

It is often asserted that legitimacy is a precondition for effectiveness. If students think their teacher is an expert, they will pay closer attention to her lessons, be more susceptible to her teachings and may also study her books with greater interest and zeal. In the context of reaching the objectives of policies aimed at transforming routines or changing behaviour, the legitimacy of the policy instrument or the administering agency may be of great significance with regard to compliance with the altered standard. In reorganizing the production process to curb pollution, it may be of great importance for the plant's management to be convinced that global warming is a real problem and that the government's policy is unavoidable and quite effective. This conviction may promote compliance with the standard.[15]

Vice versa, in some cases success breeds legitimacy. If the administrative authority can show that speed limits do in fact reduce car accidents, complaints about increased travelling time may evaporate. Following either line of reasoning we conclude that there may be a positive interaction between effectiveness and legitimacy.

In the same way, the lawfulness of an administrative decision is an important precondition for its effectiveness. One of the most convincing arguments to get people to do things they normally do not want to do – such as paying taxes – is to stress that everyone in a comparable situation has to do the same. The fact that the administrative decision (the final tax assessment) has a legal status guarantees impartiality and equality before the law. This legal status makes the policy instrument relating to tax collection more effective.

On the other hand, in some administrative practices the unlawfulness of the administrative decision seriously frustrates its effectiveness. When decisions which are aggravating to some parties – such as the introduction of a speed limit – are unlawful, it is easy for those opposing the decision to convince the courts that the administrative authority was not authorized to make the decision or failed to follow the correct procedure. If the court rules that the speed limit is null and void, the municipality no longer has the authority to enforce it. Following either line of reasoning we conclude that there may be a positive interaction between the lawfulness of a decision and its effectiveness.

The legitimacy of an administrative decision may also make it efficient. When citizens or companies comply with government standards spontaneously and without coercion, the government does not have to spend money on additional instruments such as grants, fines, supervision and individualized contracts or on secondary processes such as litigation and enforcement. Administrative decisions that are legitimate are more likely to gain the cooperation

---

15 Ingram & Mann (1980).

of target groups affected by the regulations in question. One of the main ideas behind experiments with interactive decision-making is that participation in the decision-making process leads to more commitment and better compliance on the part of the citizens affected by the decision.

From this *optimistic* perspective on interactions between the four normative criteria of success, we only see win-win relationships. Unfortunately, everyday practice in public administration seems to present a somewhat less rosy picture. In the first place there is the observation that substantive standards and formal procedures drastically reduce administrative authorities' leeway. Because of their limited discretion, administrative authorities are unable to opt for the best decision, lose time in procedural technicalities and miss the boat.

Secondly, the law often requires a degree of precision for all decisions which is actually only defensible in a few of these decisions. Thirdly, by making clever use of legal protection small but passionate minorities may seriously delay and complicate administrative decisions. Recently the administrative burden of legal procedures has received widespread attention. According to this *pessimistic* perspective the interaction between lawfulness on the one hand and efficiency, effectiveness and legitimacy on the other hand is negative. Instead of win-win relationships, the pessimistic perspective emphasizes the trade-offs: if lawfulness is enhanced, by implication efficiency, effectiveness and legitimacy will be adversely affected.

When hypotheses conflict we have a research problem. Two avenues of approach present themselves. We can examine existing evaluation studies to tally the number of times the optimistic win-win hypothesis is borne out against the number of times the pessimistic zero-sum game hypothesis applies. The other, more theoretical approach is to further specify the circumstances in which the pessimistic hypothesis is plausible and the circumstances in which the optimistic hypothesis seems to fit. Until both avenues have been explored, there is no academic argument to prefer the optimistic perspective to the pessimistic perspective.

3.3 Should administrative authorities be selective in their efforts?

Increasing the effectiveness of administrative decisions may require interventions directed towards society, whereas increasing the efficiency of decisions may require a reform of the internal organization. Increasing the legitimacy of administrative decisions may entail more interaction and participation, whereas increasing the lawfulness of administrative decisions may entail more distance, objectivity and adherence to the letter of the law. These are quite different remedies. The idea that by implementing one remedy we can increase performance on all four criteria is attractive but unlikely. If this is the case and public resources are scarce, administrative authorities must make a choice: where are they to start; which deficient criterion should be addressed first? De

Vries states that many public officials suffer from the so-called Atlas syndrome. Like the mythological figure, they think that they have to shoulder all the problems of the world. They want efficiency and effectiveness as well as lawfulness and legitimacy. Atlas's motto is: everything perfect at the first attempt.[16] While the aspiration to be Atlas can be inspiring, the task itself can be quite tiring and depressing. De Vries concludes that the public administrator has no other choice than to optimize one quality criterion at a time, at the risk of making sacrifices with regard to the three other aspects.[17]

But which of the four aspects of administrative quality should be given priority? It seems rational to devote attention to the aspect that has been neglected the most in the recent past. But if the administrative authority emphasizes one aspect of administrative quality in the next period, it will inevitably have to make sacrifices with regard to the opposite aspect.

De Vries claims that there are specific negative relationships between the four aspects of administrative quality. For example, if the administrative authority wants to bridge the gap between the desires and expectations of the public on the one hand and current policies and decisions on the other, it emphasizes the problem of legitimacy; the remedy is greater democratization and more opportunities for citizens to participate in administrative decision-making. But what sacrifice will increasing the extent of democratic participation entail? The most important trade-off is loss of efficiency. Therefore in the following planning period the administrative authority will be faced with the necessity of cutting back on expenditure.

But what is the direct result of cutting back on government spending? The direct result is a reduction in effectiveness. If the administrative authority has to cut back on expenditure it will focus its energy on internal, organizational issues of management, reform and reorganization. Its external performance will be neglected.

Loss of public service quality will elicit protest from the public. When the government budget has found a new balance after a successful retrenchment, there will probably be a compelling call to increase the effectiveness of administrative decisions. When governments are under pressure to improve their effectiveness in the short term, they are also under pressure to deregulate and to realise quick gains by unorthodox interventions. According to De Vries's *policy-generation theory*, what will be the victim of this pursuit of short-sighted effectiveness? The answer is the lawfulness of administrative decision-making. Deregulation and unorthodox interventions in society create legal uncertainty and new equalities.

In the next policy phase the administrative authorities will strive to regulate the administrative decision-making process at the risk of increasing alienation between the expectations of the broader public and the legal rights and duties guaranteed within the legal system. The only way out in the subsequent policy

---

16 This was the title of the Dutch book preceding this publication: *Alles in een keer goed*, Deventer 2005.

17 De Vries (1999); De Vries (2002); De Vries (2005).

phase is an increase in democratization. This brings us back to the beginning of a new cycle of four policy phases.

The theory of policy generations is comprehensive and inspiring. There are empirical data to support it. If we assume this theory is valid, we may also draw a conclusion about the programming of academic evaluations. If the administrative authority is in a policy phase in which one of the four aspects of quality is emphasized, academic policy researchers should concentrate their research efforts on precisely the opposite criterion. We can illustrate the implications of this research strategy in the following way.

Imagine that the administrative authority under study is focusing its decision-making on the issue of short-sighted effectiveness. In this policy phase academic researchers should concentrate their research efforts on the insecurity and inequality among target groups which result from deregulation and unorthodox societal interventions. In the subsequent policy phase, when administrative authorities invest in legal quality, the evaluators should focus their research on the growing alienation between the rights and duties laid down by law and people's real needs and expectations in their daily lives.

4 Discussion

There are four dominant perspectives on the evaluation of administrative decisions. These perspectives differ fundamentally. Legal scholars are inclined to conceive of administrative decision-making as the application of general law to specific cases. Policy analysts see administrative decisions as interventions in ongoing societal processes, aimed at reducing problems or attaining policy objectives. Political scientists see administrative decision-making as something akin to cutting Gordian knots. An administrative decision puts an end to any debate for or against and starts the phase of implementing whichever alternative gained majority support. Economists see administrative decisions as investments in the total welfare of society.

These four different conceptions of the nature of administrative decisions are accompanied by four different evaluation criteria. Legal scholars examine whether the authority in question has applied the rules lawfully. Economists want to find out if the government's investment has proved cost-effective. Political scientists will determine whether demonstrations of power are really accepted by the parties involved in the succeeding phases of implementation and compliance by the public. Policy analysts want to know if the intervention chosen by the administrative authority has been effective. In collecting the relevant data and drawing their conclusions, the four communities of professionals use different methods and different concepts.

While researchers investigating the quality of administrative decision-making have difficulty understanding each other, the public officials themselves have difficulty identifying their priorities and allocating their limited resources (attention and money). Both researchers and practitioners are in need of hypotheses concerning the relationships between the four aspects of sound administration. Management consultants often opt for a positive perspective and assert that the four criteria are engaged in a win-win interaction. Academic evaluators often opt for the more cynical perspective and claim that the four criteria are captured in a negative spiral. Any improvement regarding one quality criterion will be offset by sacrifices regarding the other three. According to them, public officials are like Sisyphus caught in a zero-sum game.

However, our knowledge of the interaction between the four aspects of administrative quality is modest. Although some authors suggest there are no observable relationships between the four normative aspects, we are inclined to conclude that it is possible to find empirical evidence of interactions between the levels of efficiency, legitimacy, effectiveness and lawfulness. But if we conclude that there are in fact observable interactions, what is the nature of these interactions? Optimists claim that these are typically win-win relationships, whereas pessimists believe they are zero-sum relationships. Empirical findings would probably fall in between these two extremes. The policy-generations theory provides a promising lead to study the interactions between the four normative aspects of administrative quality in a dynamic perspective.

Three observations seem to be relevant to our research. Firstly, we must realize that in optimizing the legal quality of administrative decision-making administrative authorities depend on the extent to which administrative decision-making is efficient, effective and legitimate. Secondly, we must bear in mind that improvements in legal quality may be offset by deteriorations in efficiency, effectiveness or legitimacy. Thirdly, perhaps we should be more aware of dynamics than we have been in the past. Successful improvements regarding one aspect of administrative quality may entail sacrifices regarding others. Ultimately this will lead to calls for reform and policy change. By focusing on the dark side of this antithesis, research might be able to help to keep the public administration boat upright.

CHAPTER 3

Factors for legal quality of administrative decision-making

J. de Ridder

1 Introduction: rules are tools?

Rule application – determining the rights, entitlements or wrongs of parties in individual cases – is a special branch of the legal profession and of legal scholarship. The subject of what constitutes 'good' or 'right' mode for this kind of administrative decision-making has been widely debated over a long time. One central issue has always been the tension between the rule of law and the administrative discretion needed in order to provide tailor-made solutions. This issue goes all the way back to nineteenth-century German discussions of bureaucracy and the *Rechtsstaat* – the state under the rule of law.[1] A hundred years ago these discussions gave rise to the first 'administrative procedures' legislation in Germanic countries; a way of submitting administration to the rule of law that since has become prevalent throughout the western world. However, this common basic trait, found in most administrative systems, cannot conceal the differences in approach and emphasis when it comes to putting the concept of *Rechtsstaat* into practice.

There is, for instance, a remarkable discrepancy between main tendencies in the international literature about administrative decision-making and the prevailing discussions in the Dutch legal community on the same topic. In the Anglo-American literature a dominant theme is what often is termed 'responsive regulation'.[2] Rules and regulations are considered to be tools to solve problems.[3] Certainly, administration should comply with basic legal standards such as equality, fairness and proportionality, and ensure that decisions are not made arbitrarily. Yet, the application of rules in single cases ought to provide for tailor made solutions. Compare this with the Dutch approach to regulation of the administration. Only relatively recently an administrative procedures act came into force.[4] While this act was designed to regulate administrative decision-making, in practice it has become above all the legal base for suing administrative authorities for improper administration. No judge-free haven for public authorities is the creed. It is not certain whether this juridification of administrative decision-making has in fact led to any improvement in administrative practices. It might even be argued that it has led to administrative authorities using circumventing tactics in order to make administrative judge-proof.[5]

The rules-are-tools tendency in the Anglo-American literature might be regarded as a healthy reaction to an overly legalistic bureaucratic administrative practice – a reaction that also includes an emphasis on non-legal instruments such as administration-by-negotiation and mediation and a denunciation of

---

1 Beetham (1974).

2 Ayres & Braithwaite (1992); Braithwaite (2002).

3 Sparrow (2000).

4 The Dutch *Algemene wet bestuursrecht* (General Administrative Law Act) was passed in 1992 and came into force in 1994.

5 Herweijer, De Jong & De Ridder (2005).

adversarial procedure.[6] However, all this scholarly writing does not seem to have much of an impact on American legal practice.[7] In comparison, the Dutch attempt to bridle public authorities by means of rules and courts may be considered an overdue reaction to the rather loose administrative morals that had been typical of much Dutch administrative decision-making. Here, administrative practice often seemed to be far removed from the law in the books. To be sure, principles of proper administration had been developed in case law long before they were codified in the *Algemene wet bestuursrecht* (General Administrative Law Act). Rules were regarded both as safeguards against powerful authorities and as tools for these same authorities.[8] Nevertheless, it took a long time before systematic regulation of the administration was inacted. The fact that the Netherlands lack any bureaucratic tradition whatsoever[9] certainly has a lot to do with this late juridification of public administration. Rules are reins, rather than tools, seems to be the present day conviction of much of the Dutch legal community. However, in the everyday reality of public administration, a tool view of rules is at least as important as the awareness that laws are there to be complied with. In order to grasp the concept of legal quality of administrative decisions in the Dutch context, one has to be aware of this rather sharp distinction between administrative practice and administrative law.

Making administrative decisions is behaviour: behaviour in the sense that the social sciences attach to that concept.[10] It is people in organizations deliberating and choosing and acting. Decision-making is also a legal phenomenon: within a legal framework as laid down in the *Algemene wet bestuursrecht*, decisions are made by legal entities called 'administrative authorities". As legal entities they create situations with legal consequences. In the same vein, the legal *quality* of administrative decisions is determined within the legal framework: essentially it boils down to conformity to the law and to precedent. The assessment of the legal quality of a decision therefore corresponds with the potential ruling of a judge. While the legal appraisal of administrative decisions belongs entirely within the legal realm, the explanation of observed legal quality does not. Legal quality results from behaviour: from the choices of people, administrators and politicians, choices of *actors*, more generally speaking. In order to understand administrative behaviour it is necessary to identify *factors* that influence such behaviour. Such factors include both properties of actors who make choices and circumstances under which they make them. The central question to be dealt with here is: which of the factors that influence administrative behaviour determine the legal quality of the decisions that result from that behaviour? The core of this contribution will be an exploration of factors that are likely to

---

6 Kagan (1991).

7 Kagan (2001).

8 'Instrument en waarborg'(Tool and Safeguard) is the subtitle of a classic handbook on Dutch administrative law. De Haan, Drupsteen & Fernhout (1978).

9 Daalder (1985).

10 Simon (1973).

have a bearing on administrative quality. However, in section 2 we will first take a closer look at administrative decision-making itself.

In the following sections several factors will be discussed that are likely to have consequences for legal administrative quality at the administrative floor shop. Most day-to-day administrative decisions are prepared and made by people employed by administrative agencies. Therefore to a large extent legal quality is a result of the choice behaviour of these public servants. What determines their choices? Generally speaking, there are three ways in which choices of actors in collective environments such as administrative organizations may be influenced.[11] The first has to do with the beliefs and attitudes that constitute people's 'premises of choices'. These may have been moulded by *unobtrusive* controls such as training, culture building and socialization. For instance, a public servant who has had thorough legal training is likely to have a different approach to administrative decision-making than an economist or a civil engineer. The second way for organizational control of administrative decision making is the choice behaviour itself. There is a variety of *obtrusive* controls the organization can apply: for example operational rules, hierarchical instruction and supervision. The *Algemene wet bestuursrecht* contains provisions about operational rules (labelled *policy rules*) and hierarchy (labelled *mandate* regulation). The third way is mechanization: choice behaviour is largely or even entirely subjected to the constraints of decision algorithms executed by machines. Obviously present-day government agencies which are responsible for bulk-processing applications such as social security claims and other claims for financial support use IT on a large scale. These three ways of influencing behaviour will constitute a point of departure in our exploration of the factors that influence legal quality. However, before proceeding to our discussion of factors and circumstances, we will present an anatomy of administrative decision-making.

2 The regulation of administrative behaviour

Making administrative decisions is administrative behaviour. Administrative law regulates administrative behaviour. That is, administrative law is supposed to further certain methods of administrative decision-making and to thwart others. We know that the effects of legal rules on behaviour are not straightforward, to say the least. The simple assumption that rules determine actions, an idea that was prevalent in early research on the relationship between regulation and behaviour, has been convincingly refuted.[12] Compliance is not necessarily the normal situation, and the opposite, so called deviant behaviour, cannot be regarded as a special case requiring special explanation. Compliance and non-compliance are just two of many possible workings of legal rules. Theories have been developed that explain rule-following as one potential

---

11 Perrow (1972), p. 23.

12 Griffiths (1978).

outcome of a complex social process. This applies both to compliance on the part of individual citizens and compliance on the part of bureaucratic 'specialists' such as decision-makers on public agency shop floors.[13] Of all the factors that make up that complex social process, a prime one is the match between the administrative behaviour to be regulated and the rules that are meant to regulate that behaviour. That match is mutual: the question is not only to which extend behaviour complies with the rules, but also to which extend the rules fit the issues and choices which are regulated. In this section we will explore some of the intricacies of this correspondence.

Our analysis begins with the concept of a *legal relationship*. The relationship between an administrative authority and a citizen – which we will refer to as an administrative relationship – is always partly a legal relationship. This is to say that an administrative relationship is always governed by one or more legal rules. Furthermore, if a dispute arises within the relationship, in will usually be possible to bring that dispute before a court. Nevertheless, relationships between government agencies and citizens typically go far beyond their legal aspects. The 'legalness' of administrative relationships may vary widely. Sometimes the legal aspect is dominant and everything that takes place between the administrative authority and the citizen is fixed in rules and regulations. In other instances of administrative relations, the legal aspect is hoovering in the background, to be activated only when a conflict arises.[14] One of the properties of an administrative relationship is therefore its *quantity of law*.[15] Roughly speaking, the quantity of law of an administrative relationship is the extent to which rules and courts determine the interactions and their outcomes in that administrative relationship. It should be noted that quantity of law does not depend on the number of relevant rules or the amount of relevant case law – even though regulatory expansiveness is also an important issue. What concerns us here is the degree and intensity with which law is an active part of administrative relations.

From a rule of law point of view, one might be inclined to think that the quantity of law in an administrative relationship is large and constant. Every decision has to be prepared according to administrative procedure laid down in the *Algemene wet bestuursrecht*. Every decision has to be a realisation of the substantive norms formulated in the relevant statutes. However, research has shown that this is often not or not entirely the case. Decisions approving additional schooling for people receiving social assistance have been made without much consideration for the relevant substantive norms.[16] Street-level bureaucrats dealing with applications for building permits typically play down

---

[13] Griffiths (2003), especially section 5.2.3.

[14] From studies in the sociology of law we know that this is a typical feature of contract relationships (social relations governed by contract rules); contracts are only activated when other ways of solving issues arising in the relationship have been exhausted. Macaulay (1984).

[15] Black (1976).

[16] Marseille (1993).

the legal side of the process of granting permits.[17] They strive for what they call 'good permits' – i.e. permits that are in line with professional standards – and they will be quick to emphasize that construction faults in a building are not due to a lack of legal quality in the decision to grant the permit, but to a lack of engineering skills. However, the quantity of law increases rapidly if the building plan in question is controversial or does not comply with professional standards or planning requirements. 'In situations like these we play hard ball', one public official said in a research interview. In this case 'playing hard ball' means using the whole gamut of legal instruments so as to ensure compliance with all policy standards and requirements. The *Informatiebeheergroep*,[18] an agency that is characteristically bulk-processing administrative decisions, professes to have up to 90% 'smooth cases'; the decisions involved can be dealt with entirely on the basis of the algorithms in its decision computers. A minimal amount of law, laid down in the computer programs, governs the legal relationships in hundreds of thousands of entitlements. Here the amount of law rapidly increases if the information submitted with the application is flawed or contradictory, or if a case is out of the ordinary and does not fit into any of the computer program's pre-structured categories.

From the rule-of-law point of view it could appear plausible that the larger the quantity of law in an administrative relationship, the higher the quality of the administrative decision in question will be. However, one might well argue the opposite. From studies of contractual relationships we know that contracts usually contain many rules concerning the reciprocal rights and duties of the parties to the contract, but that these contracts usually remain dormant in the actual relationship between those parties.[19] If for example a delivery is overdue or does not meet expectations, or one party is temporarily unable honour a payment obligation, parties to contracts generally prefer to solve their issues through negotiations, in their joint interests. Expanding the amount of law in the relationship by activating a contract through enforcement with litigators and courts is costly and the outcome is relatively uncertain. The amount of law in relationships governed by contracts is therefore changeable, depending on the circumstances. The amount of law is limited both under conditions of far-reaching interdependency and in situations of total mutual independence. In the latter case the exit option (changing partners) is usually much cheaper than enforcing the contract. In the former situation, breaking up the relationship is much more costly than any possible gain from contract enforcement. More generally, in most contract relationships the amount of law is limited to start with: contracts are typically incomplete, covering only a small portion of all possible future events.[20]

---

17 Aalders (1984); Niemeijer (1991).

18 The Dutch *Informatiebeheergroep* (IBG) is the executive agency for financial support for students.

19 Macaulay (1963); Macaulay (1966).

20 Couwenberg (2003); Tirole (1999).

These more general insights from contract law studies can be applied to administrative relationships. Dutch administrative regulation shows a tendency to be exhaustive, setting out to cover all possible situations. The legislators who created the *Algemene wet bestuursrecht* attempted to implement the principles of legality and legal certainty to the fullest degree, writing 'complete contracts' into the act. Where substantive norms in specific legislation leave the administrative authority discretion, the room for choice is filled up with policy rules and guidelines. Nevertheless, just as in relationships governed by contracts the actual amount of law in administrative relations may be minimal, while the quality of the decisions made in those relations is at least satisfactory.

There is yet another catch in the complicated relationship between administrative law and administrative behaviour. Broadly speaking, administrative relationships are regulated by four kinds of rules. Each of these categories represents its own kind of administrative quality. First of all there is the collection of regulations that form the core of the rule of law system: the set of rules that protect citizens against the abuse of power by administrative authorities. This set of first-order principles includes general rules such as the exclusion of arbitrary administration, the principle of equal treatment, the principle of legal certainty, and the principal of legitimate expectations. These standards are universal and may be found in most systems of administrative legislation worldwide. Infringements of these basic principles constitute a most serious threat to the legal quality of administration.

Then there is a second category of rules: substantive norms that stem from policy choices about the allocation and distribution of resources and about prohibitions and incentives. Physical planning rules and regulations concerning social welfare fall into this category. Administrative compliance with such rules is a hallmark of legal quality. But at the same time, from the point of view of regulators policies are elusive. Policies attempt to keep in line with real world developments and require flexibility of administrative behaviour. Flexibility can be built into regulatory systems by means of administrative discretion. Yet, whenever there is discretion, administrative choice must again be guided by the first-order principles. Adherence to these principles promotes a steady administrative course and decision-making by precedent, and is therefore to some extent at odds with administrative flexibility. Here, the match between administrative behaviour and administrative regulation becomes precarious.

The third category of administrative rules has to do with order, civil decency and propriety. They might be termed the 'rules of engagement' in administrative relationships. Examples include time limits to ensure prompt decision-making, entitlement of parties to be heard, procedural rules concerning the preparation of decisions, and the like. These rules are less universal than the first-order principles and the substantive norms. In some legal systems such as that in Great Britain, many of these quality requirements are not so much a matter laws that attribute rights to individual citizens for specific forms of treatment. Instead they are written into citizen's charters which create collective rights for a citizenry as a whole. They are of the type: 'At least 90% of all applications must be dealt with within two weeks'. In this way an administrative agency commits itself to making an effort to avoid unnecessary procrastination while preserving the option of extensive preparation in cases that require far more than the average term. Too much procedural standardization in administrative law may stand in the way of an individual procedural approach to administrative decision-making.[21]

A fourth category of rules originates from professional guidelines and standards.[22] It includes emission guidelines, standards about what constitutes ALARA and 'present technology', standard reference specifications for construction, general criteria for using the frequency spectrum, etc. These rules are juridifications of technical guidelines used by professionals when applying their professional expertise. This kind of juridification can be traced back to first-order principles such as legal certainty, equal treatment and legitimate expectations. The standard for the quality of decisions is primarily a technical matter (for example fire safety or prevention of environmental damage). From the point of view of professional administrative behaviour these technical guidelines are self-evident, while they may look ludicrous once clad in the legal wrappings of admininistrative regulation.[23] Administrative deficiencies in this area are primarily technical in nature, but because thof their juridification they may translate into issues of legal quality as well.

As we have seen, administrative relations are governed by various kinds of rules in varying degrees of intensity. The likelihood of a match between administrative rules and administrative behaviour varies with the quantity of law and the kind of rules. Standards of quality for administrative behaviour and administrative decisions may vary accordingly.

3 Bureaucracy: a judicial culture

Once upon a time there was a *Rechtsstaat* without democracy and without courts. The rule of law government affairs was ensured by something called 'bureaucracy'. Administrative decisions were the product of public bureaucracy, without involvement of politicians or judges. It was decision making by bureaucrats, professionals whose expertise it was to apply general rules in individual cases. Where did bureaucratic administration come from?

---

21 Recently, some authoritative spokesmen have voiced criticism of the regulation of administrative procedures in the Netherlands, claiming that administrative procedures have become too standardized and no longer allow sufficient room for procedural solutions geared to specific circumstances. See for example Herweijer, De Jong & De Ridder (2005).

22 Bröring (1993).

23 A famous example (used by Vice President Al Gore in his Reinventing Government campaign) were the six pages of US General Services Administration rules, listing all the specifications a federal ashtray had to comply with.

Some have suggested that bureaucracy is a by-product of the *Rechtsstaat* – the state under the rule of law.[24] Legal quality of administrative decisions would have called for such a specialised decision machine.. From this perspective, bureaucratic administration is always the perhaps disagreeable but also unavoidable companion of a government based on the rule of law. From a historical perspective however, there is more to be said for the opposite view: the bureaucracy introduced and elaborated the rule of law,[25] thus creating the *Rechtsstaat*.

From the late eighteenth century onwards, in most continental countries an organization of professional civil servants carved itself a position between the government (the prince) and the citizenry, and eventually emerged as the principal institution for the dispensation of public justice. Bureaucracy was a great success: the miracle of the nineteenth century. Not only in the German and Austrian empires – the two outstanding examples – but in most parts of the continent, the bureaucratic state under the rule of law became the core of public administration. Pre-Weberian German literature glorified this administrative invention. Bureaucracy shaped the principles of legal certainty and equality before the law. It placed constraints on the arbitrary exercise of power and it purged the handling of public affairs from. In doing so, a body of administrative law was created which made governmental decisions more predictable and fair. Legislation regulating administrative procedures codified bureaucratic practice and the legal arsenal of the bureaucracy became more and more refined. These developments took place in many countries in Europe. The ultimate triumph of bureaucracy was in Sweden, where the state bureaucracy's monopoly on administrative decision-making was laid down in the constitution.

In the United States, after a history of layman administration, bureaucracy, and in its wake the rule of law, also gained a foothold when the young constitutional lawyer Woodrow Wilson advocated the separation of politics and administration. His famous article[26] was based on a scanty review of German authors. Ironically, the situation in the United States was the opposite of that in the large monarchies in continental Europe. Unlike Europe, America had lots of judges and lots of democracy. On the other hand, America had a very poor administrative system and not really a 'law-based state'. The bureaucratization of the federal administration found its completion in the Administrative Procedures Act of 1946. State administrations followed suit.

What explains the immense success of this administrative device? For one thing, bureaucracy offered far more advantages than drawbacks for both parties in administrative relationships – that is the sovereign and the citizen. Citizens were charged with some fixed obligations that they could no longer escape, but these charges were equally distributed and predictable and no longer the result of arbitrary decisions of some ruler. Obligations now were knowable; public

---

[24] Donner (1984).

[25] Strictly speaking, the 'rule of law' is an Anglo-American concept, whereas bureaucracy and the *Rechtsstaat* are continental concepts. *Rechtsstaat* literally means 'law-based state'.

[26] Wilson (1887), p. 197-222.

authority was to be exercised within the confines of the law. As for the other party – while rulers lost some of their power to the bureaucracy, in exchange they gained the certainty that individual citizens would fulfil their obligations under the law and that they would be able to count on a constant source of revenue. These trade-offs are what can be characterized as the political economy of the bureaucratic *Rechtsstaat*: an exchange which produced a new allocation of rights and obligations that was more advantageous for all parties involved.

The bureaucratic state administration had several specific features which explain why it was so effective in fulfilling its mediating role between rulers and citizens. We know the so called 'characteristics of bureaucracy' primarily from the reconstruction made by Max Weber in the early twentieth century. By that time the bureaucratic *Rechtsstaat* was already past its prime. Weber himself played an active part in the reforms leading to a democratic *Rechtsstaat* which would eventually break the bureaucracy's monopoly on administrative decision-making.[27]

One set of features primarily concerns us here: classic bureaucracy was run by a corps of civil servants with a very specific attitude. Their stated interest was to do justice, *sine ira et studio*: without prejudice, unequal treatment or other forms of arbitrary rule. Their oath of office obligated them to the rightful execution of the laws.The culture of these civil servants was more similar to that of the present-day judiciary than to the culture of the modern public service. Administrative decision-making implied creating law. Whereas nowadays bureaucracy is associated with too many rules, classic bureaucracy had far more discretion than might be expected. Discretion was applied on the basis of bureaucratic judgement, in two or three instances if so required. If a citizen felt slighted by a primary decision, he could find recourse in administrative appeal – with all its advantages of administrative appeal such as adjudication ex officio, integral assessment and substitute decisions. In many ways the bureaucratic ideal comes close to what Kagan calls the *judicial mode* of rule application.[28]

Due to the fact that for a long time The Netherlands lacked a strong central government, this country never had a bureaucratic tradition.[29] The most bureaucratic sections of the civil service were the Tax and Customs Administration and the Public Prosecutor's Office. Because public affairs in the Netherlands always had been a negotiated environment, political dominance was strong long before politics were democratized. To this day, political dominance of administration prevailes.[30] Nowhere in Europe is the primacy of the political realm so overrid-

---

27 Beetham (1974).

28 Kagan (1978). Kagan distinguishes three other, less attractive modes of administrative justice: the *legalistic mode* ignores the purpose of the rules that are applied; the *unauthorized discretion* mode ignores formal compliance with those rules; *retreatism* does both.

29 Daalder (1985).

30 To be sure, in the eighties and nineties of the 20th century, autonomous agencies became popular for a while. Yet the reason for this popularity was primarily economic; it was considered to be a way for introducing market oriented management in the civil service.

ing as in the Netherlands; Wilson's dichotomy of politics and administration are not to be found in this country. Nevertheless, even here for a long time the prevailing conviction was that high-quality administrative decision-making requires a high-quality public administration. Struycken, a leading scholar on administrative law in the early twentieth century, put so much emphasis on the need for a good administrative organization to ensure sound administrative decisions that he denounced legal protection against the administration as superfluous and possibly harmful. Instead, he believed that the quality of the administration of justice should be assured by the careful selection and training of public servants – an approach totally in line with the bureaucratic model.[31] It seems certain that views such as Struycken's prevented the establishment of an administrative court system throughout most of the twentieth century.

According to this view, the legal quality of administrative decision-making should be ensured primarily on the input side of the administrative system. Legal protection and other modern methods of promoting and safeguarding quality, such as citizens' charters and benchmark systems, all apply on the output side. The *Algemene wet bestuursrecht* and its predecessors shifted the emphasis from input to output, and it cannot be denied that some of Struycken's fears have been realized. Administrative relationships have changed in nature: to an increasing extent administrative agencies and citizens have become two independent parties, each pursuing its own interests, and administrative procedures have became more adversarial. Under the *Algemene wet bestuursrecht*, administrative agencies have become not so much servants of administrative justice as well as agents of specific interests; at least, this is the opinion of some observers.[32] While courts can correct some administrative wrongs in individual cases, the effect of legal protection on the overall legal quality of administrative decision-making is questionable to say the least. In order to gain more insight into some factors that may have a more structural bearing on legal quality, we must turn back to the properties of the administrative apparatus: bureaucracy and beyond.

4 Individual public servants: attitudes and professions

In present day writings, the classic bureaucrat often is depicted as an automaton – a small cog in a large machine constructed of rules and hierarchy.[33] However, this view does not do justice to the responsibilities and achievements of public bureaucracies. As noted before, the bureaucratic *Rechtsstaat* was also confronted with sometimes large gaps between general rules

[31] Struycken (1910). 'Through better organization of the civil service and through redesigning and improving legal and administrative procedures, the already present public spirit of the civil service can be unfolded in full'.

[32] Damen (1994).

[33] Mintzberg (1979).

and individual cases, which is why discretionary powers were an important feature of the administration of justice. Beyond that, the typical bureaucrat was a professional, trained in the values of his discipline and imbued with a culture of public spirit and esprit de corps. Not decisions in individual cases were the object of control by superiors, but the *premises* on which those decisions were based: knowledge, expertise, a sense of purpose, shared values.[34] These premises were shaped by education and training, by organizational 'indoctrination' and by communication processes within the organization.[35] The classic bureaucrat's decision premises comprisex all the values of the bureaucratic *Rechtsstaat* and were remarkably similar to the principles of proper administration now written into law in most advanced nations.

As we have seen, the Netherlands never had a real bureaucracy. The Tax and Customs Administration came most nearby, with its own training institute for high-ranking officials, its comparative admission examinations, and its esprit de corps and professional zeal. However, these elements all began to fade after a university degree in tax law was introduced in the 1960s and Tax and Customs Administration officials were recruited from the graduates of this programme. To some extent local government employees also had some of the characteristics of the classic bureaucrat. Regional associations of municipalities ran their own training institutes, which produced public servants with an attitude focused on the administration of justice. During the past decades all of these training institutions have disappeared in rapid succession. Public servants with specific public service training have made way for employees with a general education who lack the enculturation in the public service. Administrative agencies now have to transfer that culture to their new recruits themselves, and generally this is not the highest priority for human resource management in the public service.[36]

For employees in a public agency there are at least three competing factors which may adversely affect an attitude focused on the administration of justice: the employee's selfinterests, the employee's professional background if it is not legal, and the employee's political convictions and policy views. The most important factor in this context is the professional orientation other than that of the traditional bureaucrat. A professional is a member of a group of people with the same knowledge and skills; the group distinguishes itself by a high level of expertise and knowledge and by the capacity to exclude people from that group.[37] Examples of professional groups of this sort are spatial planners,[38] police officers and physicians. One consequence of the exclusiveness of a professional group is that its members have a strong orientation towards the norms, values and opinions of their particular group. Public servants with a strong professional

34 Simon (1976).

35 Perrow (1979), p. 45.

36 Visitatiecommissie juridische functie en wetgeving (2007).

37 Benveniste (1987).

38 Faludi & Van der Valk (1994).

affiliation might be inclined to favour the norms of their profession above public service norms. One study showed that of all the professional groups working at Dutch national ministries members of the medical profession were the most prone to deviant or autonomous behaviour.

It is not only the professional or technical orientation of public employees that may threaten an agency's culture of administrative justice. That culture itself may shift in a different direction. In the past the introduction of new ways of dealing with public affairs, such as an economic approach or the policy analysis movement, changed agencies that had traditionally been legally oriented. A relatively recent worldwide change in thinking about government organizations was the 'Reinventing Government' movement.[39] Although this concept meant many different things to many different people, the core idea was to introduce business-style attitudes and techniques to public management.[40] There are indications that this 'reinvented government', while fostering risk-seeking and entrepreneurial attitudes, had an adverse effect on the judicial mode of careful consideration and thorough attention to individual cases.[41]

A special instance of the new market-oriented public administration is the hybrid agency. Hybrid agencies are public organizations that combine both public (budgeted) activities and market (for profit) activities.[42] For some time in the 1990s this concept enjoyed a favourable reception amongst politicians and high-ranking civil servants in the Netherlands. Its obvious drawback is the operation of Gresham's Law: bad money drives out good money. Or more specifically – activities that generate money in the market for a government agency drive out activities that are publicly funded anyway. Public tasks – in particular the administration of justice – are neglected because of the lure of the market. A case in point is the operation of the Information Management Group – the Dutch student support agency, which for some time was a prime example of a hybrid organization.[43]

To sum up this section, we may conclude that the culture of administrative justice is no longer prevalent in public agencies. At best, it is competing with other professional orientations and sometimes it is entirely absent. In some cases it is driven out by an exaggerated emphasis on business-style public administration, as in hybrid agencies. Preserving legal quality of administration under these circumstances requires specific measures. One of these measures is to distribute legally trained public servants throughout the public service rather than confining them to separate legal units. Another is to give all civil servants in an agency some basic legal training, so as to create a pervasive awareness of the legal aspects of public administration throughout the whole agency.[44]

---

39 Osborne & Gaebler (1992).

40 Nathan (1995).

41 Rouban (1999).

42 In 't Veld (1995).

43 Van Thiel (2000).

44 Visitatiecommissie juridische functie en wetgeving (2007).

5 The organization of administrative justice

Legal awareness is primarily an attribute of people on the 'shop floor' of government organizations: public employees working in public agencies, making choices which to a large extent determine the legal quality of the administration. Among the factors which may enhance or encumber administrative justice at the shop floor are properties of the organizational structure of the agency in question. We will confine ourselves here to a discussion of three important structural features: division of labour combined with task specialization, outsourcing, and hierarchical control.

5.1 Division of labour and task specialization

If the attitude of administrative justice is not a self-evident component of an agency's culture and of the public servants' premises of decision, then the administrative law approach is just one administrative specialization among many others. Administering justice will be a specialization that has to compete with other specializations for resources, political and management support, favourable slots in the agency's decision-making processes and – ultimately – an adequate impact on the outcomes of decision making. The legal quality of the agency's decisions is likely to be higher if the legal speciality in the organization is well equipped to take on this competition. At least two factors influence the capacity for competition: relative investments in the organization's legal function and the institutional position of the legal speciality.

In the Netherlands, for a long time investments in public agencies' legal personnel lagged far behind other investments in agency quality such as the introduction of IT. In the wake of 'reinventing government', government agencies that deal with bulk-processing of administrative decisions, introduced relatively low normative costing for individual decisions, rulings on objections and the handling of appeals, in an attempt to keep down overall organizational costs. At the end of the twentieth century, several spectacular legal mishaps, particularly in the area of implementating European regulations, forced the central government to rethink the position of the legal remit within the ministries and their implementing bodies. A thorough investigation was commissioned which a few years later resulted in a critical analysis of the institutional position of law in government organizations.[45] A second inquiry, seven years later, showed that the institutional position of law had improved considerably and that investments in the legal function were adequate.[46] This same inquiry also found that for bulk-processing of administrative decisions, devices such as internal contracting with executive agencies represented a considerable improvement: costs were controlled while satisfactory standards of legal quality were preserved. Similar studies for local governments are lacking, but casuistic material relating to

---

45 Visitatiecommissie wetgeving (2000).

46 Visitatiecommissie juridische functie en wetgeving (2007).

specific policy areas suggests that for many local authorities investment in legal human resources is not the highest priority.

The second inquiry found that the organizational position of the legal function in the ministries varies widely depending on the government agency. It may be embedded within shopfloor-level work units, it may be institutionalized in separate organizational units, or the agency may combine the two in various ways. When embedded in shopfloor-level work units, legal capacity may be part of the training of all public servants, or it may be entrusted to dedicated legal officers. In some cases specialized legal units at the shopfloor level collaborate with other units in preparing administrative decisions.[47] Some ministries have a chief legal officer who oversees all of the ministry's legal activities. However, even if a ministry has a chief legal officer, this officer lacks the authority to exercise proper legal control. This contrasts with the position of the chief financial officer, who has veto rights and sanctions which can be used to enforce budgetary discipline. Even though legal discipline in the Dutch ministries has improved greatly over the past five years, it is felt that a central legal authority could fill in the missing link between a ministry's top management and the legal function which is scattered throughout the organization.[48]

In local government organizations, the position of chief legal counsel was traditionally held by the town clerk, the highest-ranking official in the municipal organization and chief adviser to the mayor and aldermen and the municipal council. The town clerk had legal staff available. The widespread introduction in the 1980s of so-called integrated management split the municipal organization into a number of sectors, each with a manager who exercises full control over all administrative functions, including the legal function. The sector agencies typically have developed into 'semi-autonomous fields', in which external administrative law is often adopted only with difficulty, if at all.[49] In many local governments it is now hard to identify the legal function as a separate institutional specialty.

5.2 Outsourcing

An entirely different way to position the legal function in a government agency's workflow is *outsourcing*. This solution was boosted by the Reinventing Government movement, which saw contractualism as one of the most advanced modes of organizing government activities.[50] Outsourcing legal activities is no longer limited to hiring lawyers in difficult court cases. Law firms are routinely consulted in all kinds of legal entanglements. In local government bodies, external legal advisers often take care of entire legal tasks such as settling claims for damages stemming from spatial planning. Indeed, in this

47 Visitatiecommissie juridische functie en wetgeving (2007), section 3.2.

48 Visitatiecommissie juridische functie en wetgeving (2007), section 3.2.

49 Griffiths (2003), section 4.3.

50 Fortin & Van Hassel (2000).

regard the legal function does not differ from other administrative functions such as financial management. In central government ministries, awareness of the drawbacks of too much outsourcing of legal activities is growing. The loss of core knowledge about legal issues and legal imperatives is just one of these drawbacks; the abating of a culture of administrative justice is another. In local governments, such awareness does not seem to be present as yet.

5.3 Hierarchy

Another feature of the 'reinvented' government organization is output management: the quality of administrative actions is measured and accounted for on the basis of specifics of the output of administrative processes. One important precondition for successful output management is that the output is in fact measurable. Outputs that are measurable are referred to as 'inspection goods'; outputs that are difficult or impossible to measure are referred to as 'trust goods'. There is a vast literature about the consequences of attempting to measure outputs that are in effect trust goods. Usually the specifics of such outputs are reduced to some measurable indicators, while the essence of the administrative results is completely disregarded. Another effect is that an administrator who is held accountable for output measured in this reductionist way will tend to behave in such a way that the reduced requirements are fulfilled. This is called the *control paradox*. Managers who attempt to exercise hierarchical control by means of output measures may end up with much less than they bargained for.

Administrative justice is in essence a trust good. Numbers of decisions, the time taken to prepare decisions, numbers of objections and numbers of appeals are all measurable indicators of legal quality; but if too much emphasis is placed on these and similar measures, attention may be diverted from the essence of administrative decision-making – which is doing justice. On the other hand, hierarchical control that is not satisfied with merely checking measurable output data but monitors the legal quality of administrative decision-making in a professional way may enhance such important aspects of legal quality as legal certainty and equality.

To sum up the discussion above: a number of organizational characteristics seem to be of pre-eminent importance in safeguarding the legal quality of administration. First of all, from the human resource management perspective, adequate investments in legal personnel are required. Empirical evidence shows that this is far from stating the obvious. Moreover, the legal function has to be organized *into* the organization, at different levels. At the shopfloor, administrative justice should be integrated into the daily routine of administrative decision-making. At the management level, a chief legal officer or official with some similar position should exercise integrated legal control. At intermediate levels, specialized units can provide legal expertise. Outsourcing legal activities can enhance legal quality if those activities are limited to two categories of cases: the entirely routine and the entirely singular. The first category can be dealt with more efficiently without loss of quality, while the second will require expertise that could never be mustered by the agency itself. Outsourcing of other legal activities might very well lead to loss of legal expertise or even to the loss of an administrative justice culture in the agency. When exercised solely on the basis of numbers, hierarchical control will lead to loss of quality.

6 The environment of administrative decision-making

6.1 Technical environment

A large part of present-day administrative decision-making is automated, especially when decisions are bulk-processed. Decisions are then largely produced by computers, by means of digital techniques. The details of individual cases are standardized and fed into the computer. The relevant rules are converted into an algorithm – a finite set of instructions which the computer uses to apply the rules in each individual case. The use of automation in administrative decision-making works two ways. On the one hand, regulations in the disguise of computer algorithms are very precise. The more precisely a rule is formulated, the more built-in certainty there will be about the decision that will be made in an individual case. Automation of decision-making therefore provides more legal certainty and in that respect enhances legal quality. On the other hand, translating rules into computer language inevitably entails a reduction in complexity – sometimes a considerable reduction. There is no doubt that the introduction of automated decision-making has influenced the content of regulations.[51] A computer is less capable of taking the relevant distinguishing features of the individual case into consideration. Automation of decision-making will therefore result in less equal treatment and in that respect will diminish legal quality. Beyond that, if public servants at the shop floor are confronted with intuitively unacceptable outcomes of computer decision making, they will be inclined to "play the machine", for instance by feeding it tampered data, in order to gain a more desirable result.[52] If this is the case, automation of bureaucratic processes will – paradoxically – lead to more arbitrary administration and therefore reduce legal quality.

6.2 Political environment

As mentioned before, the primacy of political authority is an overriding attribute of the Dutch governmental system and of Dutch constitutional law. It is so much taken for granted that people seldom realize that from an international point of view the Netherlands is exceptional in this respect. In

---

[51] Zouridis (2000).

[52] Zuurmond (1994).

most modern administrations it would be unacceptable for a minister to intervene in the tax administration's decisions concerning tax assessments in individual cases. In the Netherlands it is entirely within a minister's jurisdiction to do so. The same applies to many other kinds of decisions in individual cases. In other legal cultures, not only *Einzelfall* legislation (for one special case) but any political intrusion into single cases is barred. As usual, many of these cultural differences can be explained by historical developments; most countries had independent bureaucracies long before the democratic *Rechtsstaat* with its political control of the bureaucracy came into being. Still, in most countries some measure of bureaucratic independence has been retained in order to buttress the separation of powers and to sustain the system of administrative checks and balances, thus upholding prerequisites for administrative justice. In legal cultures other than the Dutch one, it is assumed that political involvement in administrative decision-making at the individual case level may have adverse consequences for the legal quality of administrative decisions.

The literature suggests that this assumption is highly plausible. Research has shown, for instance, that political interference in individual cases – which is typically ad hoc rather than systematic – leads to *legalism* in shopfloor administrative behaviour. Public employees are inclined to *go by the book* in order to cover themselves against political pressure.[53] Even though both terms have, in this context, a derogatory meaning, to a certain extent these responses enhance compliance with the law. However, political meddling may also have the opposite effect: it may lead to diluting the rule of law. Politicians, to a greater extent than public servants, experience incentives to get things done, to satisfy their constituencies, even if it requires decisions that put a strain on compliance with the law. Research has shown, for instance, that a large percentage of municipal authorities issue building permits which violate relevant rules on a more or less regular basis.[54] This *contra legem* behaviour was found to be due largely to the political preferences of aldermen.

6.3 Society at large

A significant characteristic of the societal environment of administrative agencies is *uncertainty*. Studies in the sociology of law have shown that the quantity of law, and more specifically the number of court cases, sharply increases under conditions of uncertainty. It takes time for te regulated to adjust their habits and choices to new regulations; they need a while to reconsider their positions and to choose new courses of action. All of this goes hand in hand with increased levels of conflict, resulting in legal disputes and an increased demand for judicial intervention. Administrative agencies react to this uncertainty in a variety of ways. Sometimes they try to restore certainty as soon as possible; this leads to higher levels of legal activity in order to get the new

53 Prottas (1979); Kagan (1978).

54 De Ridder, Dijkstra & Kemkers (2002).

rules properly established. The administrative agency may also attempt to avoid the new rules, especially if they have been handed down from above, and to carry on administrative business as usual.[55] Thus changes in policies and regulations and the uncertainty this causes may lead to increased legal awareness and to higher levels of legal quality. Yet it may also have the opposite effect, i.e. administrative avoidance, which in turn leads to a reduction in the legal quality of administrative decision-making.

The section above can be summarized by a number of conclusions. The automation of routine decision-making is likely to enhance legal quality; however, in the case of non-routine decisions automation leads to a relatively large reduction in complexity and as a result legal quality is reduced. Political interference or potential political interference in administrative decision-making is likely to make shopfloor public employees more inclined to go by the book. The ensuing legalistic mode of working has a moderately positive effect on legal quality. However, a large amount of political pressure may force shopfloor public employees to give up on administrative justice altogether and to replace it with opportunistic administration. In that case legal quality will be low. Lastly, uncertainty in an administrative agency's social environment may be seen as a challenge, to be met by increased legal quality. If the agency in question lacks the culture or the resources to meet this challenge, it may avoid uncertainty and change and attempt to continue in its established ways. This administrative inertia will decrease legal quality.

7 Concluding remarks

This article discusses circumstances and factors that may influence the quality – and more specifically the legal quality – of administrative decision-making. A minimal concept of legal quality is administrative compliance to the law. A maximum concept of legal quality is administrative justice. It is not clear whether administrative compliance always results in the level of administrative quality suggested by the phrase 'administrative justice'. Administrative law is a normative model of administrative decision-making. As a model it is complex, but not nearly as complex as the administrative reality with its myriad of administrative relationships which it represents. Therefore it can never be entirely certain whether administrative compliance is equivalent to administrative justice. Kagan's terms 'going by the book' and 'legalism' suggest that compliance with the law can be stretched too far.

Moreover, administrative quality is more than just legal quality. There are many other aspects of quality; administrative decisions must meet economic, technical and professional standards and must be goal-oriented.[56] Tensions between these different quality requirements may easily arise. The clas-

---

55 De Ridder & Kemkers (2002).

56 Snellen (1987); Diesing (1962).

sic tension between legal certainty and administrative flexibility which was mentioned in the introductory section is just one example. There is an intrinsic tendency in administrative law to bring policies, economics and techniques within the realm of the law, harnassed by general legal standards. This increases the amount of law – legal *quantity* – but not necessarily legal *quality*. In fact, recent experience has led to the opposite view, namely that more rules tend to lead to a reduction in administrative quality. The response in terms of policy is deregulation. In its report on 'The future of the *Rechtsstaat*', the Dutch government's Advisory Council on Government Policy concluded that the juridification of public administration will have to be reduced; detailed regulations should be replaced by open standards and administrative discretion.[57] In a response to the report the Dutch government applauded this view. Deregulation will alter the minimalconcept of legal quality in administration; compliance to law will become more difficult to identify. The maximum concept of administrative justice will, however, remain the same.

[57] Wetenschappelijke raad voor het regeringsbeleid (2002).

CHAPTER 4

Legal factors of legal quality

H.E. Bröring & A. Tollenaar

1 Introduction

Legal quality is a characteristic of administrative decision-making that is based on the law. This essay discusses how the law influences legal quality; in other words, what legal factors determine the legal quality of decision-making?

At first glance, looking for the legal factors of legal quality may seem a strange tautology, since the law is part of both the independent variable and the dependent variable in the supposed connection between 'legal factors' and 'quality of decision-making'. In the first place the law is a measure of legal quality: by definition unlawful decision-making is of poor quality. However, in this article we are only concerned with analysing developments in law which influence legal quality.

One of the first problems in describing legal factors is that a very great diversity of relevant factors are conceivable; it is impossible to mention all these factors and to describe their connection with legal quality. We have therefore been compelled to limit ourselves by classifying various legal factors into three categories which we will distinguish below. The factors in each of these categories arguably have an influence on legal quality.

The first category consists of factors connected with the relationship between the government and members of the public in administrative law (the administrative relationship). In the Netherlands this relationship is codified in the *Algemene wet bestuursrecht* (General Administrative Law Act) which came into force in 1994. This codification may be regarded as an essential development as regards the quality of decision-making. One of the arguments for drawing up this Act was that codification of procedural rules in particular would raise the quality of decision-making. In this context the object of study is the legal quality of the concepts used by the legislators to codify the legal relationship between citizens and administration in the *Algemene wet bestuursrecht*; thus the first group of factors whose influence on legal quality will be examined consists of the *core concepts* used in the codification of the *administrative relationship*, and their current interpretation.

Due to the codification of the administrative relationship the plethora of legal concepts has been reduced to the general concept of the 'decision'.[1] There is an intrinsic tension in the law between the general and the specific.[2] In the specific sections of administrative law a wide variety of legal concepts – all 'decisions' within the meaning of the *Algemene wet bestuursrecht* – and legal standards are to be found. Within this diversity a few general tendencies can be observed. Changing *legal concepts* and *legal standards* constitute a second category of legal factors which influence legal quality.

The administrative court is charged with the supervision of compliance with legal standards, but supervisory bodies also play an important role in this

1 Art. 1:3 *Algemene wet bestuursrecht* (General Administrative Law Act).

2 Not only in administrative law but also, for example, in private law. See De Jong (2003).

context. The third category of legal factors therefore consists of those related to *monitoring* compliance with legal standards and the way this monitoring is shaped in administrative law.

The main points of our contribution have been outlined above. However, at this point it seems appropriate to make two important qualifying comments to put this article into perspective. Firstly it should be noted that a legal factor is usually the reflection in the law of a societal development taking place in the abstract relationship between the public and the government. From the perspective of the law, these societal developments can be regarded as exogenous;[3] they have to do with changes in civil society, individualization and citizenship, which may lead to changes in the relationship between the public and administrative authorities. The changes may entail more responsibilities being allocated to citizens, with the government acting only when civil society fails.

Societal developments may influence the categories of legal factors we have distinguished. Different, more reciprocal legal concepts are better suited to the developments referred to above, and the European law dimension has an influence on the relative importance of legal standards in the government's task. And finally, the emphasis on the citizen's own responsibility has consequences for legal protection and therefore also for the way compliance with legal standards is monitored by the administrative court.

A second, partly related point is that ultimately the legal factors may not be the most decisive factors in determining legal quality; the influence of legal factors should not be exaggerated, precisely because these factors are often the result of developments taking place in society. Moreover, the social context also has an influence on the assessment of legal quality itself, since legal quality is a concept in which several legal standards conflict with each other. For example, the standard of legal certainty, which demands speed, may conflict with the standard of due care, which requires more investigation – and thus more time. It is not clear which of the two standards should take precedence and which of the two defines legal quality.[4] Moreover, beyond the perspective of legal quality there are also other qualities, such as effectiveness or efficiency, against which legal quality can be weighed. Legal quality is not always convincing outside the legal perspective; other values are regarded as more significant.

An example of a situation in which the standards of legal quality are evidently shifting is the rise of mediation in administrative law.[5] Greater effectiveness and efficiency are achieved if parties can agree through negotiation on juristic acts which are acceptable to both. Precisely in this negotiation process objective lawfulness is regarded as less significant than finding a solution which is acceptable to the parties involved. In certain circumstances even a solution

---

3 Wetenschappelijke raad voor het regeringsbeleid (2002).

4 At this juncture time and timeliness seem to be of great importance. This can be deduced for example from the way uncertainty as to the established facts is accepted in administrative law. See Schuurmans (2005).

5 See Donner (2004).

which is legally defective may be accepted, so long as the parties have reached agreement as to the solution.[6]

2 Administrative relationship and core concepts

The object of the administrative relationship is the *decision*[7] and the relationship is shaped by the administrative body and the interested party concerned as opposite poles. The first category of legal factors which may influence legal quality has to do with the scope of the administrative relationship. Developments in this area are connected with the discussion about the desired level of legal protection, since legal protection is available to interested parties in that they may raise objections to or appeal against a decision made by an administrative body.

Two developments can be pinpointed in this group of factors. Firstly a certain subjectivization can be observed, which in the legal debate is reflected by the interpretation of two core concepts: the concept of the 'decision' and the concept of the 'interested party'. A second development is that the boundary between the public and the private domains is shifting because the public law organizations which shape administrative relationships are also legal entities under private law. This leads to a certain amount of interaction between public law and private law standards.

2.1 Narrowing down the administrative relationship: subjectivization

In his inaugural lecture Schlössels points out the relative value of the concept of the decision in the light of adequate legal protection.[8] Legal protection is available not only against administrative acts which can be regarded as 'decisions',[9] but also against other acts if the court thinks it is important that it should be possible to raise objections and appeal against these acts even though they do not come under the definition of 'decision'.[10]

Administrative law is focusing more and more on the parties involved in the administrative relationship and less on the juristic acts which take place

---

6 It can even be concluded from *Hoge Raad* (Supreme Court) 9 December 2005, *AA* 2006, p. 825, with note by Zwemmer, that an agreement determining a legal relationship with the Tax and Customs Administration which partially contravenes the law is null and void only if the agreement is so much in breach of what the law – as a whole – prescribes on the matter concerned that the parties could not rely on compliance with it.

7 It is precisely in its focus on the decision as its object that administrative law differs for example from municipal law.

8 Schlössels (2003), p. 28.

9 As defined in Art. 1:3 of the *Algemene wet bestuursrecht*.

10 Pront-Van Bommel (2002), p. 62; See De Wijkerslooth (1999), p. 92-93.

between them, at least from the point of view of adequate legal protection.[11] This means that in order to examine the legal quality of decision-making it is not the product – that is, the decision – that must be studied but the legal relationship between the parties. In itself this is quite difficult, because a very large number of interactions and actions take place between the parties which bear very little relation if any to the actual juristic act (the decision).

The subjectivization of the administrative relationship is also shown by the interpretation of the concept of the interested party. A question which is constantly asked is whether too many citizens have access to the administrative court. This is a widely perceived problem, but to date no clear solution has been presented.[12] A topical question is whether it is appropriate to apply some form of relativity to the interested party concept.[13]

A restriction of the interested party concept based on the doctrine of relativity perfects the subjective legal relationship. In the legal administrative relationship the doctrine of relativity boils down to a restriction of the claim that can be made by the citizen vis-à-vis the administration for compliance with legal rules which are partly intended to protect the citizen's interests.[14] Views on the restriction of the breadth of the interested party concept range from outright rejection[15] to cautious proposals in that direction.[16]

To a certain extent core concepts such as decision, administrative body and interested party are vague in content. Nevertheless, there is not a great deal of latitude in interpreting them. While the boundaries of the interested party concept are ultimately determined by standards and legal policy, without legislative intervention changes in the definition of the concept can be effected only gradually and in a relatively marginal sense. For example, restriction of the interested party concept by introducing the relativity requirement into the concept would require legislative intervention.

2.2 Blurring of the boundary between the domains of public and private law

The second trend in the administrative relationship is the blurring of the boundary between the domains of public and private law. Government tasks are no longer performed only by state, provincial and municipal bodies and other legal entities governed by public law, but also by private organizations. Independent administrative bodies are flourishing on the borderline between public and private law. Various attempts to gain an overview of the number of independent administrative bodies have repeatedly resulted

11 Commissie Rechtsbescherming VAR (2004).

12 Commmissie evaluatie Awb II (2001), p. 18-19.

13 De Poorter (2004), p. 62 ff.

14 Pront-Van Bommel (2002), p. 117.

15 Pront-Van Bommel (2002), p. 138-139; De Poorter (2003), p. 28.

16 Schueler (2003), p. 28; See also Verheij (2006), p. 99-112.

in impressive lists of unknown and in some cases unsuspected administrative bodies.[17] By assigning certain government tasks to private organizations the government is in danger of losing sight of the range of its activities.

The proliferation of the kinds and numbers of independent administrative bodies illustrates the changes in the legislators' political focus. On the one hand independent administrative bodies may result from governmentalization, when the legislators recognize public interests in private law relationships and assign public law tasks to legal entities governed by private law. An example of this is the *Stichting Toezicht Effectenverkeer* (Securities Board of the Netherlands). As the *Autoriteit Financiële Markten* (Netherlands Financial Markets Authority) this private board has become a legal entity governed by public law. Occasionally the involvement of a public interest is only recognized by the court and it is only in retrospect, in a specific conflict brought before the administrative court, that it becomes evident that administrative law is applicable. This occurs with boards charged with the allocation of subsidies or benefits, such as the *Stichting Silicose* (Silicosis Foundation) benefits.[18]

A trend which is the opposite to governmentalization is that towards shedding public tasks by assigning them to private organizations. Privatization may also take the shape of constructing independent administrative bodies – private organizations set up for the sake of efficiency.

The existence of independent administrative bodies shows that the boundary between government and non-government is blurred. In addition to the question of legal protection, another question with regard to independent administrative bodies is to what standards they must comply. To what extent must independent administrative bodies comply with the principle of legality and with standards of public access? When the chips are down – that is, when a specific conflict is brought before the administrative court – it has to be clear whether or not an administrative body is involved. No matter what trends there may be towards convergence in standards, the question of whether or not an administrative law relationship is involved must be answered unequivocally.[19]

3 Standards and legal concepts

The second category of legal factors which influence legal quality consists of legal standards and legal concepts. These have to do with develop-

[17] *Algemene Rekenkamer* (Court of Audit) (2000). The term used, 'rechtspersoon met een wettelijke taak' (legal entity with a statutory task) overlaps to a large extent with the independent administrative body. See also Kloosterman et al. (2002).

[18] *Raad van State* 27 August 2003, *AB* 2004, 10 with note by Verheij (*Stichting Silicose*). Another example is the *Stichting financiële hulpverlening vuurwerkramp* (Foundation for financial aid relating to the fireworks disaster) in *Raad van State* 19 May 2004, *JB* 2004/256 with note by Peters).

[19] Wetenschappelijke raad voor het regeringsbeleid (2002), p. 132. Ultimately a kind of reciprocity arises whereby public law standards also apply in private law relationships and vice versa.

ments in the way the administrative relationship is shaped in practice. What legal concepts are used and what legal standards play a role in this context?

Traditionally standards have been set through legislation. Special Acts, sometimes supplemented by lower-level legislation, indicate the standards with which citizens and government authorities must comply. Ideal-typically, these standards are in optimal accordance with the principles of legal certainty and legal equality.[20] The legislation process guarantees knowable standards, so that ultimately the court is able to establish what is lawful. Moreover, the abstract character of legislature safeguards universal rules and therefore legal equality.

However, alternatives to legislation are developing, such as standardization by the administrative body itself in the form of policy rules, or standardization by or in conjunction with the target group in the form of interactive regulation, self-regulation and agreements. The relevance of these alternatives to legal quality becomes clear when they interpret principles such as legal equality and legal certainty in different ways.

These alternative legal concepts are used mainly for the sake of values which have nothing to do with any legal discourse, such as functionality, efficiency and legitimacy. The idea of functionality also underlies the tendency to replace concrete juristic acts – usually issuing permits – by general rules.[21] Tailor-made provisions are replaced by universal rules, often with the argument that this reduces the pressure of rules for the public – often companies.[22] The consequence of this trend is a shift from preventive towards repressive monitoring, with an increased role for punitive administrative law.

3.1 Developments in legislation

Legislation seems to be becoming a less and less appealing legal concept. This has to do with criticism of classic rule-of-law principles such as legal equality and legal certainty. The principle of equality is felt to be oppressive.[23] A differentiated approach is required to tackle calculating behaviour by members of the public which is detrimental to the public interest, and this is impeded by the general standards laid down in legislation. More open standards and a broader scope for executive administrative authorities are solutions used to combat this problem in legislation techniques and they lead to de-emphasization of the principle of equality.[24] Zijlstra & Van Ommeren strongly condemn this

[20] Scheltema (1996).

[21] For a comparative product study see Houweling (2006).

[22] This mechanism has been observed in environmental legislation. Another example is the proposed replacement of the *gebruiksvergunning* (permit to use a public building) with the *Besluit brandveilig gebruik bouwwerken* (Decree on Fire Safety in the Use of Buildings) (see *TK* 2006/07, 29 383, no. 63, p. 17 ff.).

[23] Government's vision 'De Andere Overheid', *TK* 2003/04, 29 362, no. 1; See also Tollenaar (2004).

[24] Raad voor Maatschappelijke Ontwikkeling (2002), p. 34; Wetenschappelijke raad voor het regeringsbeleid (2002), p. 111. For a government position see the policy document 'Bruikbare rechtsorde', *TK*

tendency;[25] they say that if differentiation is needed in certain cases it should be incorporated or made possible in the legislation itself.

It appears that the principle of legal certainty is not a constant factor either – at least the law is not a good source of legal certainty. Vague standards and a complicated stratification of standards of conduct make the law obscure – not only to the public but also to the court.[26] A lack of legal certainty must be compensated for; to an increasing extent government authorities are expected to take an active role in designing policy and providing information about the way in which administrative powers are exercised. This is highlighted not only by the codification of policy rules but also by the rise of new legal concepts such as contracts and agreements.

3.2 Standardization by administrative authorities: policy rules and 'pseudo policy rules'

The observation that the legislators are failing in their legislative task is anything but new.[27] However, the solutions adopted to try to compensate for this failure are new – for example the way standardization is approached by administrative authorities. To the extent that the administrative authority has latitude or freedom in exercising an administrative power, it will inevitably make use of supplementary rules. Policy can be established and made known by means of decisions, but policy may also consist of guidelines, internal instructions, model decisions, etc.

Standardization by an administrative authority has taken the specific shape of the codification of policy rules. In the Netherlands an administrative body is legally authorized to establish policy rules so long as they refer to matters within its field of competence. An administrative body may also lay down policy rules pertaining to the administrative competence of another administrative body, but to do so it needs special authority. If the authority to lay down policy rules is absent, the rules laid down are referred to as guidelines or 'pseudo policy rules'.[28] It is precisely because of the legal basis for the establishment of policy rules that some observers see major similarities between policy rules and universally binding regulations.[29]

The importance of policy rules increases as legislation grows vaguer. Sometimes the task assigned by the legislators to administrative bodies is so complex

2003/04, 29 279, no. 9, p. 18.

25 Zijlstra & Van Ommeren (2003).

26 This is why Scheltema, for example, questioned the principle of legality: Scheltema (1996).

27 Loeff & Struycken made reference to this. Van der Hoeven (1989).

28 *Centrale Raad van Beroep* (Central Appeals Tribunal) 19 November 2003, *AB* 2004, 119 with note by Bröring, and Bröring (1993).

29 Ruiter (1986), p. 65-70, and Bröring (1993), p. 387-400. In legal practice it has also proved difficult to make a distinction between the two. See *Raad van State* 1 February 2006, *AB* 2006, 152 and *Raad van State* 9 August 2006, *AB* 2006, 366 both with notes by Tollenaar.

that it is almost impossible for them to carry out this task lawfully without having laid down policy rules. In this sense the whole collection of rules which apply in the exercise of an administrative power seems to be a constant factor. When the legislators withdraw, this does not necessarily lead to a reduction in the number of standards, but it does often lead to a change in the way standards are manifested. Ultimately, in administrative bureaucracy people are looking for a digital answer to the question: may I do it or not? An interesting phenomenon in this context is the ongoing IT-ization in which this digital answer is laid down. Depending on the data input, the computer system produces a certain answer. Bovens & Zouridis rightly question how this relates to the classic administrative task which demands that every decision must take account of the concrete circumstances of the case so that any automatic application of rules is inappropriate.[30]

3.3 Standardization by the target group: interactive standardization and self-regulation

In addition to standardization by the government, standards are set by or in conjunction with those for whom the standards are intended – the target groups. A distinction can be made depending on the extent to which the government and the public are involved in the establishment of the standards. If the standards are set in a reciprocal process between the target group and the government, they are laid down in contracts or agreements in which the administrative authority agrees to exercise its power in a certain way and the citizen agrees to observe certain rules of conduct. Negotiation with the authorities about what standards are to apply fits in with the evolution of citizens from silent subjects to responsible parties, capable of protecting their own interests. Interactive standardization may, for example, take the form of a reintegration agreement between an individual who is returning to the labour force and the administrative body, in which both parties assume certain obligations.[31]

If the administrative authority is not involved in the development of the standards, the process is one of self-regulation. Several versions of this process are conceivable. Often members of the public are assigned a duty of care, or the granting of a permit is made dependent on possessing a certificate. This certificate is part of a number of standards agreed to without any government intervention, laid down for example by the profession concerned. A private certifying institution monitors compliance with these standards. This means that the role of the government has become very indirect.

Often when standards are laid down by members of the public, those involved belong to fairly well-defined professional groups whose actions influence a public interest; an example is the health care sector. The name of anyone who gives medical treatment in the Netherlands must be entered into a central

---

[30] Bovens & Zouridis (2002).

[31] *Central Raad van Beroep* 30 September 2003, *AB* 2004, 100 with note by Faber.

register.[32] A care provider must provide responsible care (Article 40 *Wet op de beroepen in de individuele gezondheidszorg*: Individual Health Care Professions Act). What 'responsible care' entails is laid down in numerous protocols drawn up by the profession itself; moreover, these protocols are enforced primarily by disciplinary measures – that is, by the profession itself.[33] Public law may then intervene by striking off a name from the register in combination with prosecution under criminal law.[34]

This self-regulation covers a fairly closely-defined group with specialized knowledge. The duty of care laid down in the proposed *Woningwet* (Housing Act) is less clear. Licences are to be granted to citizens who in principle are not professionals but who will be confronted with a far-reaching duty of care for health and safety in connection with a prospective construction or demolition process. This implies that the non-professional citizen has knowledge of quite complicated technical standards, which are moreover not always knowable.[35]

3.4 Growth of punitive administrative law

Developments in the way standards of conduct are set also have consequences for the way in which compliance with these standards by individual citizens and businesses is monitored. To an increasing extent the enforcement instruments at the disposal of administrative authorities consist not only of remedial sanctions but also of punitive sanctions such as administrative fines. This development indicates that not only is the boundary between public and private becoming blurred (see 2.2), but also the boundary between administrative law and criminal law. More and more skirmishes are breaking out on the borderline between the two areas of law, especially now that attempts are being made to increase the scope of criminal law by enabling the public prosecutor to impose punitive measures without the intervention of the court.[36] In future extra attention will have to be paid to the supervision of citizens' and businesses' compliance with their obligations. Questions arise, for example, as to how criminal law safeguards are to be implemented when administrative bodies impose punitive sanctions. Is the administrative court adequately equipped and sufficiently active to take on the task of the criminal court?

---

32 Art. 3 and 4 of the *Wet op de beroepen in de individuele gezondheidszorg* (Individual Health Care Professions Act).

33 Medical disciplinary rules are governed to a considerable extent by public law because the organization and procedure of the disciplinary tribunal are regulated in some detail in the Health Care Professions Disciplinary Regulations Decree.

34 Art. 7 and 6 of the *Wet op de beroepen in de individuele gezondheidszorg*.

35 See proposed Art. 1a of the *Woningwet* (Housing Act), see *TK* 2002/03, 29 392, no. 2. For criticism, see Teunissen (2004), p. 418-424 and Otto's response to it Otto (2004), p. 1750-1751.

36 For supposed differences in quality between administrative law and criminal law see Bröring (2005) (see http://irs.ub.rug.nl/ppn/296307858).

3.5 Influence of European law (internationalization)

In the shifting relationship between rule-of-law values, the European-law environment of administrative law has acquired a special meaning. From the perspective of European law, the core standard is the effective implementation of European law regulations. This means that standards set by national law must fulfil certain requirements, since national law must ensure the effective implementation of European law standards. These requirements will probably not be met if a European directive is not implemented in an Act but only incorporated in an agreement or a policy rule.

Moreover, to an increasing extent national principles are interpreted from a European perspective; examples are the nationally operating principle of legitimate expectations and the principle of respect for the discretion of the administrative body. Promises made by an administrative body cannot be enforced if European interests require conformity to European regulations.[37] It has also become clear that in certain circumstances European law limits the freedom of the administrative authority not to reassess repeated requests on their contents but to treat them summarily. If an administrative authority's refusal to grant a repeated request contravenes a European interest, it will result in an obligation to reconsider a previous decision.[38] On the basis of European law limits are placed on the discretion of administrative bodies.

4 Monitoring

The final category of factors which influence legal quality have to do with the way the actions of administrative bodies are monitored under law.[39] In a certain sense monitoring by the court and the supervisory body amounts to a legal quality system. Interested parties can appeal against a decision through the administrative court, while on a somewhat more structural basis, external monitoring is carried out by supervisory bodies.

4.1 From supervision to legal protection and back again

In the 20th century external supervision in the Netherlands developed mainly within the administrative hierarchy. As a legal remedy a member of the public was able to question the correctness of administrative decisions by appealing to an administrative body higher up in the hierarchy

37 Jans et al. (2002), p. 216 ff., and the case law referred to there.

38 Case C-453/00 *Kühne & Heitz* [2004] ECR I-837, *AB* 2004, 58 with note by Widdershoven.

39 Internal quality checks, including complaint procedures and administrative appeals, are not taken into consideration here.

(administrative appeal).[40] This higher administrative body had the power to completely reconsider the challenged decision. The citizen could then appeal to the Crown against this higher authority's decision. The judgment in the ECHR Benthem case put an end to this system.[41] Administrative appeal has been replaced – or supplemented – by legal protection through the administrative court.

The change from administrative appeal to legal protection through the administrative court means that monitoring has become more and more focused on the product of the decision-making process. The administrative court is only interested in the decision at hand and the conflict about it between citizen and administrative authority.[42] However, in addition to monitoring at the product level there is also a need for monitoring at the process level; after all, the observation that the administrative authority has made a wrong decision raises the question of whether the administrative authority always makes the wrong decision or whether this is an incidental failure. The logical consequence of shifting legal protection to the administrative court is an expansion of the number of supervisors monitoring the exercise of administrative powers, particularly by lower administrative bodies. The administrative bodies higher in the hierarchy have lost their monitoring function, but have been compensated by being assigned more and more supervisory powers. The fact that to an increasing extent standards relating to administrative law have been codified in universal statutory rules is evidence that supervision is an expanding component of administrative law.

4.2 Legal protection, supervision and legal quality

The developments in legal protection and supervision outlined above have at least two consequences for the legal quality of decision-making. The way the administrative court judges government actions is determined by its perception of its task, which is that in the first place it must try to resolve the conflict at hand.[43] The administrative court's aim is not by definition to assess whether the decision is in accordance with objective law. Instead, it responds to the grievances brought forward by the interested party appealing against the decision. The consequence is that in the dispensation of administrative justice the question answered is not whether, in view of the legislation and of general principles of proper administration, the citizen has received what he or she is

---

[40] There are exceptions: the *Centrale Raad van Beroep* (Central Appeals Tribunal) has existed for over a hundred years.

[41] ECHR 23 October 1985 (Benthem), *AB* 1986, 1 with note by Hirsch Ballin, *NJ* 1986, 102 with note by Alkema.

[42] Cf. the trend towards subjectivization described in 2.1.

[43] Brenninkmeijer et al. (eds.) (2003), specifically the contributions by Marseille and Bröring in this volume.

entitled to, but whether the citizen's objection to the decision justifies changing that decision.

The administrative court seems to be less and less inclined to focus on the substantive correctness of a decision; instead, in assessing a decision it focuses mainly on formal standards, which after all often take the sting out of a conflict. The important thing is the way the citizen was treated, how the decision was prepared and conveyed. In assessing the decision the administrative court takes administrative discretion into account[44] and is therefore more likely to reverse a decision on the grounds that it does not understand the decision in question (lack of motivation) than on the grounds that the decision in question is substantively incorrect.[45] After a formal reversal it is again up to the administrative authority to make a better decision, though no judgment has been made as to the substantive quality of the decision.[46] In new legislation there is evidence of an opposite tendency; adaptations of administrative procedural law through ongoing deformalization (Article 6:22 *Algemene wet bestuursrecht*) and universal introduction of what is known as the 'administrative loop' are intended to move the main focus back to substantive quality.[47]

Since the administrative court cannot be regarded as being capable of providing full quality assurance as regards decision-making, the question arises whether other mechanisms are to be found in the law to safeguard these aspects of quality. If legal protection does not provide a guarantee that administrative bodies exercise their powers in such a way that citizens can obtain what they are entitled to, then supervision by higher administrative bodies might be expected to serve as a safeguard mechanism. However, supervisory bodies do not assess concrete decisions but the organization of decision-making procedures in an administrative body. A supervisory body monitors the presence of the organizational preconditions for making the right decision. The result is a formalization of the administrative task, manifested in the establishment of policy rules.[48] However, a favourable judgment on the part of the supervisory body as regards the organization and the working procedures described says nothing about whether or not the policy has been applied in a specific case. In other words, supervision also partially fails to assess substantive quality.[49]

---

44 Especially since the report prepared by the Van Kemenade Committee: Kemenade (1997).

45 *Raad van State* 11 April 2003, *AB* 2003, 281 with note by A.T. Marseille.

46 It is conceivable that a decision of poor substantive quality is repeatedly annulled on formal grounds, replaced by a decision which is substantively identical, and then again annulled on formal grounds. For an example of this see Zwart (1999), p. 90 ff.

47 Draft bill, General Administrative Law Act Adaptation.

48 For example, the VROM (Housing, Spatial Planning and the Environment) inspection is focused mainly on whether policy and policy rules are in place. Tollenaar (2006).

49 Cf. De Ridder (2004), p. 39 ff.

5 Summary and conclusions

In terms of the law, legal quality is influenced by the way in which the administrative relationship has been codified with the help of core concepts, by developments in legal concepts and legal standards, and finally by developments in the way compliance with legal standards is monitored. As regards the core concepts, a salient feature is that the legislators are considering introducing the relativity requirement into the interested party concept. However, the most interesting legal factors are related to changing usage of legal concepts and to developments in monitoring compliance.

To an increasing extent standards are set outside formal legislation. The law itself does not provide a complete answer to the question of what is lawful in a specific case. Nevertheless, in the application of bureaucratic rules the need is felt for a regulation system which leads to binary answers. Regularity and standardization are in fact typical features of all organizations of a certain size.[50]

The use of alternative legal concepts as the law becomes vaguer suggests that there is a regulation constant, based on the need to reduce uncertainty for both the administrative authority and the public. This regulation constant leads to digitization in the form of a regulation system which offers only two answers: the decision is viable or it is not. Shades of grey are not conducive to reducing uncertainty. There are several factors which influence this phenomenon. For example, the number of parties involved in the decision-making process and the frequency of the decision-making process are factors which may well result in universal rules. The regulation constant leads to the conclusion that deregulation is no more than a cosmetic operation whereby standards laid down in legislation are exchanged for standards laid down in other legal instruments such as protocols, policy rules or agreements.

Due to the increasing significance of alternative and extralegal standardization, the question arises of how these legal concepts relate to rule-of-law principles such as legal certainty and legal equality. Alternative, extralegal standards do not lead to the same legal quality of decision-making but do create different relationships between certain aspects of quality. On the one hand alternative or extralegal standards may lead to better quality, for example because of their positive effect on efficiency in the form of a reduction in enforcement costs. On the other hand alternative legal concepts may also lead to poorer quality, for example as regards legal equality, legal certainty or enforceability.

Monitoring and supervision are also important factors in determining legal quality. The shift from a complete review on the basis of objective law to a limited review of the subjective administrative relationship is compensated by administrative supervision which focuses on the whole process of the exercise of an administrative power. The relationship between the court, the supervisory body and legal quality is complex. The administrative court assesses legal quality mainly on the basis of procedural standards, and its assessment of quality is

[50] Cf. Donner (1987), p. 125.

therefore incomplete. The assessment of legal quality by supervisory bodies is often also focused on procedure, but at the organizational level. Moreover, the supervisory body's focus on working procedures and policy leads to a higher degree of standardization, which means that the individual dispensation of justice is lost. More supervision does not automatically lead to improved legal quality.

An examination of the legal factors determining legal quality raises questions as to exactly how changes in the law influence the way administrative bodies make decisions. It is important to produce empirical evidence for the influence of legal factors, since it is striking that the academic publications studied for this contribution were rarely based on empirical evidence. In particular, assertions about broadening or narrowing of the administrative relationship tend to be based on incidents which have been the subject of a large amount of social and political attention.

In describing the legal factors, a striking aspect is that the law is becoming narrower and narrower. In spite of attempts to move in the opposite direction, there is evidence of increasing juridification or formalization of the administrative relationship. This is a social trend which is inspired by the aim to reduce uncertainty. Reduction of uncertainty leads to making standards more stringent rather than more blurred. Universal legal standards are becoming increasingly concrete and specific. However, in this process regulators run up against the boundaries of what can be regulated. The automatic reflex is then to take refuge in open standards, substantiated by the law by invoking an underlying sense of justice. In the process of making standards more stringent, reasonableness and fairness act as a lubricant in the search for the most just decisions. This is a constant in law; standards are made more and more stringent by being made concrete and if possible codified, but this is automatically corrected by the sense of justice.[51]

[51] This same phenomenon is also to be found in private law, where reasonableness and fairness, in spite of or owing to detailed legislation, are also dominating the assessment of lawfulness to an increasing extent.

CHAPTER 5

How can mediation be implemented in the current administrative decision-making process?

H.D. Tolsma

1 Introduction

Mediation is a process whereby an independent third party is brought in to supervise the parties involved in a dispute in their attempts to find a solution to that dispute. In Japan and China this method of conflict resolution has traditionally been more dominant than judicial proceedings. In the late 1960s rising pressure on the legal system in the United States led to a search for methods of alternative dispute resolution.[1] There have been positive experiences with the mediation method not only in the United States but also for example in Australia and New Zealand. These favourable reports have reached Europe; several European countries are exploring ways of implementing mediation in the legal system. Many countries have regulations relating to mediation in matters of civil law. For example, Belgium, Germany and England have legal provisions which enable a case which has been submitted to the court to be referred to mediation. In England and Germany experience has also been gained with compulsory mediation in family law cases and property disputes.[2] There is also interest in mediation at the European level. The European Commission has drawn up a draft directive with the objective of promoting mediation in cross-border conflicts in civil and commercial cases.[3]

In European countries there is no regulation of mediation in the domain of administrative law. However, this does not mean that in administrative cases no attention is paid to this method of dispute resolution. In the Netherlands experience has been gained in various areas of administrative law in resolving administrative disputes under the supervision of a mediator – for example in disputes between administrative authorities and citizens in matters of social security law or taxation law. In administrative disputes relating to environmental law, in which often several parties with conflicting interests are involved, mediation has also proved to be an effective instrument to resolve the dispute between the parties.[4] Since April 2005 Dutch courts have also had the option of referring administrative disputes to mediation.

The mediation method has several advantages in comparison with the current administrative decision-making system. If disputes can be resolved within the framework of the decision-making process itself, judicial proceedings can be avoided and decisions can be implemented more quickly. Citizens can use permits sooner, without having to wait for long-drawn-out legal proceedings with uncertain outcomes. Avoiding judicial proceedings reduces the pressure on the administrative courts and contributes to the efficiency and effectiveness of the administrative decision-making process. Unnecessary juridification of

1 Brown & Marriot (1999), p. 12. 'Alternative Dispute Resolution or ADR may be defined as a range of procedures that serve as alternatives to litigation through the courts for the resolution of disputes, generally involving the intercession and assistance of a neutral and impartial third party.'

2 De Roo & Jagtenberg (2003).

3 COM (2004) 718 final.

4 Wiggers-Rust (ed.) (2000).

disputes can be prevented by mediation. Mediation offers ways of improving the quality of the administrative decision-making process.

This chapter explores possible ways of implementing the mediation method in the current administrative decision-making process. In the first place mediation could be integrated into the decision-making process by making it compulsory for the parties involved. The parties would have to participate in a mediation process before access was granted to judicial proceedings. A proposal from the German literature concerning compulsory mediation will be discussed below (Section 2). In the second place, mediation could be integrated into the decision-making process if administrative authorities had a legal duty to strive toward consensus with the parties concerned. Two questions raised in this context are: on what legal standard might this duty be based, and in what circumstances would the duty apply? (Section 3). An essential element of mediation is that the parties negotiate and search together for a solution to the dispute. The third topic discussed is to what extent the element of mediation can be implemented in a legal system in which administrative authorities have special purpose powers (Section 4). The chapter concludes with a few final comments (Section 5).

2 Compulsory mediation?

One way of integrating mediation into the administrative decision-making process is to make this form of dispute resolution compulsory for the parties involved. If there is a dispute between an administrative authority and a citizen about a particular decision, then the parties would first have to attempt to resolve the dispute by mediation before they were given access to judicial proceedings. In view of the advantages in comparison with the current decision-making process, compulsory mediation seems justifiable.

Vetter has worked out a detailed model for the implementation of compulsory mediation. In this model a preliminary stage preceding a judicial stage is combined with the concept of mediation. An original feature of his proposal is that the mediation process should be completely integrated into the objection process.[5] A dispute between an administrative authority and a citizen who has an objection to a decision made by that administrative authority must be dealt with under the supervision of a mediator. This point of departure is different from that of current practice in which mediation is only used to support or assist the statutory decision-making process. According to Vetter a mediative preliminary stage would not lead to objections on the basis of European law or the constitution. Nor does he see any problems in connection with the voluntariness of the parties, which is one of the core tenets of mediation. The obligation to participate in mediation must be distinguished from the ultimate result of

[5] Vetter (2004), p. 190-196.

the process. An obligation to participate does not mean an obligation to reach consensus. Another possible objection to compulsory mediation is that not every dispute is suited to mediation. If the parties are not prepared to negotiate, or if the legal decision is obvious from the outset, then clearly mediation will not be successful. However, Vetter considers that even in these cases an attempt at mediation is worthwhile. In his opinion a mediator should see disputes of this sort as a challenge![6]

In addition to these basic principles the proposal also includes a number of procedural aspects.[7] The preliminary procedure is to be initiated by the citizen involved in the dispute. Parties with direct interests or third parties can respond to the initial decision within one month by submitting a petition in writing. In the initial decision the administrative authority must include a list of mediators from which the parties concerned may choose three. Then the administrative authority must designate one of these three mediators. In principle a successful mediation attempt will culminate in an administrative agreement.[8] The parties must attend the negotiations in person. If the applicant fails to appear and does not have a valid excuse, the consequence is that the petition will be deemed to have been withdrawn. If the representative of the administrative authority fails to appear, the mediative preliminary stage will be deemed to have failed and the applicant will be given access to judicial proceedings. In this case the costs will in principle be paid by the administrative authority.

Vetter's proposal has met with criticism in the German literature; his critics doubt whether compulsory mediation would really be so effective.[9] Their doubt stems from the fact that in practice only ten percent of administrative legal disputes are considered suitable for mediation. If mediation were made compulsory for all cases, the danger would arise that the parties in the dispute might regard the mediative preliminary stage merely as a necessary intermediate step before judicial proceedings.[10] In Dutch civil law it was shown at an earlier stage that this is a real danger. Even when the Dutch Code of Civil Procedure was introduced in 1838, the Dutch legislators rejected the system whereby the parties had to attempt to reach a settlement before commencing legal proceedings because this obligation was regarded as a mere formality. Recently there have been experiments with compulsory mediation in family law in England. The results are not favourable; it proved that parties' willingness to co-operate was not improved by the fact that they were compelled to participate in mediation.[11] In cases which are not suitable, mediation might also clash with the German

---

6 Vetter (2004), p. 201.

7 Vetter (2004), p. 222-231.

8 German administrative law includes a provision pertaining to administrative agreements (§ 54 *Verwaltungsverfahrensgesetz*).

9 Lotz (2005), p. 424; Pitschas (2004), p. 401.

10 Siegel (2005), p. 573.

11 Pel & Spliet (2003), p. 1901.

statutory precept of 'acceleration of proceedings' (*Beschleunigungsgebot*).[12] The idea that during the objection process the emphasis should be on trying to reach an amicable settlement does meet with approval.

Like the German critics, I am of the opinion that not all disputes are suited to mediation. I think the method of dealing with a dispute in an administrative decision-making process should depend on the particular situation. Not all cases are suited to a decision-making process focused on reaching consensus. It is neither efficient nor effective to use mediation in disputes to which it is not suited. If a party is not prepared to co-operate with an attempt at mediation, the dispute should be dealt with through a decision-making process which focuses on the traditional hierarchic and unilateral method of decision-making. An assessment will have to be made for each case as to which method is the most suitable to resolve the dispute. If the parties opt to try to reach an amicable settlement, the assistance of a mediator to supervise the negotiations between the parties will not be needed in all cases. In a situation in which a public servant is confronted with a citizen who objects to a decision, the public servant can also make use of mediation skills and endeavour to reach an amicable settlement. Mediation is suitable for dealing with complex cases – for example a dispute pertaining to environmental law in which several parties have interests and several decision-making pathways must be traversed. Sometimes an individual who wants to expand a business needs not only a planning permit but also an environmental permit and a permit under the Dutch *Wet verontreiniging oppervlaktewateren* (Pollution of Surface Waters Act). Neighbours who have objections to the expansion of the business may initiate proceedings against every decision. Moreover, a dispute may have been carrying on for years, so that emotions play a role. The mediation method provides a way to deal with all the objections to the various decisions and to search for a resolution of the dispute in one co-ordinated process. The help of an independent mediator is to be recommended in view of the complexity of the case. In less complex cases the assistance of a mediator is unnecessary. In certain cases an informal method of dispute resolution may be more efficient and effective. If mediation is made compulsory, these other methods, which involve the mediation skills of the administrative authority itself, will not be utilized.

3 Legal duty to strive toward consensus

The use of mediation – or mediation techniques – can be incorporated into the decision-making process if the administrative authority has a legal duty to strive toward consensus. But on what standard can this legal duty be based and how far would it extend? In what circumstances would an admin-

[12] According to the provisions of § 10 *Verwaltungsverfahrensgesetz* administrative procedures must be carried out simply, effectively and quickly.

istrative authority have a legal duty to strive toward consensus in the administrative decision-making process?

It is clear that at present there is no *direct* legal duty to strive toward consensus in the administrative decision-making process; nor is there any regulation of the use of mediation or mediation techniques in the administrative decision-making process. To what extent could an *indirect* legal duty be based on existing administrative regulations and case law relating to the preparation of decisions?

In preparing decisions administrative authorities must comply with certain standards. In the Netherlands the general standards which must be observed in preparing a decision are laid down in the *Algemene wet bestuursrecht* (General Administrative Law Act). One of the standards on which an indirect legal duty on the part of the administrative authority might be based is the general duty of care. The duty of care is laid down in Article 3:2 of the *Algemene wet bestuursrecht*, which says that in preparing a decision an administrative authority must gather the necessary knowledge about the relevant facts and the interests to be weighed. The question is to what extent, on the basis of this standard, the administrative authority has an indirect duty to strive toward consensus. Dutch case law shows that it is seldom assumed in administrative courts that an administrative authority has an indirect legal duty to strive toward consensus in the decision-making process. I will quote two judgments which are interesting in this context. The first is a decision by the Chair of judicial division of the *Raad van State* (Council of State), 23 September 1986, in response to the introduction of cutbacks in child protection and youth welfare work.[13] The judgment of the Chair was as follows:

> '(...) in Our opinion the principle of the duty of care on the part of the government should have led to consultation with the appellants about a new funding system and in particular about the size, pace and distribution of the ensuing measures aimed at further reduction of costs, and to attempts to reach agreement with them on these matters.'

The second case is a judgment by the Chair of the judicial division of the *Raad van State*, 28 June 1993.[14] In this case a dispute had arisen between neighbours about a cat which was causing a nuisance in the neighbourhood. After complaints from the neighbourhood the administrative authority had ordered the owner to keep the tomcat inside enclosed premises. The owner did not agree with this decision and submitted an objection. The appeal court's judgment was as follows:

> 'In these circumstances the respondent in this case might (...) have been expected, before deciding to serve the notice now at issue, to examine whether the neighbours' complaints might not to a large extent have been dealt with effectively

[13] Chair *Raad van State* 23 December 1986, *tB/S* 1986, 210 with note by De Waard.

[14] Chair *Raad van State* 28 June 1993, *AB* 1994, 422.

> by mediation in finding a – less far-reaching – settlement between the appellants and the neighbours involved (...).'

In these two cases the court expressly draws the administrative authority's attention to its task of striving toward consensus in the decision-making process. In addition to these examples there are several cases which refer to an indirect duty on the part of the administrative authority to strive toward consensus. By virtue of Article 3:2 of the *Algemene wet bestuursrecht*, in principle the administrative authority has the duty to examine whether, and if so how, the costs incurred by the parties concerned can be limited.[15] If a business has to be relocated as a consequence of a routing decision in the framework of upgrading a road, then preparation with due care entails that the administrative authority must examine ways of limiting the adverse effects, for example by providing support for the relocation of the business. This duty to investigate, based on Article 3:2 of the *Algemene wet bestuursrecht*, may mean that if a party in the dispute proposes a solution to the dispute, this solution must be examined. If a party indicates that a certain alteration of a decision will satisfy its objections, the administrative authority must refer to this proposed solution in giving the grounds for its decision.[16] An important component of the requirement of due care is the duty to hear the parties involved before taking a decision. The *Algemene wet bestuursrecht* contains legal provisions for various stages of the decision-making process, including references to the duty to hear the parties.[17] The legislator stated explicitly that one of the functions of hearing the parties concerned during the objections stage was that it gave the administrative authority an opportunity to 'search for a solution to the problems which have arisen'.[18] Then the legislator goes on to explain that a solution does not necessarily consist of meeting the objections. The administrative authority may also show the party concerned a different way of reaching the desired result, or consultation may lead to a compromise that would not have been found without the hearing. In other words, the administrative authority should take an active approach and should not regard the hearing as a formality during which it merely listens to what is brought forward. Occasionally the court draws an administrative authority's attention to this function of the hearing. In a dispute between a permit holder and third parties about changes to the exit situation on an industrial estate, the administrative authority had failed to involve the permit holder in the hearing.

[15] See for example *Raad van State* 25 January 2001, *AB* 2001, 147 with note by De Gier, and *Raad van State* 5 November 1998, *JB* 1999/7 with note by Seerden.

[16] Cf. *Raad van State* 14 January 1999, *JB* 1999/30 with note by Schlössels. See also *Raad van State* 13 February 2001, *JB* 2001/87 with note by Schlössels.

[17] Art. 4:7 and 4:8 of the *Algemene wet bestuursrecht* (General Administrative Law Act) regulate the duty to hear the parties during the preparatory stage. Art. 3:15 of the same act states that the parties concerned must be able to put forward their views on a draft decision. Art. 7:2 of this act regulates the duty to hear the parties during the objection process.

[18] *TK* 1988/99, 21 221, no. 3, PG Awb I, p. 329. See also *TK* 1998/99, 26 360, no. 1, p. 21.

According to the Administrative Law Division a response from the permit holder to the arguments brought forward by the third parties 'might have facilitated a solution to the problems which had arisen'.[19]

In my opinion the administrative authority's duty to investigate leads to several indications that in certain circumstances it should strive toward consensus in the administrative decision-making process. In order to meet the statutory requirements and norms which derive from the relevant case law, in certain cases the administrative authority will have to use elements of mediation in the decision-making process. Although these norms are formulated in terms of the classical unilateral and hierarchical method of decision-making, they provide scope for negotiation and mediation in the administrative decision-making process.[20] This reasoning is also to be found in the German literature.[21] The use of mediation or mediation techniques can therefore be implemented in the administrative decision-making process without the need for an amendment to the Act.

In what circumstances should this indirect duty to strive toward consensus apply? The use of mediation or mediation techniques in the administrative decision-making process could be stimulated if it were clear when the administrative authority should strive toward consensus. A legal duty to strive toward consensus might be implemented as follows. The administrative authority should examine whether a dispute is suited to being solved with the help of mediation or mediation techniques. In doing so it might make use of indications currently used by courts to determine whether a dispute can be referred to mediation. It is important, for example, that there is scope for negotiation, and that the parties are prepared to look for a solution to the dispute. If the investigation reveals that a dispute is suitable, then in my opinion the administrative authority should make an attempt, in conjunction with the parties concerned, to find a solution on the basis of consensus. Depending on the concrete situation, the administrative authority can opt for an independent mediator, or use mediation techniques itself. The requirement of due care provides a basis for this duty to try to reach an amicable settlement. If an appeal is lodged against a decision, the administrative court can assess, on the basis of the requirement of due care, whether the administrative authority has made sufficient effort to find a solution to the dispute. In my opinion the court should put more emphasis on the administrative authority's role in striving toward consensus than has been the case to date.

---

19 *Raad van State* 11 April 1996, *AB* 1996, 286, with note by Van Hall.

20 See De Waard (ed.) (2000), p. 229-232.

21 Härtel (2005), p. 759; Pitschas (2004), p. 400. Härtel and Pitschas propose that elements of mediation should be incorporated into the existing decision-making process. This can be done by interpreting and applying procedural decision-making norms in terms of the concept of mediation. According to this line of reasoning the duty to investigate referred to in Verwaltungsverfahrensgesetz § 24 and the duty to hear referred to in § 28 presuppose the use of mediation or mediation techniques by the administrative authority.

However, it should be noted in this context that a court can only point out the administrative authority's role in striving toward consensus in the decision-making process if the requirement of due care has been violated; a decision under public law can be made legitimately without the administrative authority using elements of mediation in the decision-making process.

4 Negotiating within the system of special purpose powers

The core component of the mediation method is that the parties negotiate with each other and try to find a solution to their dispute. It is a form of negotiated decision-making. In practising its powers under public law, an administrative authority is bound by the law and regulations. To what extent can the element of negotiation be implemented in a system in which administrative authorities have special purpose powers?

In the Netherlands, in exercising its powers an administrative authority is governed by the principle of legality and the rule of speciality. The principle of legality means that action taken by an administrative authority requires a legal basis. The rule of speciality means that an administrative authority may only exercise a power in the framework of the legislation on which that power is based. By virtue of Article 3:3 of the *Algemene wet bestuursrecht* an administrative authority may not use its power to make a decision for any other purpose than that for which the power has been given. The underlying reason for the idea that government action must be based on the law is to protect citizens against the abuse of power and unauthorized government action. In exercising a specific power, the administrative authority can act only in those interests specified by the legislation. This may be illustrated by the following example. On the basis of the Dutch *Scheepvaartverkeerswet* (Shipping Act) the Minister of Transport, Public Works and Water Management had designated a portion of the Meuse as an area where fast motor boats and jet skis could be used. Residents of the area had objected to the decision because they were afraid of serious noise nuisance. In view of the purpose of the *Scheepvaartverkeerswet* the Minister was not obliged to take the interests of residents into account. The purpose of the *Scheepvaartverkeerswet* is solely to guarantee the safety of shipping and to maintain the waterways. Protection of residents against noise nuisance is not part of the purpose of this regulation.[22] Although the objective of the system of special purpose powers is to protect the freedom of citizens, this case shows that in practice it may actually work to the disadvantage of citizens. To what extent is the power of an administrative authority to negotiate with interested parties about a decision limited by this system of special purpose powers? If the administrative authority is not authorized to take private interests into consideration, is it authorized to negotiate? Or in doing so does it violate the system of special

[22] *Raad van State* 18 September 2002, *AB* 2003, 57 with note by De Waard.

purpose powers? I will attempt to answer these questions on the basis of the following example.

A dispute arises between two neighbours about a planning permit granted by the administrative authority. The applicant has applied for the planning permit in order to build a house. The neighbour objects to the permit because he fears loss of privacy and a view. In addition, the house is to be built partly on his property. He also thinks it is a pity his neighbour failed to inform him about his building plans. The administrative authority suggests that the neighbours solve the dispute with the help of a mediator and the neighbours are prepared to co-operate with this plan. The mediation attempt is successful and various agreements are reached between the parties. To compensate the neighbour for the loss of privacy and view, a skylight will be installed in his house and the costs paid by the permit applicant. The permit applicant will also adapt the building plan of the house so that it is built within the boundaries of his own property. A new planning application will have to be submitted for this purpose. The administrative authority is willing to approve this new planning application. The agreements are laid down in a civil law agreement.[23]

How should the outcome of this mediation procedure be assessed in the light of the system of special purpose powers? The power under public law which is the main focus here is the power to grant a planning permit. Under Dutch administrative law a planning permit is subject to a rule which states that if the application meets the statutory requirements (Article 44 Housing Act) the administrative authority must grant the planning permit. In this example various objections were lodged against the planning permit: loss of view and privacy and building outside the site boundary. These objections fall under civil law, which means that in view of the rule of speciality the administrative authority may not take these interests of the neighbour into account in making its decision. In a decision-making process the administrative authority must assess the objections and then make a decision about them. If no agreement had been reached in this case, the administrative authority would have had to declare the objections to the existing planning permit ungrounded. In this example the administrative authority has no scope for negotiation within the statutory framework of the planning permit. Does the outcome of mediation violate the system of specific purpose powers? In my opinion this is not the case. In this example the resolution of the dispute resulted in civil law agreements between citizens. For the implementation of these agreements a new planning application has to be submitted to the administrative authority. The administrative authority only agreed to approve this new planning application as well; it did not negotiate about the planning permit which led to the dispute between the neighbours. In this case the resolution of the administrative dispute was sought in the legal relationship between private individuals under civil law.

---

[23] This example derives from a case which was dealt with by a mediator in the framework of a mediation project. However, some details have been altered so that it has become a fictitious example.

The example outlined above shows that the concept of 'scope for negotiation' can be interpreted broadly. In the first place it covers the administrative authority's scope for negotiating about the content of the disputed decision; in this example there was no scope for negotiation. In the second place it covers the administrative authority's scope for negotiating about a new public law decision which will be needed in the framework of the solution which has been found. As well as this scope for negotiation under public law, the administrative authority also has scope for entering into civil law agreements with citizens – and of course citizens can enter into agreements with each other.

Of course the administrative authority's scope for negotiation is not unlimited. For example, in view of the system of special purpose powers an administrative body is not authorized to reach agreements about a power under public law which is exercised by some other administrative body. By virtue of the rule of speciality, the administrative authority is not authorized to make its approval of a decision conditional on some agreement which is related to a different purpose than that for which its power has been conferred.[24] In the case referred to above, for example, the administrative authority would not have been authorized to make its approval of a new planning permit conditional on the applicant having a skylight installed in his neighbour's house to compensate for the loss of view and privacy. Another point to consider is that the administrative authority's decision-making process, which is laid down in the law, cannot be circumvented by entering into agreements. A third party who has not participated in the agreement is not bound by such an agreement. This third party retains the right to lodge an objection or an appeal against a decision taken on the basis of a solution which has been found. The parties involved in mediation run the risk of a decision made on the basis of the agreement being overturned. Therefore the administrative authority can only assume an obligation to perform to the best of its ability when agreements are reached about the exercise of a power under public law.[25] Finally it should be noted that in entering into agreements administrative authorities must observe the standards referred to in the Dutch Civil Code. An agreement which has been concluded on the basis of threat, fraud or abuse of circumstances is subject to annulment by virtue of Article 3:44 of the Dutch Civil Code.

5 Conclusion

Mediation is a subject of keen interest; the mediation method is gaining ground not only in civil law but also in administrative law. The use of mediation provides ways of improving the quality of the administrative decision-making process. It is therefore advisable to think about how to implement this method in the current administrative decision-making process. In my opinion

[24] *Hoge Raad* (Supreme Court) 3 April 1998, *NJ* 1998, 588 with note by Bloembergen.

[25] Brenninkmeijer et al. (2003), p. 223.

the idea of making it compulsory for parties to participate in a mediation procedure before gaining access to judicial proceedings goes too far. It is not necessary to make mediation a compulsory part of the decision-making process in order to attain the goal of avoiding judicial proceedings.

The use of mediation or mediation techniques in the decision-making process might be stimulated if in certain circumstances the administrative authority were to have a legal duty to strive toward consensus. My suggestion for a possible implementation of this legal duty is that in every dispute the administrative authority should seek to determine the most appropriate way of resolving the dispute. The current case law relating to Article 3:2 of the *Algemene wet bestuursrecht* provides a basis for the view that administrative authorities should try to determine whether it might be possible to reach an amicable settlement of the dispute. If a dispute proves to be unsuitable for mediation, for instance because one of the parties concerned is not prepared to co-operate, then the case should be dealt with by means of a decision-making process which relies heavily on the traditional hierarchical and unilateral method of decision-making. Depending on the particular situation, the administrative authority should not only be able to opt for the mediation method, but also to use mediation techniques itself. In my opinion the court should draw the administrative authority's attention to its role in striving toward consensus more frequently than has previously been the case.

The consequence of implementing mediation or mediation techniques in the current administrative decision-making process is that the administrative authority has to negotiate about a decision it is making. This important element of mediation may lead to tension with the system of special purpose powers. In the current administrative decision-making process, in which administrative authorities make hierarchical and unilateral decisions, the main concern is whether a specific administrative power has been exercised within the statutory framework. From this perspective it looks as though the administrative authority has very little or no scope for negotiation. The concept of 'scope for negotiation' should be interpreted broadly. In an administrative decision-making process which uses elements of mediation, the main concern is finding a solution within the statutory framework. Seen from this perspective, the administrative authority's scope for negotiation is wider because the solution to the dispute does not have to be sought solely in the content of the disputed decision. The administrative authority also has scope for negotiation with respect to any new decisions it may make and in addition it is possible to enter into civil law agreements. By using mediation or mediation techniques in an administrative decision-making process an administrative authority can actually make use of the possibilities it has at its disposal for dealing with private interests. In my opinion this does not constitute a violation of the system of special purpose powers.

In this article several topics have been discussed relating to the implementation of mediation in the current decision-making system. However, the implementation of this co-operative and consensual decision-making method in a legal system which relies mainly on the traditional hierarchical and unilateral method raises several questions. For example, in the Dutch system there is no administrative instrument in which an agreement between the parties could be laid down. Unlike in Germany, there is no general regulation of administrative agreements. A legal relationship under administrative law can only be determined by a unilateral decision made by an administrative authority. What experience has there been in Germany with this instrument and how desirable is a general regulation in the Netherlands? Another question is what the situation is as regards legal protection if problems arise again after an agreement has been reached. In the Netherlands the combination of instruments (agreement plus decision) in which the consensus is laid down leads to questions about the division of legal powers between the administrative court and the civil court. Further research will be needed to answer these questions.

CHAPTER 6

Review of final decisions in the Netherlands, Germany and Europe

K.J. de Graaf & A.T. Marseille

1 Introduction

Every decision made by a government administrative authority is presumed to be lawful; but not every administrative decision is in fact lawful. If a legal remedy is unsuccessful or if no legal remedy is lodged, then an unlawful decision will continue to apply. A government which strives to provide legal quality will try to ensure that the various administrative bodies charged with implementing government policy in concrete terms make only lawful decisions. Nonetheless, government decisions always include some which are operative but actually should not be. If an administrative authority discovers that it has made an erroneous decision which has become legally incontestable, the question arises whether it can or should do anything to change this situation and how it can optimally safeguard the legal quality of its decision-making. In a case like this the government authority is faced with a dilemma; is the notion of legal quality best represented by providing legal certainty – and thus by restraint as regards reconsidering unlawful decisions – or by safeguarding lawfulness,[1] and thus by broad powers to change previously made decisions?

In this contribution we attempt to provide insight into this dilemma and also to show how administrative bodies in the Netherlands and Germany solve the dilemma and how much leeway they are given by the court to do so. In this context a discussion of European law is indispensable. We will first explain the dilemma between lawfulness and legal certainty in more detail, for example by examining the arguments on which possible solutions may be based (Section 2). We will then deal successively with the Dutch (Section 3) and German (Section 4) solutions to the dilemma and discuss the influence of European law (Section 5). We will end with some conclusions (Section 6).

2 The dilemma: legal certainty versus lawfulness

2.1 Introduction

If an administrative body has the discretionary power to reconsider a decision which has wrongfully become incontestable, it is faced with a dilemma. Application of the principle of legal certainty would lead to upholding the erroneous decision, whereas giving priority to lawfulness would lead to changing or rectifying the erroneous decision. In the attempt to establish on what conditions an administrative authority can use its power to withdraw erroneous decisions, legal certainty and lawfulness struggle for precedence. Making the principle of legal certainty absolute means that once a decision has been made it cannot be withdrawn, because once established, legal relationships

[1] Of course the requirement of lawfulness implies that a decision should comply with the principle of legal certainty. It is therefore more correct to refer to safeguarding lawfulness. In this contribution we use the term lawfulness for the sake of brevity.

between the government and the public must be predictable and consistent. Making the requirement that decisions should be lawful absolute means that every unlawful decision should be redressed, regardless of the consequences for those involved, because compliance with the law serves the public interest.[2]

If striving towards lawfulness is allowed to play a role in addition to the requirement of legal certainty, then the principle of proportionality, which for Dutch law is laid down in Article 3:4(2) of the *Algemene wet bestuursrecht* (General Administrative Law Act), is also important. How important is the interest of redressing the erroneous decision in proportion to the interest of the parties involved being able to act in accordance with the legal status granted to them? It is only if a decision to withdraw a previous decision can be shown to satisfy this principle of proportionality that it can be said to have legal quality. An important factor is to what extent the legitimate certainty that the original decision will be maintained may be violated. The many criteria used to judge whether an appeal to the principle of legal certainty is justified must be considered in determining this.[3]

Weighing the relevant interests against each other may lead to differentiation in outcomes; for instance, a decision may be wholly or partially withdrawn, and it may be withdrawn with retrospective effect, as of the moment when it is withdrawn or as of some moment in the future. An important factor is whether the decision was unlawful or erroneous right from the outset or whether – after the decision was made – facts, circumstances or the law changed in such a way that the decision can no longer be upheld.[4] Policies can be adopted with regard to possible differentiation in the outcome of the administrative authority's consideration of the various interests involved.[5] In all of these situations the administrative authority must also consider whether, in the event that the assessment of the relative interests goes against some members of the public, it has an obligation to fully or partially compensate those involved. The principle of proportionality may mean that it does have this obligation if it withdraws a decision.[6]

---

2 See also Scheltema (1984), p. 545-547.

3 For relevant cases reports see Damen et al. (2005), p. 431 ff.

4 In the German literature these two situations are distinguished by the use of the term *Rücknahme* (§ 48 *Verwaltungsverfahrensgesetz* (VwVfG; Administrative Procedure Act) for decisions which were originally unlawful and the term *Widerruf* (§ 49 VwVfG) for decisions which were originally lawful. See Maurer (2002) p. 283.

5 For an example of policy relating to this point, see the Regulation governing the Suspension, Review and Withdrawal of Benefits of the UWV (Employees' Insurance and Benefits Office) decision, 18 April 2000, *Stcrt.* (Government Gazette) 2000, 89, last amended on 7 August 2003, *Stcrt.* 2003, 154.

6 In the Netherlands references are often made in this context to compensation for loss resulting from government decisions on the grounds of the principle of equal distribution of public burdens (*'égalité devant les charges publiques'*). See Art. 4:50(2) *Algemene wet bestuursrecht* and in comparison the limited options in § 48(3) VwVfG.

2.2 Relevant arguments

As we have seen in the preceding section, the principle of proportionality compels a government authority to weigh interests against each other if it wishes to withdraw an erroneous decision. In the following section we will discuss several relevant arguments which in Dutch legislation, literature and case law are assumed to generally play an important role in this consideration of different interests.

The extent to which the party involved knew or should have known that the decision was erroneous

The importance attached to the interest of legal certainty for the party whose legal status will deteriorate if a decision is withdrawn diminishes in proportion to the extent to which he or she could have realized that the government decision was erroneous.[7] This point of departure is to be found in several statutory provisions. For example, with respect to subsidies, the *Algemene wet bestuursrecht* provides that so long as a subsidy has not been definitively approved the authority can withdraw the subsidy if the recipient knows or should know that it was awarded erroneously.[8] If the authority based its decision on incorrect information deliberately provided by the party involved, then it can certainly be assumed that the recipient 'knew'. The phrase 'should have known' may be applicable if there is a considerable discrepancy between the decision actually made and the decision which might have been expected on the grounds of the relevant statutory provisions.[9] The capacity of the party involved is also of importance.[10]

The consequences for the legal status of the citizens involved

The withdrawal of a decision may lead to either improvement or deterioration in the legal status of those involved. If the withdrawal has only positive consequences for the applicant and there are no third parties who are adversely affected by the change, then the authority can be deemed to have the power to withdraw the decision without further ado. Nevertheless, it is not assumed that the authority has an obligation to withdraw or change a decision which it has ascertained to be erroneous for the benefit of the applicant.[11]

If the withdrawal results in an improvement in legal status for one or more of those involved but a deterioration for others, or if the withdrawal leads only to a deterioration in the legal status of the person involved (for example if a subsidy

7 Dieperink (2002), p. 57-59.

8 Art. 4:48(1)(d) *Algemene wet bestuursrecht*. See also Art. 59(1)(a) *Woningwet* (Housing Act).

9 Verheij (1997), p. 70.

10 Van Meegen (2001) p. 19-32, p. 26; *Centrale Raad van Beroep* (Central Appeals Tribunal) 17 April 1979, *AB* 1980, 269 with note by Smits; *Raad van State* (Council of State) 2 September 1999, *BR* 2000, pp. 321-322.

11 This can be indirectly concluded from case law deriving from the *Raad van State* regarding Art. 4:6 *Algemene wet bestuursrecht*. See Bröring & Marseille (2002).

is withdrawn), the authority cannot exercise its power without further ado. As we have already seen, the authority must then examine whether the operation of the general principles of proper administration, especially the principle of legal certainty, impedes the exercise of this power. One important factor is how extensive the damage will be for the party who has acquired an excessively favourable legal status if the decision is changed. The greater the damage, the greater the relative importance of this party's legal certainty will be in proportion to the interests of a potential third party who is adversely affected by the authority's erroneous decision.

To answer the question of whether an interested party can invoke the principle of legal certainty in order to avert a withdrawal which affects him or her adversely, it is important to establish to what extent the interested party has been able to act on the previous decision; however, this is not a prerequisite for a successful appeal to the principle of legal certainty.[12]

How much time has passed

By making a decision the authority makes it clear that it has completed the process of deliberation as to the question of whether and if so how it will exercise a power. It is not appropriate for a decision to be reversed on the grounds of progressive insight. The authority is deemed to be answerable for the lawfulness of its decision.

Nevertheless, the interested party does not have absolute certainty that the authority will not withdraw its decision. The principle of legal certainty does not seem to be a direct impediment to withdrawing a decision – at least up to the point where there is no longer any legal remedy against an erroneous decision;[13] and of course the authority still has its general power to withdraw decisions. But in exercising this power a valid point of departure may be that the more time has passed, the more importance should be attributed to the interests of the legal certainty of the party involved in proportion to the interests of the lawfulness of decisions.[14] This principle is one of the grounds for setting a time limit of five years for withdrawing a decision to approve a subsidy; in principle this period begins on the date on which the approval is made known.[15]

The nature of the power by virtue of which the erroneous decision was made

Administrative powers come in many shapes and sizes. One relevant distinction is that between discretionary and non-discretionary powers. In the literature on administrative law it is assumed that this distinction is of importance in

12 See Nicolaï (1990), p. 366; De Sterke (1989).

13 Konijnenbelt (1975), p. 104 (under d).

14 Chair *College van Beroep voor het bedrijfsleven* (Trade and Industry Appeals Tribunal) 20 July 1989, *AB* 1990, 88 with note by Eijlander; see also Konijnenbelt (1975), p. 105; Verheij (1997), p. 73; see also Art. 4:49(3) *Algemene wet bestuursrecht* and in comparison § 48(4) VwVfG.

15 Art. 4:49(3) *Algemene wet bestuursrecht*. For comments see Den Ouden, Jacobs & Verheij (2004), p. 116-118.

determining on what grounds the power to withdraw a decision is based. If the original – erroneous – decision was the result of exercising a non-discretionary power and the statutory regulation in force does not include explicit grounds for withdrawing a decision, then the authority does not have the power to withdraw that decision.[16] Nevertheless, cases are known in which an extralegal ground for withdrawing a non-discretionary decision is indicated.[17] In addition, if a discretionary administrative power has been exercised erroneously and the statutory regulation in force also includes provisions about withdrawals, the intention of the Act may be incompatible with revoking the decision on other grounds. Although the administrative body cannot be denied the power to reverse a decision, even if it is on different grounds from those referred to in the special Act, this power would seem to depend more on the intention of the Act than on the nature of the power exercised (non-discretionary or discretionary).[18] After all, no matter how much freedom the authority had in making the decision, as soon as the decision has been made its validity is no longer affected by the nature of the power on which it was based.

The legal standards which the decision must meet

A final significant factor which should be mentioned is the nature of the legal standards which a decision must meet. In one specific area this certainly seems to be making itself felt. Because of the principle of community loyalty laid down in Article 10 of the EC Treaty, there may be more pressure to withdraw decisions which contravene European law than decisions which contravene national law; in fact, in some cases it seems that the administrative authority even has an obligation to withdraw such decisions.[19] It is not inconceivable that the same sort of obligation should be assumed to exist in relation to erroneous decisions which contravene legal rules concerning public order – rules which are not to be applied at the discretion of the parties.

2.3 Conclusion

In Dutch administrative law there is a curious but not really surprising asymmetry between the attention paid to standards applying to the exercise of a power to withdraw a decision to the detriment of one or more of the parties involved and the attention paid to reversals in favour of the parties involved. The most attention is focused on the scope of the administrative authority's power to reverse something which has been permitted or granted to

---

16 See Van Wijk, Konijnenbelt & Van Male (2002) p. 382.

17 *Raad van State* 30 December 1999, *AB* 2000, 47 with note by Schreuder-Vlasblom (important interests, public order and safety); Chair *College van Beroep voor het bedrijfsleven* 20 July 1989, *AB* 1990, 88 with note by Eijlander (fraudulent acts); cf. Dieperink (2002) p. 57.

18 De Haan, Drupsteen & Fernhout (1998) p. 38-39.

19 See Section 5; see also Case C-453/00 *Kühne & Heitz* [2004] ECR I-837, *JB* 2004/42 with note by N. Verheij; see also Jans & De Graaf (2004).

the detriment of the party or parties involved. Although various legislative processes in the Netherlands show that the legislators are more and more inclined to give precedence to lawfulness by determining that administrative authorities have an obligation to withdraw what they have erroneously permitted or granted,[20] the focus is repeatedly on considering the relative importance of the interest of proportionality and the general principles of proper administration, especially the principle of legal certainty.

In the section above we have examined various relevant, universal arguments which may be able to help administrative authorities in confronting the dilemma between lawfulness and legal certainty. The question is how the administrative court assesses the administrative authority's deliberations in regard to this dilemma. Below we will discuss Dutch and German law in turn and examine the influence of European law on the dilemma.

3 The Netherlands

In the Netherlands there is no general legal regulation of an administrative authority's withdrawal of decisions it has previously made. Any provisions in special Acts pertaining to the possibility of withdrawal standardize the administrative authority's power to withdraw decisions.[21] In many cases special Acts do not include provisions regarding the withdrawal of decisions and if the case in question involves a discretionary power, the power to withdraw a decision is implicitly assumed to exist. In such cases the power is governed solely by the general principles of proper administration.

Dutch administrative law does include a regulation pertaining to requests made to administrative authorities to use their power to withdraw decisions. This regulation is to be found in Article 4:6 *Algemene wet bestuursrecht*.[22] Strictly speaking this provision applies only to the situation in which someone whose application has been refused by the authority asks the authority, after the time limit for filing objections or appealing has expired (or after an unsuccessful objection or appeal procedure), to reconsider its refusal, and not to a situation in which the request to reconsider concerns an *ex officio* decision. However, the standard laid down in Article 4:6 *Algemene wet bestuursrecht* is also applied

---

[20] See *TK* 2003/04, 28 916, nos. 2 and 3; see also Hoekstra (2004), p. 1 ff.

[21] There are plenty of examples: Art. 59 *Woningwet* (Housing Act) (withdrawal of building permit), Art. 4:48-4:51 *Algemene wet bestuursrecht* (withdrawal of a subsidy decision), Art. 8.23 *Wet milieubeheer* (Environmental Management Act) (withdrawal of environmental permit) and Art. 76 *Wet werk en inkomen naar arbeidsvermogen* (Work and Income According to Labour Capacity Act) (withdrawal of unemployment benefits).

[22] It is conceivable that a special Act might provide a regulation which is different from Art. 4:6 *Algemene wet bestuursrecht*. Whether Art. 11(4) Social Security (Coordination) Act contains a regulation of this kind was answered in the negative by the *Centrale Raad van Beroep* (28 July 2005, *RSV* 2005/256, *USZ* 2005/341 with note by editor).

when a request is submitted to reconsider a decision made by the administrative authority *ex officio*.[23] In judging a request to reconsider a decision a crucial factor is whether the applicant refers in his or her request to 'new facts that have emerged' or 'circumstances that have altered'.[24] These are facts or circumstances which have arisen after the previous decision was made or which could not be brought forward before the decision was made.[25] If new facts or altered circumstances are mentioned in the application for withdrawal of the decision, reconsideration is mandatory. If not, the administrative authority may invoke its power, laid down in Article 4:6(2) *Algemene wet bestuursrecht*, to deny the request for reconsideration with reference to the original decision. How much leeway does the court give the authority in this context?

The Dutch legal system has several supreme administrative courts. The two most important are the *Raad van State* (Council of State) and the *Centrale Raad van Beroep* (Central Appeals Tribunal). These two administrative courts have different views on the leeway an administrative authority has in deciding about requests made by citizens to use their powers to withdraw and change decisions.

3.1 The Dutch *Raad van State*

The case law of the *Raad van State* shows that the administrative authority's power may never lead to an obligation to grant a request for reconsideration in spite of the absence of new facts that have emerged.[26] Various arguments are put forward to support this view. The first has to do with legislative history. It is assumed that the legislators did not want administrative authorities to have this obligation and that this is why the court is not allowed to review an administrative authority's use of Article 4:6(2) *Algemene wet bestuursrecht*. If the court were to do so, this would lead to case law criteria concerning the use of the power to reconsider, and that is exactly what the legislators did not want. 'The legislator wanted the administrative authority's use of its discretion to be immune from judicial review'.[27]

The ne bis in idem principle is also used to support administrative authorities' absolute freedom in assessing requests to reconsider, the reasoning being that the court should not express an opinion on a response to a request to reconsider a decision if the decision in question has already been appealed without success. According to the *Raad van State*, 'the general legal principle which is

[23] It is not always clear whether an application should be regarded as a repeated application or a new application. See for example *Central Raad van Beroep* 25 November 2005, *RSV* 2006/46 and *Raad van State* 3 May 2006, *JB* 2006/186.

[24] From this point onwards, if a reference is made to 'new facts that have emerged', it should be taken to include 'circumstances that have altered'.

[25] See for example *Raad van State* 4 April 2003, *AB* 2003, 315 with note by Vermeulen, *JB* 2003/139 with note by Van der Linden, ABRvS 14 September 2005, *AB* 2006, 50 with note by Ortlep.

[26] Chair *Raad van State* 3 May 2001, *AB* 2001, 198 with note by Marseille.

[27] Schreuder-Vlasblom (2006), p. 126. All quotations are translated.

defined in relation to administrative decision-making in Article 4:6 *Algemene wet bestuursrecht* and according to which the same case cannot be tried more than once also applies to the administration of justice, and except for recourse to legal remedies available by virtue of the law the same case cannot be brought before the court a second time. The legal provisions for lodging an appeal are incompatible with a situation in which lodging an appeal against a decision about a repeated application results in the court judging the case as though the appeal were against the previous decision.'[28]

The ne bis in idem principle does not apply to requests to reconsider decisions which have never been contested. In cases like this the administrative authority's freedom is defended with reference to the time limits for lodging legal remedies. The reasoning is that if the party concerned has failed to lodge a legal remedy on time, the fact that the time limit has expired constitutes an unbreachable barrier to challenging the decision. The administrative court has no discretion on this point. If a party turns to the court after the time limit has expired, the court *must* refuse to consider the case. The possibility of obtaining a judicial judgement concerning a decision which was not appealed on time by means of a request to reconsider would be detrimental to strict observance of the time limits.[29]

The consequence of the *Raad van State*'s point of view is that a refusal on the part of an administrative authority to make use of its power to withdraw a decision, no matter on what grounds, will always be respected.

3.2 The Dutch *Centrale Raad van Beroep*

In the past, case law of the *Centrale Raad van Beroep* relating to the discretion an administrative authority has in using its power to withdraw decisions in response to requests has been very different from case law deriving from the *Raad van State*. If – to put it briefly – an applicant could show that the decision he or she hoped the administrative authority would withdraw was obviously erroneous and the refusal to reconsider it was at variance with the principle of proportionality, the *Centrale Raad van Beroep* deemed the refusal to grant the request unlawful.[30] The *Centrale Raad van Beroep* seemed to be gradually shifting towards the stance of the *Raad van State*,[31] but a few recent judgments show that there is after all a crucial difference between the two courts.[32] These

28 *Raad van State* 4 April 2003, *AB* 2003, 315 with note by Vermeulen, *JB* 2003/139 with note by Van der Linden, *Raad van State* 28 July 2004, *AB* 2004, 352 with note by Marseille, *JB* 2004/318.

29 *Raad van State* 16 December 1996, *AB* 1998, 32 with note by Schueler, *Raad van State* 5 September 2001, *AB* 2002, 12 with note by Marseille.

30 *Centrale Raad van Beroep* 11 January 1996, *JB* 1996/37 with note by the editor, *Central Raad van Beroep* 16 August 2000, *RSV* 2000/243.

31 *Centrale Raad van Beroep* 27 January 2006, *RSV* 2006/124, *USZ* 2006/96.

32 *Centrale Raad van Beroep* 3 March 2006, *RSV* 2006/209, *USZ* 2006/143, *Centrale Raad van Beroep* 30 June 2006, *USZ* 2006/249; for more judgments which reviewed on the grounds of the principle

judgments concerned the phased withdrawal of benefits which a few foreign employees had received by virtue of the *Toeslagenwet* (Supplementary Benefits Act). The original decisions entailed the payments being gradually reduced between 1 January 2000 and 31 December 2002 and discontinued as of 1 January 2003. A number of the affected recipients raised objections, some of these then appealed and after that appealed to a higher court. This last appeal was successful: the *Centrale Raad van Beroep* deemed the phase-out unlawful. Then several recipients whose benefits had been wrongfully phased out but who had only objected or had not lodged any legal remedy asked the administrative authority to reverse the phase-out. The authority met their requests to varying degrees. The withdrawal decisions led to several proceedings which revolved around the question of whether in denying the requests of some of those involved to reverse the decision to phase out their supplementary benefits the administrative authority had acted unlawfully.

It was clear that the requests for reconsideration were not based on any new facts that had emerged. All the requests were based solely on the hope that the administrative authority would reconsider not only for those who had gone all the way to the highest court to appeal against the original decisions, but also for those who had done little or nothing about it. The *Centrale Raad van Beroep* ruled as follows: 'In view of the fact that no new facts have been brought forward, the question arises whether it can be said that the Employees' Insurance and Benefits Office [the administrative authority, KJG and ATM] acted in violation of any written or unwritten rule of law or could not reasonably have reached the contested decision. In this context the representative of those involved has invoked the principle of equality (...).' The *Centrale Raad van Beroep* then assessed whether the administrative authority's decision not to use its power to withdraw the decision violated the principle of equality. The outcome of this assessment was negative for the applicants, but the important point is that the *Centrale Raad van Beroep* carried out the assessment. This shows that it considered that the administrative authority's reaction to the requests which were not based on new facts was nevertheless subject to assessment by the administrative court.

3.3 Conclusion

The conclusion must be that the *Centrale Raad van Beroep* is more lenient towards the citizen (and thus more strict towards the administrative authority) than the *Raad van State* in conflicts about administrative authorities' reactions to requests to reconsider final decisions even though they are not based on new facts or altered circumstances. The *Centrale Raad van Beroep* accepts that in certain circumstances the principle of equality may mean that the administrative authority has an obligation to grant such a request, even

of equality see *Centrale Raad van Beroep* 28 April 2006 (03/5390), *RSV* 2006/206, *USZ* 2006/197, *Centrale Raad van Beroep* 28 April 2006 (04/3756, 05/6083), *USZ* 2006/198.

though the party involved let the time limit for lodging a legal remedy expire, or was told by the court that there was nothing wrong with the decision he or she wanted the administrative authority to reconsider.

4 Germany

German administrative law has a general regulation concerning the withdrawal and alteration of decisions; § 48 of the German *Verwaltungsgerichtsordnung* (VwGO; Administrative Procedure Act) regulates the withdrawal and alteration of decisions which were unlawful at the time they were made (*Rücknahme*), while § 49 regulates the withdrawal and alteration of decisions which were lawful at the time they were made (*Widerruf*).

§ 51 VwGO concerns the reconsideration of a previously made decision at the request of an interested party; the term used is *Wiederaufgreifen des Verfahrens.* § 51 VwGO is closely related to Article 4:6 of the Dutch *Algemene wet bestuursrecht.* Whereas Article 4:6 *Algemene wet bestuursrecht* refers to new facts that have emerged, § 51 VwGO makes it a condition that 'new evidence is available which would have led to a decision that was more favourable for the party involved'. A limitation applies which is similar to that in the Netherlands, namely that the applicant 'due to no fault of his or her own [the applicant] was unable to put forward the ground for withdrawal in the previous proceedings'. Whereas Article 4:6 *Algemene wet bestuursrecht* refers to altered circumstances, § 51 VwGO states that the administrative authority must reconsider 'if the circumstances or legal situation on which the administrative act is based have subsequently changed in favour of the party involved'. A requirement which is included in § 51 VwGO but not in Article 4:6 *Algemene wet bestuursrecht* is the time limit within which the request must be made: 'The request must be submitted within three months. This period begins on the date on which the party involved has received notice of the grounds for withdrawal'. On the other hand, like Article 4:6 *Algemene wet bestuursrecht,* § 51 VwGO makes no reference to standardization of the administrative authority's discretionary power if there is no question of 'new evidence' or a 'change' in the 'circumstances or legal situation' on which the previous decision was based. What does this mean for the assessment of this category of requests?

In the literature it is assumed that the comprehensive enumeration in § 51 VwGO does not detract from the power of administrative authorities laid down in §§ 48 and 49 VwGO to withdraw previously made decisions, regardless of whether or not one of the grounds for reconsideration referred to in § 51 VwGO has arisen.[33] The difference between the situations which do and do not involve one of the grounds for reconsideration referred to in § 51 VwGO is that in the first case the administrative authority has an obligation to reconsider, whereas in the second case it only has the power to do so, although in certain circumstances

[33] Maurer (2006), p. 324. All quotations are translated.

this power may become an obligation.[34] The question is then whether someone who asks the administrative authority to review a previously made decision without any of the grounds for reconsideration referred to in § 51 VwGO is entitled to a decision which is '*ermessensfehlerfrei*'; and in the event that there is evidence of '*Ermessensreduzierung*', whether this party is entitled to reconsideration. This question can be answered in the affirmative. The German *Bundesverwaltungsgericht* (BVerwG; Supreme Administrative Court) ruled as follows:[35] 'Finally (...) it should be remembered that § 51 *Verwaltungsgerichtsordnung* only partially regulates the withdrawal of decisions (...). For special cases, by way of exception, it justifies an entitlement to reconsideration. In the cases it does not cover, reconsideration is also permissible in principle. (...). In special cases there may even be an entitlement to reconsideration'.

The aim of the regulation in § 48 and 49 VwGO is to serve not only the public interest, but also the interests of the individual interested party, when unfavourable decisions are involved. The legal force of decisions does not stand in the way of assuming an obligation to reconsider in certain circumstances, because this legal force is already infringed by the administrative authority's power to withdraw or change decisions. The interested party's entitlement to reconsideration is the logical consequence of this: 'The citizen's corresponding entitlement does not represent an extension, but only a constitutional complement of this infringement from a subjective legal point of view'.[36]

None of this alters the fact that if the administrative authority is asked to reconsider a decision without one of the grounds referred to in § 51 VwGO being present, the legal force of the original decision is a significant factor. In the case law of the German *Bundesverwaltungsgericht* it is emphasized over and over again that the principle of 'substantive justice' does not have precedence over the principle of legal certainty: 'The principle of substantive justice is of equal value to the principle of legal certainty'.[37] Substantive justice has precedence only in certain circumstances: 'without violating legislative freedom, in the assessment of the two principles in certain circumstances the interpretation may be that this precedence exists'.[38]

The German case law does provide examples of judgments in which the special circumstances are described in more detail, but we have not been able to find any judgments in which the German administrative court has come to the conclusion that an administrative body has wrongfully refused to review a legally incontestable decision. Special circumstances may be said to exist if 'the administrative authority has reviewed its decision in similar cases',[39] if holding

34 Maurer (2006), p. 324; Achterberg (1984), p. 198.

35 *NJW* 1981, 2595.

36 Maurer (2006), p. 325.

37 BVerwGE 28, 122, 127.

38 BVerwGE 44, 333, 336.

39 BVerwGE 26, 153, 155.

to the original decision is *'schlechthin unerträglich'* (absolutely unacceptable),[40] or if the refusal to reconsider the legally incontestable decision must be regarded as a 'violation of good faith and propriety'.[41]

Two things emerge clearly from this short investigation of German administrative law. In the first place, in German administrative law it is completely taken for granted that in certain circumstances the power – formulated in general terms – of an administrative authority to change or withdraw decisions it has made previously may lead to an obligation to make use of that power. It is striking in this context that the legal force or validity of the decision to which this obligation pertains is not regarded as an issue; the power to withdraw decisions already means that the legal force of decisions is relative, and the obligation which occasionally arises from this situation is no more than a logical consequence of that fact.

The second salient point is that in practice 'occasionally' actually means 'rarely or never'. The German administrative court has succeeded admirably in formulating in abstract terms in what circumstances an administrative authority's power becomes an obligation, but in our exploration of German administrative law we failed to come across any judgments in which an obligation of this kind was taken to exist in a concrete situation.

5 Influence of European law

After our examination of Dutch and German law we arrive at the question of how much influence European law exerts on the extent to which an administrative authority can be compelled to revoke an unlawful decision. A significant judgment in this context is that made by the Court of Justice of the European Communities on 19 September 2006.[42]

The judgment was passed in response to preliminary questions. The case which prompted these questions was an action brought by two telecommunications undertakings (i-21 and Arcor) against the German government (in its capacity as telecom supervisory body). Initially the companies had paid very high fees to acquire telecommunications permits. A third telecom company was not prepared to do this without a fight and filed a lawsuit; the German administrative court decided in its favour. The court ruled that the regulation on which the fees were based was in violation of the German *Telekommunikationsgesetz* (Telecommunications Act) and of the German *Grundgesetz* (constitution). The third company's successful appeal prompted i-21 and Arcor to request withdrawal of the fees imposed on them. The administrative authority refused, after which the two companies lodged appeals and subsequently applied for a

40 BVerwGE 28, 122, 127.

41 BVerwGE 44, 333, 337.

42 Joined Cases C-392/04 and C-422/04 *i-21 & Arcor* [2006] ECR I-8559, *AB* 2006, 411 with note by Widdershoven, *JB* 2006/288 with note by Verheij.

review by the *Bundesverwaltungsgericht*. This court ruled that the administrative authority's refusal to withdraw its previous, legally incontestable decision was not in violation of German law. However, the *Bundesverwaltungsgericht* wondered if this refusal was not at odds with Article 10 of the EC Treaty. This uncertainty led to questions being referred for a preliminary ruling. The most important of these was whether the principle of loyalty laid down in Article 10 of the EC Treaty implied that the administrative authority had an obligation to review the unlawfully imposed – but not legally contested – fees.

The opinion of the Advocate General offered hope for the telecom companies. The Advocate General set the tone by questioning the importance of legal certainty. In the administration of justice, he said, legal certainty cannot be regarded as absolute, because it may constitute an impediment to effective implementation of EU law (see par. 76). An important limitation to the principle of legal certainty is equity. According to the Advocate General, in German law this is a consequence of the fact that the principle of legal certainty must be overridden in certain cases, for instance if it is absolutely unacceptable for a legally incontestable decision to be upheld (par. 77). There is also a more objective limitation to legal certainty, which has to do with the 'foundation' and the 'direction' of the legal system. Sometimes legal certainty must be contravened for the protection of the founding principles of the legal system (par. 81). There is one important exception: the rights of third parties. If they are threatened, then legal certainty may not be infringed.

Applied to the case of the telecom companies, this means that the legal force of the original decision must be overridden if this decision contravenes 'the objectives of Community law' and leads to 'injustices contrary to its foundations, in particular the requirement of proportionality' (par. 95), unless there are grounds for justification. According to the Advocate General there is no question of such grounds in this case. On the contrary – quite the opposite seems to be the case (par. 106). It is thus open to question whether it is acceptable that certain interested parties, who had not intended to challenge an administrative decision which was not in their favour, can do so at a later stage because they find out, before the time limit for appeal has expired, that a judgment has been passed which shows that the decision they had accepted was unlawful, whereas other interested parties who had received similar decisions no longer had this option (par. 110 and 113). An additional, more fundamental argument is that 'maintaining an unlawful measure in force, irrespective of its scope and effects on the legal system, on the basis of the argument that it was "assented to" by its addressee (...) fails to take into account the essential fact that the Administration is bound by the public interest and legality' (par. 111).

All of these considerations together lead the Advocate General to the conclusion that the German court must interpret § 48 VwGO in such a way that the relevant provisions in Directive 97/13 can be fully implemented (par. 116). He then suggests that the Court answers the preliminary question as follows: 'Having regard to the duty of loyal cooperation contained in Article 10 EC, Article 11(1) of Directive 97/13 requires that assessments to individual licence fees which infringe that provision and have become final because they were not challenged within the prescribed periods should be capable of being reconsidered if, by impeding the attainment of the objectives pursued by the directive, they consolidate situations which are contrary to equity or to the principles underlying Community law. It is for the national courts to interpret their national law in a way which ensures that it facilitates such review, without prejudice to the rights of third parties.' The final sentence of the proposed answer seems crucial: if it were up to the Advocate General, the Member States would have an obligation – given the powers vested in them – to interpret their national law in such a way that community law is fully effective, even if this meant that a legally incontestable decision had to be reviewed.

In its judgment the Court of Justice does not go nearly so far. The Court focuses on the question of whether – if there is no European regulation of the matter concerned – the principles of effectiveness and non-discrimination do not imply that the German court should annul the decision to refuse to withdraw the fees.

The Court does not spend much time on the principle of effectiveness. The appeal periods in Germany gave i-21 and Arcor plenty of time to challenge the fees imposed on them. The Court goes into the principle of non-discrimination at greater length. It rules that a consequence of this principle is that if an administrative authority has an obligation under national law to withdraw a decision which is unlawful according to national law, the same obligation applies to a decision which is unlawful according to European law. An obligation of this kind exists in German law when failure to review a decision is 'absolutely unacceptable'.

The *Bundesverwaltungsgericht* ruled that the fees imposed on i-21 and Arcor were not based on a regulation which was 'manifestly unlawful' in the light of the *Telekommunikationsgesetz* and the *Grundgesetz*, and that for this reason the decision to uphold the fees was not 'absolutely unacceptable'. However, the *Bundesverwaltungsgericht* did not make the same sort of assessment in regarding the relevant European Directive. The European Court of Justice rules that the *Bundesverwaltungsgericht* must make this assessment now. Should it come to the conclusion that the regulation on which the fees were based is 'manifestly unlawful' in the light of the relevant European Directive, then it must accept the consequences which German law attaches to this qualification. We already know what these consequences are from the *Bundesverwaltungsgericht's* order for reference: the administrative authority's decision to refuse to review the fees must be deemed unlawful.

An important element of this judgment is that the Court gives a clear hint as regards the German administrative court's assessment. The Court observes that 'the objectives of that directive, which is among the measures adopted for the complete liberalisation of telecommunications services and infrastructures and is intended to encourage the entry of new operators onto the market, must be taken into account [...].' And it continues: 'In that regard, the imposition of a very high fee to cover an estimation of the general costs over a period of 30 years is such as to seriously impair competition [...].'

How big is the difference between the opinion of the Advocate General and the Court's judgment? The Advocate General's point of departure is the incompatibility of the fees with European law, whereas the Court's is the powers of the national government. The Advocate General is of the opinion that if the national government has the power to withdraw decisions which 'consolidate situations which are contrary to equity or to the principles underlying Community law', it must use that power. The Court rules that if the national rules mean that in certain circumstances the administrative authority has an obligation to revoke an unlawful decision, the court must judge whether the contradictory nature of a national regulation means that the administrative authority has an obligation to withdraw it.

The Court is more cautious than the Advocate General in two respects. In the first place, there can only be an obligation to withdraw a decision because it is incompatible with European rules if administrative authorities have an obligation under the national law system to withdraw decisions in certain circumstances. In the second place it is up to the national court to judge whether these circumstances apply in a particular case. As regards this last point, the Court's judgment conveys contradictory messages; on the one hand the judgment contains a barely concealed invitation to the *Bundesverwaltungsgericht* to rule that the decision to uphold the fees was unlawful, but on the other hand the judgment expressly gives the German court the freedom to ignore this invitation.

In the meanwhile the *Bundesverwaltungsgericht* has opted for the latter. In a judgment of 17 January 2007 it decided that the national legislation in question did not constitute manifest unlawfulness within the meaning of the relevant national law.[43] According to the *Bundesverwaltungsgericht* the concept of manifest unlawfulness implies that there was no reasonable doubt – at the time the contested decision was taken – about its infringement of the law. Applying this to the case at hand it came to the conclusion that it could not be maintained that at the time of the contested decision there was no reasonable doubt that the German telecom legislation involving high fees was incompatible with Article 11 of Directive 97/13. The incompatibility with EC law was only revealed by the judgment of the Court in *Arcor* itself, and in earlier case law pertinent to the directive.[44] According to the *Bundesverwaltungsgericht*, the complexity of the reasoning of the Court of Justice proved that the incompatibility was not at all evident. Finally, the *Bundesverwaltungsgericht*, relied on a judgment of the *Oberverwaltungsgericht Münster*[45] – which had decided that the German legislation was compatible – in

43 BVerwG 6 C 33.06. Cf. the case note of M. Taborowski in 44/5 *CMLRev.* (forthcoming) and J.H. Jans & A.T. Marseille, 'Competence *remains* competence? Reopening decisions that violate Community law', *Review of European Administrative Law* 2007 (forthcoming).

44 Joined Cases C-292/01 and C-293/02 *Albacom & Infostrada* [2003] ECR I-9449.

45 Judgment of 27 October 1999 (13 B 843/99), *MMR* 2000, 115.

reaching its decision that the national legislation in question did not constitute manifest unlawfulness within the meaning of § 48 VwGO.

6 Conclusion

In various countries administrative authorities are familiar with the dilemma between the principle of legal certainty and the basic point of departure that decisions should be lawful. The dilemma is particularly acute when it comes to the extent of the legal certainty created by an administrative authority's decisions. If a decision is not legally challenged or challenged unsuccessfully, it is assumed that it is lawful; but this is not necessarily the case. The question is to what extent the fact that an administrative authority has the power to withdraw decisions impacts on the extent to which a citizen can ask the administrative authority to review a decision it has made. In Section 2 we discussed various arguments which serve as starting points in weighing the different interests against each other. However, basically the problem remains the same: legal certainty and lawfulness struggle for precedence.

This conflict is resolved in different ways in the Netherlands and Germany. In the Netherlands one supreme administrative court (the *Raad van State*) has determined that administrative authorities have 'judicially free' discretion, whereas the other supreme administrative court (the *Centrale Raad van Beroep*) considers that the administrative authority has an obligation to make use of its power if refusing to do so would result in a violation of the principle of equality. The German court's point of departure is that in each case the administrative authority must weigh up the interests of legal certainty and lawfulness; however, the court gives the administrative authority a large amount of freedom in the way it balances these interests against each other. The influence of European law depends on the Member State involved; its consequences are greater if administrative authorities have an obligation under the Member State's national law to review unlawful decisions. Therefore in this context it seems that European law has greater consequences in German administrative law than in Dutch administrative law.

From the perspective of European law administrative authorities have a choice. They could take refuge in the judgment of the European Court of Justice, which leaves room for caution. But in striving to enhance the legal quality of their decisions, they could also base their point of view on the conclusion of the Advocate General, who has provided a differentiated framework for weighing up the interests of legal certainty and lawfulness which administrative authorities might use in assessing requests to reopen administrative decisions which have become final.

CHAPTER 7

The consequential effect of European law in respect of the requirement of due care

J.H. Jans

1 Introduction

Article 3:2 of the Dutch *Algemene wet bestuursrecht* (General Administrative Law Act) plays a central role in ensuring the highest possible quality of legal decision-making by public authorities. 'When preparing an order an administrative authority shall gather the necessary information concerning the relevant facts and the interests to be weighed,' says the provision. This requirement of *due care* gives rise to a number of factors. It puts demands on the way in which citizens are treated by public authorities (they have a duty to report and warn; they must treat the public with due respect and involve them in the consultation procedure etc.); it puts demands on the way the facts are verified (the obligation to have things investigated in depth and to obtain advice, collection of evidence); it demands due care and attention in the decision-making procedure and puts demands not least on the decision-making itself. However, little has yet been written on the meaning of this requirement of due care in legal relationships which are influenced by European law. It is now common knowledge that when European law is implemented at national level, 'direct effect' plays a central role. Interested parties can seek recourse from national courts in relation to provisions in European law (provided that these are 'unconditional and sufficiently precise') if national law conflicts with European law.[1] The other side of the fact that the national courts can provide recourse is the duty of public authorities to apply European law with direct effect. In *Costanzo,* the European Court of Justice held that:

> 'It would, moreover, be contradictory to rule that an individual may rely upon the provisions of a directive which fulfil the conditions defined above in proceedings before the national courts seeking an order against the administrative authorities, and yet to hold that those authorities are under no obligation to apply the provisions of the directive and refrain from applying provisions of national law which conflict with them. It follows that when the conditions under which the Court has held that individuals may rely on the provisions of a directive before the national courts are met, all organs of the administration, including decentralised authorities such as municipalities, are obliged to apply those provisions.' [2]

Public authorities thus have an obligation under European law to apply directly effective European law. Hence, careful decision-making by public authorities should relate also to observance of this obligation. Furthermore, Member States are liable towards the EU for all breaches of European law (whether subject to direct effect or otherwise) at all levels of government.[3] It matters not whether those bodies are part of the executive, judicial or legislative branch. Neither is it relevant whether such bodies are part of the government itself, or a regional or

[1] Cf. in detail Jans et al. (2007), Chapter III.

[2] Case 103/88 *Costanzo* [1989] ECR 1839.

[3] Cf. in detail Jans et al. (2007), Chapter VIII.

local authority. Careful decision-making with an eye to European obligations at law must therefore not only observe the obligations arising from the *Costanzo* ruling, but must also be seen as a tool for ensuring that the Netherlands, in its capacity as a Member State, meets its own obligations.

This article concentrates on what the author referred to in the title as the 'consequential effect' of European law on the requirement of due care: what are the obligations arising from Article 3:2 of the *Algemene wet bestuursrecht* aimed at preventing public authorities taking decisions conflicting with European law?

2 Duty to investigate conformity under European law of proposed decisions

There is now a reasonable body of legal precedent to substantiate the opinion that public authorities have a duty to investigate whether a proposed *decision* conflicts with 'direct effect' European law under the requirement of due care.

A ruling by the *Afdeling bestuursrechtspraak van de Raad van State* (Administrative Jurisdiction Division of the Council of State; herinafter *Raad van State*) regarding the IPPC Directive provides an appropriate example.[4] A local authority had issued an environmental permit for a pork farm. A local resident launched an appeal based on the fact that the decision contravened Article 9(4) of the IPPC Directive, in particular the obligation to utilise the 'best available techniques'. This obligation, agreed the *Raad van State*, had not been implemented in national legislation, hence there could be no guarantee that the granting of the permit would not conflict with Article 9(4) of the IPPC Directive.[5] The *Raad van State* found that the public authority should have investigated whether or not its decision and the emissions sanctioned thereunder were indeed based on the best available techniques. Because the public authority did not draw on the assessment framework for the IPPC Directive in its deliberations, the *Raad van State* came to the conclusion that the contentious decision 'did contravene the terms of Article 3:2 of the *Algemene wet bestuursrecht* that require that the public authority gather the knowledge relating to the relevant facts'. In other words, the public authority should, if necessary, investigate whether the 'normal' national assessment framework is indeed the right framework in light of potential 'direct effect' provisions in European law. Neglecting to perform such an investigation constitutes a violation of the terms of Article 3:2 of the *Algemene wet bestuursrecht* are being violated.

Raad van State precedent already suggested as much. For instance, consider a ruling handed down in 1992, in which a permit for the discharge of dangerous substances into surface water was quashed due to problems with Article 3(4) of Directive 76/464 relating to the discharge of certain dangerous substances

4 *Raad van State* 13 November 2002, *M&R* 2003/4, no. 39.

5 Cf. on the issue of direct effect of Art. 9(4) IPPC Directive: Jans & Vedder (2007), Chapter 5.

into the aquatic environment.[6] Under the terms of that Directive, the relevant permit for discharge into the surface water of so-called 'black-listed substances' may only be granted temporarily. The *Raad van State* came to the conclusion in this case that the permit had not been prepared with due care, as there was no evidence that the public authority 'had taken into account the implications in connection with the Directive in question when deciding to grant the permit.'

In the aforementioned cases, the point at issue was the potential implications that may arise from an EC Directive. The consequential effect, however, is not restricted to EC Directives. Provisions of a general nature in the EC Treaty – think of the provisions relating to the internal market and competition law – can also result in the public authority having a duty to investigate. Consider the ruling handed down by the *Raad van State* on banning the dissemination of non-native oyster seed in the eastern arm of the Scheldt.[7] The *Raad van State* ascertained that the ban constituted a 'measure of equivalent effect', in the meaning of Article 28 EC Treaty, being a quantitative import restriction. The *Raad van State*, citing Article 30 EC Treaty, recognised, however, that the ban under Article 28 EC Treaty did not preclude measures which can be justified by virtue of protection of animals and plants, given that they did not form a source of arbitrary discrimination or a disguised restriction on trade between the Member States. The State Secretary deemed the ban on dissemination justified with a view to preventing the introduction of undesirable organisms and the degradation of the eco-system in the eastern arm of the Scheldt. The *Raad van State* held in that respect that it was

> 'of the opinion that the State Secretary, by invoking the vague terms of the interests which would, apparently, have been served by the ban, and the equally vague terms of the requirement of due care had not sufficiently taken into account the aforementioned conditions under which such a ground for justification could be accepted. The State Secretary was therefore not in a position to submit any results in that respect, other than the conclusions of the workshop referred to above. Although there was enough call for further research, this was not done. The State Secretary also failed to liaise with the appropriate Irish authorities on the risks associated with importing mussels from the Irish Sea. The State Secretary also failed to provide further substantiation during the hearing. In the *Raad van State*'s opinion, the superficial substantiation provided cannot be used as justification for the restriction on the free movement of goods enforced by the ban, not least in light of the comparison which the appellant made with the risks involved in dumping waste product, some of it from extraboreal territories, and the discharge of industrial waste water into the eastern arm of the Scheldt.'

The decision was subsequently quashed on grounds including the requirement of due care. By not performing any sort of investigation into the conditions

---

6 *Raad van State* 25 September 1992, *MR* 1992/46.

7 *Raad van State* 26 February 2003, *M&R* 2003/9, no. 92.

under which a measure restricting imports could be justified, the public authority was contravening its requirement of due care.[8] This example highlights the consequential effect. It is precisely in order to prevent the decision from conflicting with the 'direct effect' ban construed by Article 28 EC Treaty, that Article 3:2 of the *Algemene wet bestuursrecht* demands careful investigation.

Even the general 'good faith' obligation of Article 10 EC Treaty may, as a consequential effect, imply a duty to investigate on the part of the public authority.[9] In a case on a breach of the Habitat Directive, the *Raad van State* decided

> 'that the sentiments behind Article 10 EC Treaty imply that in a case such as this, during the period between the submission of a list as referred to in Article 4(1) of the Habitat Directive and the approval of the list by the Commission the Member States and their bodies should abstain from activities which might seriously threaten the achievement of the result prescribed by the Directive.'[10]

As the defendant had not taken everything into consideration in the decision-making process, the decision was quashed due to careless preparation.

Another example can be found in a *Raad van State* ruling in the matter of an endorsement by the State Secretary for Public Works and Water Management of the decision to abolish several water boards.[11] That decision was allegedly in contravention of the 'River Basin Management Plan' of the Water Framework Directive 2000/60/EC, which had an implementation time limit expiring on 23 December 2003. The requirement of care, according to the *Raad van State*, implies that the question of whether correct implementation of the Directive, within the time limit, could be compromised as a result of the endorsement ought to be asked. As this could not be convincingly argued, the objection raised was dismissed by the *Raad van State*.

---

8 Cf. for a similar approach by the Court of Justice: Case C-320/03 *Commission* v. *Austria* [2005] ECR I-9871. In this case against Austria, the question arose whether measures imposing traffic restrictions on goods vehicles on the Austrian *Inntalautobahn* were in breach of Art. 28 to 30 EC Treaty. According to the Court, the Austrian ban must be regarded as an obstacle to the free movement of goods, but one that could, in principle, be justified on environmental protection grounds. However, the Court went on to apply the proportionality test. It noted that a measure so radical could only be taken if it was established that less restrictive measures were not suitable to achieve the environmental objectives. The Austrian government had failed to carry out a careful examination of possible alternatives and this failure meant that the ban was in breach of the rules on the free movement of goods. What the Court has done here is to derive a procedural duty of care principle from a substantive proportionality principle. In other words, it is not the actual existence of less burdensome alternatives that causes conflict with Art. 28 and 29 EC, but the failure to carry out a careful investigation of these alternatives beforehand.

9 *Raad van State* 11 July 2001, *MR* 2001/38.

10 This refers to the so-called *Inter-Environnement* doctrine; Case C-129/96 *Inter-Environnement Wallonie ASBL* v. *the Region of Wallonia* [1997] ECR I-7411.

11 *Raad van State* 11 July 2001, *AB* 2001, 232.

Raad van State precedent reveals that a consequential effect is also assumed outside the instance of 'direct effect' European law. A ruling on a permit issued under Article 23 of the *Besluit genetisch gemodificeerde organismen* (Decree on Genetically Modified Organisms) illustrates the potentially far-reaching scope of consequential effect.[12] Greenpeace Nederland argued among other things that a permit granted to Advanta Seeds for small-scale tests with flowering GM oil-seed rape was incompatible with Article 4 of Directive 2001/18/EC on the deliberate release of GMOs into the environment. The *Raad van State* did not, in this case, address the question of whether Article 4 of the Directive had direct effect, as it came to the conclusion that even if there was an issue of incorrect implementation national law could be interpreted in accordance with the Directive. It subsequently concluded:

> 'that interpretation of Article 26 of the *Wet milieugevaarlijke stoffen* (Environmentally Hazardous Substances Act) and Article 23 of the Decree on Genetically Modified Organisms in accordance with the Directive implies that in light of the aims of Directive 2001/18/EC, any negative consequences of the introduction must be assessed carefully on a case-by-case basis. In the *Raad van State*'s opinion, the criteria defined in Annex II of the Directive should be observed whenever an environmental risk assessment is drawn up. The respondent argued at the hearing that Annex II of the Directive is actually used when assessing applications. In the *Raad van State*'s opinion, however, it is not clear, either from the wording of the challenged decision or the documentation which forms the basis thereof, as far as they are referred to in the decision itself, whether in the case at hand the requisite careful investigation into the implications of introduction was performed, including such things as the various aspects or steps listed in Annex II. In view of this, the *Raad van State* holds that no plausible case has been made that investigation into the implications of introduction was comprehensive and that all risks associated with introduction were investigated and assessed. The decision in question thus conflicts with the terms of Articles 3:2 and 3:46 of the *Algemene wet bestuursrecht*, which state that a public authority must gather the necessary knowledge relating to the relevant facts and that the decision must be reasonably substantiated.'

In light of the above, it appears that the *Raad van State* accepts that it has an obligation to investigate a proposed decision's conformity with European law, even if there could be no recourse in national courts for the European standard which would be breached because of its lack of direct effect. Given the above, it appears that the *Raad van State* is implying that the consequential effect of the requirement of due care serves not only to comply with the public authority's obligations under the *Costanzo* ruling, but has the general function of preventing a breach of European law.

---

[12] *Raad van State* 28 July 2004, LJN: AQ5732.

In summary, it is possible to draw the conclusion that the requirement of due care obliges a public authority in the decision-making process to investigate whether the proposed decision is compatible with direct and indirect European law.

3 Duty to investigate compatibility of the national legislative framework with European law

Raad van State legal precedent shows that public authorities are not only bound to careful investigation of compatibility of their 'own' decisions with European law; they are furthermore bound to consider whether the *legislation* on which they base their executive authority is indeed compliant with European law. This question came up in all its glory in a matter which raised questions about compatibility of Article 5(2) of the End of Life Cycle Decree with Article 29 EC Treaty (prohibition of export restrictions).[13] The *Raad van State* held the following:

> In relation to the respondent's statement at the hearing, which claimed that full enforcement of the demand that car wrecking should take place within one facility could lead to conflict with Article 29 EC Treaty, the *Raad van State* made the following observations:
>
> This demand implies that car wrecks, from which dangerous substances have been removed may not be moved to another wrecking yard in another Member State. The *Raad van State* thus holds that this constitutes a restriction on exports in the meaning of Article 29 EC Treaty. Such restrictions are forbidden unless there are recognised grounds for justification within European law and the measure in question meets the requirement of proportionality. As is evident from the substance of the hearing, the respondent has not sufficiently investigated whether or not the End of Life Cycle Decree meets the criteria and, furthermore, if the conclusion is that there is a conflict, what implications there would be under normal circumstances for the matter at hand, in which there is no question of proposed movement of wrecked cars to another Member State. The *Raad van State* thus also holds that the respondent has not made a plausible case for Article 29 EC Treaty forming a justification for imposing the challenged rules.

In view of the above, the competent regional executive authority (*Gedeputeerde Staten* of Groningen), has an obligation to investigate whether the *End of Life-Cycle Decree* (enacted at government level) complies with European law. There can surely be no better illustration of provincial and municipal councils having their own responsibility for the observation of European law. Public authorities must not be guided blindly by national legislation; they ought to ensure that they are not acting in contravention of with European law as the need arises, even in

[13] *Raad van State* 26 November 2003, *MR* 2004/9.

instances in which the national legislative body might have erred. In the case at hand, the *Raad van State* went a step further, stating that the public authority also has a duty to ask itself what the implications are (when there is no question of intended shipment of wrecked cars to another Member State) if it comes to the conclusion that the End of Life Cycle Decree does not contravene Article 29 EC Treaty.

4 Obligations to consult

Under the EC Treaty, regulations and directives, *Member States* must comply with a significant number of obligations to notify the European Commission of proposed decisions and or legislation; for instance the obligation to notify in questions of state aid mandated by Article 88(3) EC Treaty and the right to maintain national provisions under Article 95(4-5) EC Treaty. I have already discussed this at length in another context; in this paper I shall limit myself to a footnote.[14] What I am concerned with in this context is the extent to which, without there being any sort of obligation under European law, public authorities have an obligation to consult as part of the requirement of due care as defined in Article 3:2 of the *Algemene wet bestuursrecht* in intra-community legal relationships. In the *Raad van State*'s view, such an obligation to consult must be taken under certain circumstances. The *Raad van State*'s ruling on the granting of subsidy by a regional authority (the governing committee of the Northern Netherlands Assembly) made this clear. The case concerned a subsidy of NLG 4m for the refurbishment of a conference/entertainment building (the Martini Plaza) in the city of Groningen.[15] A local competitor in the conference/entertainment market argued that the subsidy should be regarded as 'state aid' in the meaning of Article 87 EC Treaty, and should have been notified to the European Commission. In light of the requirement of due care, the *Raad van State* held that:

> 'The possibility of a subsidy having an impact on trade between the Netherlands and other Member States, notably Germany, given the effective radius of the economic activity benefiting from such a subsidy – in this case the holding of trade fairs – and the relatively short distance from the site to the German border cannot be ruled out. With this in mind, the executive committee should have made inquiries with the European Commission to obtain confirmation that the reporting obligation pursuant to Article 88(3) EC Treaty does not apply to the granting of subsidies, or that the same falls under the exemption clause of Regulation (EC) 70/2001, or it should have notified the Commission of its intention to grant subsidies in compliance with Article 88(3) EC Treaty.'

---

[14] Cf. Jans (1998).

[15] *Raad van State* 17 December 2003, LJN: AO0234.

Let me make it clear: the grounds for this decision are not concerned with the question of whether the European Commission should have been notified of the subsidy in question under the rules of the EC Treaty. This duty lies with the Member State, and in the case of subsidies granted by non-national authorities with the national government.[16] In the *Raad van State*'s opinion, the requirement of due care implies under *national law* that where it is possible to have a difference of opinion on the exact legal position, the obligation lies with the public authority (in this case the executive committee) to consult the European Commission on this point. In other words, if the matter gives rise to the assumption that there is an obligation to consult under European law, the consequential effect under Article 3:2 of the *Algemene wet bestuursrecht* is that the public authority has a duty to investigate whether or not the decision must be reported or not.[17]

In this context, it is also possible to refer to the *Raad van State* decision discussed above relating to the dissemination of non-native oyster seed in the eastern arm of the Scheldt.[18] The fact that, in that matter, the state secretary in question had neglected to contact the relevant authorities on the potential risks of the import of Irish Sea mussels was considered important in the *Raad van State*'s conclusion that the requirement of due care had been breached.

5 Conclusions

That European law has precedence over national law where there is conflict is, by now, common knowledge. The same can be said of the fact that the national courts can provide recourse on European law with direct effect and that public authorities must apply the same. This paper is an attempt to trace the obligations for public authorities arising from Article 3:2 of the *Algemene wet bestuursrecht* against the background of the principle of precedence and the doctrine of direct effect, precisely in order to prevent them from coming into conflict with European law. I have referred to this as the 'consequential effect' of European law on the principle of due care. It is thus not a question of an obligation which arises directly from European law, but from *national* law. This reconnaisance on the subject has revealed the following results.

---

[16] In the Netherlands, the procedure for reporting state aid is that municipal and provincial authorities use the 'State-Aid Coordination Point' at the Ministry of the Interior which relays reports to the Dutch Permanent Representation in Brussels, which, in turn, relays reports to the European Commission.

[17] I am of the opinion that such an 'obligation to verify' also arises from European law itself. It is in the nature of the case that the reporting obligation referred to in Art. 88(3) EC Treaty and Regulation 70/2001 covers 'plans to grant or alter aid' only and not potential plans of that ilk. In my opinion, the 'good faith obligation' of Art. 10 EC Treaty implies that in the event of reasonable doubt on a question of whether a specific measure falls under a Member State's reporting requirement, that Member State shall be obliged to liaise with the Commission to obtain certainty about this matter.

[18] *Raad van State* 26 February 2003, *M&R* 2003/9, no. 92.

The obligation arising for public authorities from the formal principle of care in Article 3:2 of the *Algemene wet bestuursrecht* is their duty to investigate the implications of European law on any proposed decision. The aim of this duty of investigation is to prevent the taking of decisions which are in conflict with the EC Treaty and secondary European law. It does not appear significant whether or not the relevant provisions have direct effect. However, where applicable, public authorities are also obliged to investigate whether or not the legislation on which their executive authority is based is compatible with European law. This duty also covers legislation from other authorities.

The natural conclusion is thus that under certain circumstances public authorities have a duty under the requirement of due care to organize consultation meetings. In terms of European law, an opaque legal situation could result in the public authority in question being forced to answer to the European Commission or other public authorities at home and abroad. It would be interesting to see whether this form of 'consequential effect' is an issue in other Member States of the EU. More detailed legal comparisons are therefore advisable. There is also the question of whether there is an equivalent form of 'consequential effect' in the other principles of good government.

CHAPTER 8

Quality and administration of the Dutch social security system: an impression

F.M. Noordam

1 Introduction

In many respects the Dutch social security system[1] has a bad image. The costs are too high,[2] the normative content of the legislation too low; the social security system is based on outdated views on the individual and society; social security policy stumbles from one problem to the next; the social security administrative bodies work slowly. On the other hand, most people agree that social security is still badly needed. And in proportion to the countless millions of decisions made in social security,[3] the number of critical judicial rulings is relatively limited. The same is true of the number of complaints about the social security administrative bodies submitted to the National ombudsman by members of the public. These administrative bodies seldom feature in TV programmes which focus – sometimes in a quasi-humorous way – on the operation of national bureaucracies. The era of blackbooks exposing the rudeness of the administrative bodies and their neglect of their tasks lies behind us. A few years ago an investigation conducted by the Social and Cultural Planning Office[4] showed that faith in the administrative bodies is not at a low ebb at all – on the contrary. For example, 84% of the unemployed and as many as 99% of people with old age pensions are satisfied with the payment of their benefits.[5] There is no reason to assume that this confidence has since declined.

On balance, this produces a somewhat blurred picture. Another point is that the statements made refer to different aspects of the social security system. Some are relevant to the theme of this book – the quality of the primary decision-making process in organizations which perform public tasks – while others are somewhat removed from it. I will attempt to make this blurred picture a little clearer. In doing so I will limit myself mainly to the activities of two implementing bodies, namely the *Uitvoeringsinstituut Werknemersverzekeringen* (UWV; Employees' Insurance and Benefits Office) and the *Sociale Verzekeringsbank* (SVb; Social Insurance Bank). The *Uitvoeringsinstituut Werknemersverzekeringen* implements social security provisions for employees (employees' insurance schemes) such as the *Werkloosheidswet* (Unemployment Act), a regulation for unemployment. The *Sociale Verzekeringsbank* is the implementing body of the national insurance schemes – regulations which apply to the whole population. An example is the *Algemene Ouderdomswet* (National Old Age Pensions Act). By virtue of this act all residents receive a basic pension as soon as they

---

1 For the Dutch social security system and social security law see Noordam (2006).

2 Approximately EUR 95 billion per annum is spent on social security, which is about 20% of the gross domestic product.

3 For example, the *Uitvoeringsinstituut Werknemersverzekeringen* (Employees' Insurance and Benefits Office; UWV) makes about 7 million decisions a year; cf. Nationale ombudsman (National ombudsman) (2005).

4 The Social and Cultural Planning Office of the Netherlands is a government agency which conducts research into the social aspects of all areas of government policy; http://www.scp.nl/english/.

5 Sociaal Cultureel Planbureau (2002), p. 379.

turn 65. How do the *external* bodies involved in the implementation judge the operation of the social security administrative bodies (Section 2) and what are their criteria (Section 3)? But we will also take a look at the *internal* situation: what do the administrative bodies themselves do about quality assurance with respect to implementation (Section 4)? Section 5 contains a few concluding remarks.

2 External assessors

The social security administrative bodies are surrounded by a circle of individuals and agencies which assess the way in which those bodies perform their tasks. In some cases they have put themselves forward as assessors, and in many other cases their position is a formal one, assigned to them by the law. Examples of 'self-appointed' assessors are the interested parties who do not agree with a decision made by the administrative body, for instance a decision to refuse an application for unemployment benefits. According to the interested parties' standard, the decision falls short of the mark. Other examples of self-appointed bodies are the interest groups of people entitled to benefits, such as disabled forums, unemployed unions or senior citizens' organizations. Academics sometimes fall into this category as well. The media also devote attention to the operation of administrative bodies. *Formal* assessors are the court, the National ombudsman, the Dutch *Rekenkamer* (Court of Audit),[6] supervisory bodies such as the Ministry of Social Affairs and Employment, and Parliament. I will start with the court.

2.1 The court

A judicial decision is a judgment of the way an *individual* case has been dealt with in practice, albeit that in many cases this individual case represents a set of identical – or at least similar – cases. The court assesses the administrative bodies' decisions brought before it against the benchmark of lawfulness. In 2004 this was done with regard to social security decisions about 20,000 times at district courts and 4,500 times at the *Centrale Raad van Beroep* (Central Appeals Tribunal), the highest judicial authority for legal areas pertaining to social security and the civil service.[7] The district court is the court of first instance; the *Centrale Raad van Beroep* is the appeal court in social security disputes. Over the past five years the number of judgments passed by the district

6 The Dutch *Rekenkamer* (Court of Audit), along with the *Eerste Kamer* and the *Tweede Kamer* (Upper House and Lower House), the *Raad van State* (Council of State) and the National ombudsman, is known as a High Council of State. The Court of Audit investigates whether Dutch public funds are collected and spent effectively and according to the regulations. It is independent of the government and Parliament.

7 Centraal Bureau voor de Statistiek (2006), p. 37 and p. 42.

courts and the *Centrale Raad van Beroep* in relation to social security disputes has remained fairly constant.

Essentially every judicial decision is a quality assessment. The appeals made to the court refer not only to formal and procedural points but also to substantive matters. Both in legal practice and in academic studies the focus is mainly on those decisions which constitute negative judgments of the administrative bodies' operation and legal conduct, which actually creates a somewhat biased picture of the quality of the administration; after all, in 2004 the district courts *dismissed* about two-thirds of the appeals lodged.[8] Considered over a slightly longer period, a dismissal rate of 70% seems to be fairly normal.

Although in principle every judgment is equally important in forming an opinion about implementation practice, some judgments are particularly striking. Most of these are judgments which go beyond the incident level. I will give a few examples, to which many others could be added. The *Sociale Verzekeringsbank*'s practice of denying the entitlement of widowers to a dependant's pension by virtue of the former Survivors' Benefits Act, whereas widows were granted this pension, was deemed unlawful because it contravened international law.[9] The grounds given by a predecessor of the *Uitvoeringsinstituut Werknemersverzekeringen* for imposing fines on employers because of the large number of work-disabled employees in their companies were considered by the court to be in violation of the justification principle referred to in the law.[10] The Dutch practice of refusing to allow fully unemployed frontier workers to look for work in another Member State of the EU without loss of benefits violated European law.[11] The standard fine of four months' pay imposed on employers who failed to make sufficient efforts to help their work-disabled employees to find other appropriate employment did not comply with the law. This so-called 'wage sanction' was too broad; it was not geared to individual cases as required by law.[12] These judgments caused a great deal of political and financial commotion and led to changed practices in the administrative bodies concerned or revision of the legislation in question.

2.2 The National ombudsman

The opinions expressed in the National ombudsman's reports have the same character as court judgments: in principle they refer to individual cases. But the National ombudsman is expressly authorized to go a step further than the court. He can make a recommendation to the bodies about which members of the public have complained to him as to the measures which should be taken. These measures are general in character, referring for example to the

---

8 Centraal Bureau voor de Statistiek (2006), p. 38.

9 *Centrale Raad van Beroep* 7 December 1988, *RSV* 1989/67, with case note by Keunen.

10 *Centrale Raad van Beroep* 15 January 1995, *RSV* 1996/214.

11 Case C-311/01 *Commission* v. *Netherlands* [2003] ECR I-13103.

12 *Centrale Raad van Beroep* 22 February 2006, *RSV* 2006/99.

adaptation of a certain practice connected with the complaint (Article 9:27(3) of the *Algemene wet bestuursrecht*, General Administrative Law Act).[13] In 2005 the number of complaints (petitions) pertaining to social security administrative bodies was about 1950 – 20% of the total number of complaints received by the National ombudsman that year.[14] The number of complaints is rising; in 2002, for example, there were 1460.[15] Many complaints are not investigated because they are inadmissible or because the National ombudsman is not authorized to deal with the case. The number of reports brought out by the National ombudsman about the social security administrative bodies is limited: in 2005, 21 about the *Uitvoeringsinstituut Werknemersverzekeringen* and 2 about the *Sociale Verzekeringsbank*.[16] To gain an accurate picture it is important to realize that a significant proportion of the complaints submitted do not lead to a report because the administrative body later met the complainer's wishes, sometimes but not necessarily after intervention by the National ombudsman. In substantive terms these cases can be regarded as justified complaints. The majority of the complaints are about the long processing duration and the careless, ill-mannered or indolent way citizens have been treated by the staff of the administrative bodies. Over and over again it becomes clear that processing duration and treatment of the public are the persistent weak points of big bureaucracies. The National ombudsman is particularly critical with respect to the *Uitvoeringsinstituut Werknemersverzekeringen*. When presenting the Annual Report 2005 the National ombudsman emphasized that citizens can get into serious financial difficulties as a result of the slow processing of their applications.[17]

Several municipalities have municipal ombudsmen. If there is a municipal ombudsman, then in accordance with the distribution of tasks the National ombudsman is not authorized to deal with municipal cases. The municipal ombudsman holds the same sort of inquiry as the National ombudsman. An example of an inquiry by a municipal ombudsman is the report by the ombudsman of the municipality of Amsterdam dated 3 July 2006.[18] According to this report the municipality's information provision, working method and decision-making process relating to so-called home visits in the framework of the implementation of the *Wet werk en bijstand* (Work and Social Assistance Act) was 'improper'. The home visit is an instrument used to check whether an interested party who has submitted an application for social assistance may be cohabiting; cohabitation is a contraindication to entitlement to social assistance.

---

[13] An example is the National ombudsman's recommendation dated 2 December 2002, *RSV* 2003/43, that steps should be taken to ensure that a complaint about overstepping the time limit within which a decision has to be made is dealt with in accordance with the relevant provisions of the *Algemene wet bestuursrecht*.

[14] Nationale ombudsman (2005), p. 13.

[15] Nationale ombudsman (2002), p. 13.

[16] See http://www.nationaleombudsman.nl/rapporten/rapporten/2005/sociale_zaken.asp.

[17] Press Release, National ombudsman; 19 April 2006.

[18] The report can be found on http://www.gemeentelijkeombudsman.nl.

2.3 The Netherlands Court of Audit

The Netherlands Court of Audit, the body which – to put it briefly – monitors the income and expenditure of the Dutch national government, occasionally also investigates the administration of social security and brings out a report on it. Examples are the report *Opsporing en vervolging van fraude* (Detection and prosecution of fraud) brought out in 2000 and the report *Alleenstaande ouders in de bijstand* (Single parents on social assistance) brought out in 2003. One of the conclusions of the fraud report was that over one-quarter of the fraud cases failed to lead to administrative or criminal penalties.[19] The second report showed that municipalities made less effort to help single parents to find work than other people entitled to social assistance.[20] The Netherlands Court of Audit conducts inquiries of this kind in the framework of its legal mission, which is to review and improve the lawful, effective, efficient and honest operation of public administration.

2.4 Supervisory bodies

The supervisory bodies produce a stream of reports and assessments, some of which are connected with the cycle of accountability of the social security administrative bodies vis-à-vis the supervisory body and – ultimately – the political representative bodies (parliament, municipal council). The former Social Insurance Supervisory Board's[21] annual assessments of the implementation of the social security laws are well known. These assessments culminated in the issue of declarations of lawfulness in which the Social Insurance Supervisory Board gave its opinion regarding the lawfulness of the implementation of the social security laws by the administrative bodies of the employed persons' and national insurance schemes. The Social Insurance Supervisory Board's assessment was focused on financial-legal aspects; the main concern was whether the administrative bodies' expenses and receipts in the year in question had been effected in accordance with the legislation and regulations. An unqualified opinion was given if the error percentage was less than 1%. If the error percentage was 3% or more an adverse opinion was given. A distinction was made between financial errors and formal errors (without financial consequences), for example errors consisting of disregard for correct procedures.

For many years in succession the opinion given regarding the performance of the body implementing the employed persons' insurance schemes was mainly negative. The number of errors was always much too high. By contrast, the Social Insurance Supervisory Board gave a positive assessment regarding the performance of the *Sociale Verzekeringsbank*, with the exception of the

---

19 Netherlands Court of Audit press release, 14 December 2000.

20 Netherlands Court of Audit press release, 14 May 2003.

21 Now: Inspection Service for Work and Income.

implementation of the National Survivors' Benefits Act, which did not meet the standard of lawfulness.

After the *Wet structuur uitvoeringsorganisatie werk en inkomen* (Structure of Administration Agencies (Employment and Income) Act) – a legal regulation of the implementation structure of the employed persons' insurance schemes – had come into force, in 2003 the annual external declarations of lawfulness were abolished. The emphasis shifted even further towards *self-accountability* on the part of the administrative bodies. Accountability for the lawfulness of implementation plays an important role in this context. This accountability is still very much focused on financial aspects; the accountability report is accompanied by an audit report in which an accountant gives an opinion regarding the lawfulness of the acquisition and expenditure of resources by bodies including the *Uitvoeringsinstituut Werknemersverzekeringen* and the *Sociale Verzekeringsbank*, and the lawfulness of implementation by the municipalities. Since 2003 the most important party to which the social security administrative bodies have had to account for themselves has been the Minister of Social Affairs and Employment. In turn, the Minister reports to Parliament. With regard to implementation, the Minister breathes down the necks of the administrative bodies, which are legally separate from the departmental organization.[22] For the execution of his supervisory task he enlists the aid of the Inspection Service for Work and Income, which is a departmental body, although the Inspection Service is some distance away from the Minister; a somewhat ambiguous construction.

As far as lawfulness is concerned, the *Uitvoeringsinstituut Werknemersverzekeringen* still oversteps the 1% error margin, a level which involves many many millions of euros. Promptness of the provision of benefits also still often fails to meet the legal standards, as was shown by the Minister of Social Affairs and Employment's report on the implementation of the *Wet structuur uitvoeringsorganisatie werk en inkomen* in 2005. While the *Sociale Verzekeringsbank*'s unlawfulness ratings remained within the legal limits in 2005, the promptness of their provision of benefits still required improvement.[23]

The origins of many investigations held by supervisory bodies lie in the supervisory body's annual investigation plan. Others are linked to incidents which have occurred during the year. The supervisory body itself may decide to initiate an investigation, but it may also be requested to do so by the responsible minister. An example of the second case is the investigation undertaken by the Inspection Service for Work and Income at the request of the Minister of Social Affairs and Employment into the way the *Uitvoeringsinstituut Werknemersverzekeringen* treats its clients. This investigation (2006) resulted from concern in Parliament and on the part of the minister about the persistent stream of

---

[22] The bodies concerned are so-called independent administrative bodies which – at least theoretically – enjoy a high degree of autonomy. However, legal reality and everyday practice show a different picture; a typical feature is the strongly proactive role of the Minister of Social Affairs and Employment.

[23] *TK* 2005/06, 26 448, no. 271, pp. 4 and 9.

complaints about the careless and discourteous treatment of clients on incapacity benefits by staff of the *Uitvoeringsinstituut Werknemersverzekeringen.*[24]

I will mention a few examples of investigations relating to the provision of social assistance. The municipality of Amsterdam's implementation of the *Algemene bijstandswet* (Social Assistance Act) fell far below the standard for years. This led to the placement of a departmental official at the Social Services of the municipality of Amsterdam – a ministerial intervention without any legal basis – and the repeated imposition of financial sanctions[25] on the municipality of Amsterdam. The Inspection Service for Work and Income followed the municipality's attempts to get its implementation under control again closely.[26] An example of a completely different nature is an investigation by the Inspection Service for Work and Income into the outsourcing of the implementation of the *Algemene bijstandwet* by the Dutch municipality of Maarssen to a private institution. The work outsourced included the assessment of applications for social assistance – the so-called assessment of claims. Outsourcing was a politically sensitive issue, especially with regard to the assessment of claims, a core component of implementation of the Act. Outsourcing the assessment of claims was deemed to contravene the regulation then in force; the assessment of claims belonged in the public domain. After intervention by the Minister of Social Affairs and Employment the municipality of Maarssen stopped outsourcing the implementation.[27] In the present *Wet werk en bijstand* (Work and Social Assistance Act) the assessment of claims is explicitly reserved for the municipal bodies responsible for implementing the Act. Other components of the implementation, such as the payment of the benefits, may be outsourced.

2.5 Parliament

Parliament also sometimes conducts an inquiry related to the quality of the implementation of social security. A notorious example was the parliamentary inquiry into the operation of the social security administrative bodies in the early 1990s (1992-1993). One of the conclusions of the parliamentary committee of inquiry (Buurmeijer Committee) was that the administrative bodies of the time, the now no longer existing industrial insurance boards, had not operated effectively in realizing the objectives of the legislators. Among other things, there was evidence of unlawful implementation ('application of the Act not in accordance with the law') of the provisions of the *Wet op de arbeidsongeschiktheidsverzekering* (Disablement Benefits Act), an insurance act for employees.[28] The industrial insurance boards' policy was determined to a

24 Inspectie Werk en Inkomen (2006).

25 The sanctions consisted of reductions in the national government's financial compensation of social assistance expenditure by the municipality of Amsterdam.

26 Cf. Inspectie Werk en Inkomen (2003).

27 Aanhangsel Handelingen (Appendix) to *TK* 2001/02, no. 686.

28 Enquêtecommissie uitvoeringsorganen sociale verzekeringen (1993), p. 23.

high degree by social partners, employers' organizations and employers' unions, which were thought to have been using the *Wet op de arbeidsongeschiktheidsverzekering* improperly for years as a redundancy scheme. This rather harsh political judgment on the part of the Buurmeijer Committee led to the decision by the Lower House of the Dutch Parliament that the social partners should no longer be allowed to bear the responsibility for medical examinations and assessments of the degree of incapacity of individuals who claimed to be eligible for benefits by virtue of the *Wet op de arbeidsongeschiktheidsverzekering*. This was the beginning of the removal of social partners from social security ten years later, a fundamental change in the structure of implementation, which had always been dominated by social partners ever since the first appearance of social security in the early twentieth century.

Generally speaking Parliament's involvement with the quality of implementation is less spectacular. As we have seen, Parliament is notified of the accountability reports drawn up annually by the social security administrative bodies for the Minister of Social Affairs and Employment and the minister's opinion of these reports. Parliament is also involved in the periodic evaluation of new legislation. An example is the evaluation carried out in 1999 of the Social Security Benefits (Fines, Measures, Recovery and Collection) Act. In 1996 this act introduced a strict system of sanctions (cuts in benefits, punitive fines) for persons entitled to benefits who failed to meet obligations such as the obligation (for unemployed persons) to accept appropriate work and the obligation to promptly provide the administrative bodies with any information which might be relevant to their entitlement to benefits. The report *Straffen met beleid* brought out by the former supervisory body, the previously mentioned Social Insurance Supervisory Board, is important in this context. This report concluded, among other things, that the staff of the administrative bodies ignored the legal obligation to impose sanctions, mitigated sanctions, or failed to impose sanctions on grounds not based on the law.[29] It was also established that it was very likely that the Social Security Benefits (Fines, Measures, Recovery and Collection) Act had contributed to a greater degree of inequality in the application of the sanctions instrument.[30] As far as the authority and effectiveness of the Social Security Benefits (Fines, Measures, Recovery and Collection) Act were concerned, these were clearly fatal conclusions.

2.6 Third party assessors

Sometimes assessors enlist the aid of third parties to gather data, to analyse a problem or to make recommendations. For example, in 1993 the Minister and the Secretary of State for Social Affairs and Employment set up a committee of inquiry into the application of the *Algemene bijstandwet* (Social Assistance Act) (Van der Zwan Committee). This was prompted by indications

[29] College van toezicht sociale verzekeringen (1999), p. 16.

[30] College van toezicht sociale verzekeringen (1999), p. 15.

that there was a considerable amount of 'improper use' of the *Algemene bijstandswet*, the social security safety net dating from 1965. The committee was to examine the severity and scope and the underlying causes of this improper use and make recommendations as to how to make the *Algemene bijstandswet* less vulnerable to abuse. On the basis of file investigation[31] the committee concluded that in practice, 'across the board and in the vast majority of municipalities', implementation was typified by inadmissible shortcomings – not exactly a favourable assessment. The committee's findings and recommendations led to fundamental, often rather bureaucratic alterations in the new *Algemene bijstandswet* which was being debated by the Lower House of Parliament at the time. Recently this act – and most of those alterations – were laid aside when the present Algemene bijstandswet came into force: the *Wet werk en bijstand* (Work and Social Assistance Act).

The government sometimes also asks third parties to assess the primary decision-making process. An example is the investigation conducted by Winnie Sorgdrager, former Minister of Justice, at the request of the *Uitvoeringsinstituut Werknemersverzekeringen*, which led to a report titled *De last van bezwaar*.[32] This report dating from 2004 examines not only the objection procedure but also the relationship between the objection procedure and the quality of the primary process. Sorgdrager's conclusion about the quality of the *Uitvoeringsinstituut Werknemersverzekeringen* is considerably more positive than that of the Minister (see 2.4). While acknowledging that improvements are possible and necessary, she characterizes the *Uitvoeringsinstituut Werknemersverzekeringen* as 'an organization which performs well'.[33] The Minister is probably the one who is right, although Sorgdrager does seem to have the benefit recipients on her side (see 1).

2.7 Jurisprudence

In jurisprudence relatively little interest has been shown in the quality of the primary decision-making process. The focus of attention is on the legislation and case law, which – from the point of view of the primary decision-making process – can be regarded as quality factors (4.3). For example, in the framework of the first evaluation of the *Algemene wet bestuursrecht* empirical research was conducted into the operation of several social security administrative bodies. Also relevant in this context are the studies conducted by the University of Groningen for the Social Insurance Supervisory Board with regard to the *Algemene wet bestuursrecht* and the social security contributions for employees, the *Werkloosheidswet* (Unemployment Act), and the *Algemene Kinderbijslagwet* (Child Benefits Act) dating from 1997. An important finding was that in general the administrative bodies investigated acted in accordance with the provisions

---

31 Enquêtecommissie uitvoeringsorganen sociale verzekeringen (1993), p. 1.

32 Sorgdrager (2004).

33 Sorgdrager (2004), p. 35.

of the *Algemene wet bestuursrecht*. Their compliance was 'very satisfactory'.[34] In 2002 the results were published of a new evaluation of the *Algemene wet bestuursrecht*. One of the conclusions which can be drawn from this evaluation is that the administrative bodies very frequently fail to make decisions within the legal time limits,[35] a conclusion which sounds familiar. In a recent legal essay about the wage sanction in the *Wet op de arbeidsongeschiktheidsverzekering* (Disablement Benefits Act) already referred to (section. 2.1), the author concluded that the way this sanction was applied by the *Uitvoeringsinstituut Werknemersverzekeringen* was unlawful.[36] Some time ago the *Centrale Raad van Beroep* endorsed this opinion.[37] The legislation has now been adapted.

3 Assessment criteria

The various assessors apply their own criteria – which are not always explicitly formulated – in assessing the primary decision-making process. Apart from *policy-related* criteria (as applied for example by the Buurmeijer Committee), other standards by which the decision-making process is judged are those of *lawfulness, effectiveness, cost-effectiveness* and *propriety*. Sometimes these standards are laid down explicitly in the law; for example Article 37 *Wet structuur uitvoeringsorganisatie werk en inkomen*, Article 76 *Wet werk en bijstand* (Work and Social Assistance Act), Article 9:27 *Algemene wet bestuursrecht* and Articles 213 and 213a *Gemeentewet* (Municipalities Act). The Netherlands Court of Audit also applies the standard of *integrity*, but this standard is not referred to in the law. It is only relatively recently that attention has been paid to the concept of integrity in public administration; the concept came to the fore in the early 1990s.

From a legal point of view lawfulness is the dominant standard, and with respect to lawfulness the court is the obvious authority. Formally the court is always right. This does not alter the fact that the court may make a legally incorrect decision – but for the time being a decision of this kind is still binding. Some parties may be of the opinion that a judicial decision which is formally correct is nevertheless flawed, and that a different decision, which meets the wishes of the citizen to a higher degree, is desirable. Criticism of this kind may be found in academic circles, legal assistance agencies and stakeholder organizations. The administrative body may also consider a court ruling incorrect or undesirable, but for the time being it must comply with the ruling. Generally it will in fact do so, but there are exceptions. An example is that the administrative bodies do not comply with the judgment of the Supreme Court – the highest court in the Netherlands – of 11 July 2003, *Rechtspraak Sociale Verzeke-*

[34] See e.g. College van toezicht sociale verzekeringen (1997), p. 10.

[35] Commissie evaluatie Awb II (2002), p. 25.

[36] Noordam (2004), p. 447.

[37] *Centrale Raad van Beroep* 22 February 2006, *RSV* 2006/99.

ring 2003/242, because, like the Minister of Social Affairs and Employment, it considers the Supreme Court's views on the social security legislation applicable to international postings incorrect. They declared this publicly, which constitutionally speaking may be regarded as a rather strange move.[38]

4 Administrative bodies and quality

4.1 Introduction

The administrative bodies are paying an increasing amount of attention to the quality of implementation. For example, the importance of good quality in implementation is highlighted in the mission statement of the *Sociale Verzekeringsbank*. In terms reminiscent of 'marketing speak', the *Sociale Verzekeringsbank* says of itself: 'Service-oriented and socially aware, the SVB aims to be the best implementor of state financial schemes for individuals'.[39] This is a relatively recent development, which implies that in many cases the administrative bodies are still working on the professionalization of the quality aspect. This is certainly true of an institution like the *Uitvoeringsinstituut Werknemersverzekeringen*, which has only existed for a few years (2003) and is the product of a merger of five other implementing organizations. The *Uitvoeringsinstituut Werknemersverzekeringen* had to get all these component parts, each with its own corporate culture and administrative system, heading in the same direction as soon as possible. At the same time, in this instable organizational environment, it had to implement several major legislative operations, which also had drastic staffing and organizational consequences. The key word in the professionalization of the quality aspect is quality management. The administrative bodies' long-range plans are chock-full of ambitions, which for the *Uitvoeringsinstituut Werknemersverzekeringen* and the *Sociale Verzekeringsbank* are partly a result of the very detailed agreements about, for example, 'implementation performance indicators' which are reached between the *Uitvoeringsinstituut Werknemersverzekeringen* and the *Sociale Verzekeringsbank* and the Minister of Social Affairs and Employment on this score.[40] These agreements illustrate the limited independence of these independent administrative bodies in practice (cf. 2.4). In their annual reports the administrative bodies give detailed accounts of their achievements with respect to implementation. Performance is compared with the long-range objectives. Attention is paid to the organization of quality within the institutions, to the problems involved in coordinating the various components of the organizations with their decentralized branches, to measuring the quality of production, to benchmarking and certification by the Inter-

---

[38] Cf. Aanhangsel Handelingen (Appendix) to *TK* 2003/04, no. 172.

[39] Sociale Verzekeringsbank (2004), p. 11. http://www.svb.nl/internet/uk/about_the_svb.

[40] See *TK* 2003/04, 26 448, no. 98, pp. 6-7.

national Organization for Standardization, and to social policy. This last aspect reflects the importance of 'satisfied' employees.

4.2 A broad concept of quality

The concept of quality used by the administrative bodies is a broad one; it is not limited to 'correct' implementation in the legal or financial-legal sense, in other words quality in the sense of *lawfulness* – the quality concept highlighted in this volume. The administrative bodies' concept of quality also includes – at least – the idea that implementation should be *effective, cost-effective, prompt* and *client-oriented*.[41] It is not clear what the precise interrelationships between these aspects are; nor is it clear whether there is any particular hierarchy, although sometimes the lawfulness of implementation is referred to as the primary aspect of quality. For example, the *Sociale Verzekeringsbank* states in so many words that its main objective in carrying out its tasks is to meet the standards of lawfulness which apply.[42] But there are also examples where lawfulness has disappeared from the scene.[43] If lawfulness is the main priority – as in the case of the *Sociale Verzekeringsbank* – this does necessarily imply that lawfulness always has priority, for instance over cost-effectiveness. Cost-effectiveness is a standard which may conflict with the standard of lawfulness. For example, double-checking decisions relating to benefits claims promotes lawfulness, but does not rate highly as far as cost-effectiveness is concerned. This is a policy dilemma for the administrative bodies, but not for others, such as the individual interested party or the court; their only point of reference is lawfulness.

Within the domain of the *Uitvoeringsinstituut Werknemersverzekeringen* (Employees' Insurance and Benefits Office), effectiveness may for instance be related to the objective of getting people off benefits and into employment. This objective is translated into percentages of successful reintegration projects, which vary among different target groups. Sometimes specific numbers of benefit claimants returning to employment are mentioned. For example, within its general objective of achieving as low as possible a number of people on social assistance, the municipality of Groningen aims to have 665 individuals return to mainstream jobs and 415 to subsidized jobs.[44] Cost-effectiveness has to do with the relationship between production (numbers of people on benefits, numbers of reintegrations, etc.) and the human and material resources required to achieve this production. Cost-effectiveness can be expressed in the costs of

---

41 See for example UWV (2003) p. 17. The Uitvoeringsinstituut Werknemersverzekeringen (UWV; Employees' Insurance and Benefits Office's) annual reports also show that quality and quality management are essential aspects of implementation.

42 Sociale Verzekeringsbank (2004) p. 21.

43 Cf. Dienst Sociale Zaken en Werk gemeente Groningen (2003) issued by the Department of Social Affairs and Employment of the municipality of Groningen, which no longer expressly refers to lawfulness as an independent aspect of quality.

44 Dienst Sociale Zaken en Werk gemeente Groningen (2003), p. 17.

implementation per client (party entitled to monetary benefits or other services; employer legally bound to pay national insurance contributions). Promptness, in legal terms an aspect of lawfulness, is the clearest, most measurable factor. It relates to the promptness of the decisions which are to be made, usually in response to an application for benefits. But promptness may also be involved in cases in which the initiative to make a decision lies with the administrative body. For instance, the *Uitvoeringsinstituut Werknemersverzekeringen* aims to determine 99% of the premium invoices – for the employee insurance contributions to be paid by employers – by 31 December of the year in question.[45] Sometimes special standards of promptness are formulated for relatively independent components of the decision-making process. *Client orientation*, the broadest quality standard from a systematic point of view, is interpreted in quite a variety of ways. The most important aspect of client orientation is whether or not the clients are satisfied with the service provided by the administrative body (by telephone, in letters, etc.). But other matters may also fall into this category, such as information, the use of Internet to apply for benefits, how much input interested parties have in the choice of a reintegration company, and the organization's periodic consultation with stakeholder groups about certain aspects of the implementation. In some cases, namely in those related to the treatment of parties entitled to benefits and parties legally bound to pay national insurance contributions, client orientation is reminiscent of the standard of propriety in the *Algemene wet bestuursrecht*. The administrative bodies also formulate certain objectives – sometimes very specific ones – relating to this aspect. For example, the *Uitvoeringsinstituut Werknemersverzekeringen* and the *Sociale Verzekeringsbank* aim to achieve a level of customer satisfaction of about 6.5 (out of 10).[46] The municipality of Groningen keeps things a little more general: it aims at 'satisfied clients'.[47]

4.3 The organization of quality

Quality is not something to be taken for granted; quality can be created. The administrative bodies have to organize the level of quality they want themselves or that is required by third parties. The successful organization of quality requires administrative bodies to have insight into the factors which may have a positive or negative influence on the quality of implementation (both processes and products).

Which *quality factors* influence the quality of implementation? As we have seen, the factors involved are those which are thought to have a positive or negative influence on the quality of implementation. Whether this is in fact the case

45 Since 2006 the UWV has no longer been responsible for collecting the contributions for employees' insurance. This task is now performed by the national tax office.

46 Uitvoerinsginstituut werknemersverzekeringen (2004), p. 14 and Sociale Verzekeringsbank (2004), p. 23.

47 Dienst Sociale Zaken en Werk gemeente Groningen (2003), p. 17.

will have to be investigated in further detail. An interesting point is whether it is possible to distinguish factors which are typical for social security organizations as opposed to factors which are universally important in determining the quality of administrative organizations.

The most important thing is that the administrative body in question is convinced of the importance of quality and is also prepared to deploy sufficient human and material resources to achieve it. It is equally obvious that the organization must have expert staff at its disposal. In addition, there must be practicable regulations which also provide a certain minimum of stability – standards which social security legislation certainly does not meet in all cases. It is impossible to imagine 'benefits factories' like the *Uitvoeringsinstituut Werknemersverzekeringen* and the *Sociale Verzekeringsbank* without automation. Approximately 90% of the implementation of the *Algemene Kinderbijslagwet* (Child Benefits Act) is done by computers. The implementation process and the monitoring process related to it must be abuse-proof. Automation is of assistance here as well (linking of databases). Too much dependency on other organizations may have an adverse effect on an administrative body's own implementation process. An example is the role of the Centre for Work and Income specified in the *Wet structuur uitvoeringsorganisatie werk en inkomen*. The Centre for Work and Income is responsible for collecting the applications for benefits submitted by unemployed people and people who have to rely on social assistance for the *Uitvoeringsinstituut Werknemersverzekeringen* and the municipalities.[48] The fact that the Centre for Work and Income is in charge of this initial stage may lead to problems in the next stage of the process, namely the assessment of these submissions by the *Uitvoeringsinstituut Werknemersverzekeringen* and the municipalities, for example due to incomplete data collection by the Centre for Work and Income; it may also have an adverse effect on the promptness of the decisions the *Uitvoeringsinstituut Werknemersverzekeringen* and the municipalities make, for instance if the Centre for Work and Income is late in sending on the files. Complex legal problems, many individual assessments, many transfer points and a high level of policy freedom are not conducive to raising the quality of implementation. The same is true of other factors such as work pressure, the dominant management style in the organization, the quality of the employment terms and working conditions, continual overhauls and the – sometimes pathological – interference of politics in the organization and details of implementation.

The aim of the organization of quality is on the one hand to exclude factors which have an adverse effect on quality and on the other hand to strengthen the factors to which a positive effect can be attributed. The administrative bodies can do a lot themselves, by promoting staff expertise, organizing the work in a different way, applying internal and external benchmarking, investigating areas of poor quality in their implementation and introducing quality charters.

In this context administrative bodies must be on the alert for any signals suggesting lack of quality. Cases of fraud, anonymous complaints about imple-

---

[48] http://www.cwinet.nl/nl/about_cwi.asp.

mentation, rulings by the court and the National ombudsman, recommendations made by clients' participation councils – committees of people entitled to benefits which are linked to the administrative bodies and have an advisory role –, criticism by stakeholder groups and media reports (with parliamentary questions following like Pavlovian reactions) can all be regarded as *quality signals*. Complaints play a particularly prominent role; they can be regarded as criticism of the quality of implementation, but also as free advice from experts by experience. At the same time, the significance of complaints is limited, even though about 50% of complaints are upheld.[49] The reason is that most complaints are about the duration of processing applications and the treatment of interested parties by the staff of the administrative body concerned.[50] These are classic, persistent implementation problems and experience has shown that little benefit is to be gained from them.

The administrative bodies themselves also regularly investigate certain aspects of their implementation. The outcomes of these investigations are also seen as quality signals. In 1992 a report was published of an investigation conducted by the Social Services of the municipality of Groningen. This report, which aroused a great deal of publicity, stated that in about 30% of social assistance cases there was evidence of fraud. This investigation was an important trigger for the formation of the Van der Zwan Committee, also referred to in 2.6. It should be noted that by no means all internal investigations are made public. Administrative bodies also occasionally call in external agencies to investigate their organizations, which may lead to the rearrangement or outsourcing of tasks, changes in procedures and – more generally – to changes in or an overhaul of the organization. This type of investigation also has to do not only with fashion but with quality (of the organization).

4.4 Learning and improving

Organizations should learn from quality signals, but generally the learning process does not take place spontaneously; it too needs to be organized. In this connection it should be borne in mind that while many signals do not go further than the incident level, some of them indicate *structural* quality defects, which should be a reason to take action. Improvement entails adapting procedures, training staff, cracking down on management contracts and altering quality objectives or formulating new ones. The important thing is to define points which need improvement and to draw up improvement programmes in order to redress the detected shortcomings. The actions involved are voluntary ones, a product of the modern quality management mantra of 'ongoing learning

49 Uitvoeringsinsituut Werknemersverzekeringen (2006), p. 47.

50 60% of the complaints submitted about the UWV had to do with the duration of processing and the treatment of clients. Uitvoeringsinstituut Werknemersverzekeringen (2006), p. 25. For the *Sociale Verzekeringsbank* (Social Insurance Bank) the percentage was over 50%. Sociale Verzekeringsbank (2004), p. 47.

and improvement'. In the background a role is played by the formal correction mechanism which is at the disposal of the supervisory bodies and those politically responsible. Acting in violation of the acknowledged quality criteria may lead to all sorts of negative consequences for the administrative body in question: unfavourable publicity, closer monitoring, being placed under guardianship, receiving instructions, financial sanctions, dismissal of administrators, in short a further reduction in the relative autonomy of the administrative bodies.

5 Concluding remarks

What is the situation in the Netherlands at present as far as the quality of implementation in the social security sector is concerned? It is not difficult to present a rather negative picture based on the material available. Just combine the findings of the Van der Zwan Committee, the 25% of appeals to the court which are upheld, the chaos which reigns at the Social Services of Amsterdam, the findings of the National ombudsman, the *Uitvoeringsinstituut Werknemersverzekeringen*'s inadequate lawfulness scores year in year out, and the large number of well-founded complaints lodged by members of the public about the processing time taken by the administrative bodies and their treatment of the public. The *Uitvoeringsinstituut Werknemersverzekeringen* in particular does not look too good. But it is questionable whether this method produces an accurate and representative picture. The evidence involved actually consists of no more than impressions. There has been no systematic, sufficiently independent investigation of the quality of the primary decision-making process over a broad area. Therefore it is not possible to make well-founded judgments on the basis of the material discussed. Moreover, the picture we have outlined is incomplete. For example, the important sector of the social health insurance schemes has not been discussed and the municipal social insurance regulations only marginally. The fact that the various assessors work according to their own quality concepts, that the interrelationships of those quality concepts are unclear, that there is no systematic overview of the factors which determine the quality of implementation, and that there is a lack of insight into the influence of these factors means that it is impossible to make universal judgments; it also means that research is badly needed. Moreover, it is relatively easy to indicate even more gaps in our knowledge about the issue of 'quality and social security'.

In making a qualitatively defensible quality judgment of implementation it is important not to judge a snapshot but to look at the long-term picture, so that it becomes clear whether the shortcomings observed are mere incidents or structural defects. Incidents cannot always be avoided, but structural shortcomings can be rectified. However, this requires insight into the factors which have a positive or negative influence on the process of primary decision-making and the way these factors operate. At present this insight is not present to a sufficient extent.

In recent years the social security administrative bodies have – rightly – been paying a lot of attention to quality assurance. Formulating annual quality objectives, measuring and evaluating performance, judging by results, and developing and implementing improvement programmes have become standard features of administrative bodies' culture. Client orientation and client satisfaction, concepts which admittedly are not always defined, are the ultimate goal. So long as the report ratings are good and the target values are achieved, then the implementing body and the monitoring bodies are satisfied. A perspective of this kind may lead to dutiful obedience to the rules, in the knowledge that the intended rating will then be attained. This leaves little room for an administrative attitude of helpfulness, service, turning a blind eye to violations in certain circumstances, and actively 'tracking down' interested parties (to ensure people do not miss out on what they are entitled to). The current goal of maximum efficiency in the implementation of social security regulations is not conducive to this kind of attitude either. In fact, it is questionable whether there is any room at all for a somewhat more 'sympathetic' style of implementation, which would be in line with the concept of a service-oriented government. After all, in many cases social security entails applying rules which can lead to only one outcome. Then there is little freedom in policy and assessment. Nevertheless, this does not mean that sympathetic implementation is impossible. At the same time, 'sympathetic' does not imply that the legal boundaries may be overstepped.

It is good to see that in striving towards quality the administrative bodies do not limit themselves to the primary decision-making process, with lawfulness as the most important assessment indicator. The administrative bodies' quality assurance covers a wider area. Often 'supra-individual' concerns are involved: reducing the number of people claiming disablement benefits by 10%, a certain percentage of successful reintegrations, catching up with backlogs of work, a politically desirable reduction in implementation costs, etc. The efforts which administrative bodies have to make in these areas may be of considerable influence on the quality of the primary process.

Finally, the administrative bodies should be assessed in a reasonable manner. Again I would like to point out the many millions of decisions per year which are irreproachable. Moreover, the administrative bodies themselves are not always in control. For instance, sometimes the legislation produced by the Ministry of Social Affairs and Employment is weak, but the administrative bodies have to make the best of it. Over the past decades major changes have taken place in the social security system at a rapid pace, and a large number of significant changes are still forthcoming. These are all factors which generate mistakes in implementation. Another fact which should be borne in mind is that the administrative bodies are the first in line and may be corrected by other players – the court in particular – which are in a much more comfortable position, having wisdom in hindsight. These corrections imply that the administrative bodies have acted unlawfully. Formally this is correct, but an approach of this kind is not always just. Justice is a joint product of three responsible parties: the *legislators* supply the raw materials, the *administrative body* provides the ingredients and the *court* prepares the meal and ultimately serves it. If the meal does not go down well, it is not necessarily the fault of the ingredients. The legislators and the court certainly do not always supply the desired quality either.

CHAPTER 9

Quality in Dutch asylum law: from 'strict but fair', to 'fast but good'?

H.B. Winter & K.F. Bolt

1 Introduction

The quality of primary decision-making in Dutch aliens law has been a bone of contention for many years, especially with regard to asylum cases. There are many sources which testify to problems in this branch of law. The problems were particularly severe under the revised *Vreemdelingenwet* (Aliens Act) which came into force in 1994. Case law, evaluation studies[1] and other literature[2] all provide evidence that the quality of aliens law decisions in the Netherlands left much to be desired. One of the two main objectives of the *Vreemdelingenwet 2000* (Aliens Act 2000) was to raise the quality of decisions relating to applications for asylum. The other main objective was to speed up the administrative decision-making process. To this end the objection procedure, which provided asylum seekers whose applications had been rejected with an opportunity to ask the administrative body concerned to reconsider the decision, was abolished. In the course of this objection procedure, the asylum seeker in question often had a chance to explain his or her objections at greater length at a hearing. It was thought that doing away with this review procedure would lead to faster decision-making with respect to individual files; the bureaucratic capacities of the Dutch *Immigratie- en Naturalisatiedienst* (IND, Immigration and Naturalization Service) could be used for the primary decision-making process and disputes would be brought before a court sooner, so that both the administrative body and the asylum seeker would have a clear and definite answer sooner. However, it was thought possible that doing away with the administrative review would have a significant disadvantage, namely that the quality of the asylum decisions presented to the court would be poorer. In order to limit this possible reduction in quality, a 'notification of intent' was introduced into the application procedure. The administrative body first issues an intended decision to which the asylum seeker and his or her legal aid lawyer can respond by submitting their view of the situation. Then a definitive primary decision is made, which can be appealed to the district court.

The *Vreemdelingenwet 2000* aimed to speed up the decision-making process and at the same time to improve quality.[3] There seems to be a certain tension between these two goals. Faster decision-making may well have a negative impact on the care taken in preparing decisions. In this contribution we will examine which factors apart from the speed of decision-making may influence the quality of decision-making in asylum cases. These factors can be divided into legal and non-legal factors. In section 2 we will focus on the legal factors, which are mainly connected with interventions by the legislator. But not only legal factors are relevant – especially in asylum law. In section 3 we will address

---

1 Visser & Homburg Regioplan Onderzoek (1995); Berenschot (1995).

2 See for example Bröring & Winter (1996), p. 11-29; Borger, Winter & Scheltema, (1996); Doornbos & Sellies (1997); Hoogvliet (2001).

3 See the explanatory memorandum to the bill and the memorandum in response to the report, *TK* 1998/99, 26 732, nos. 3 and 7 respectively.

the structure of the decision-making process and other non-legal factors which determine the outcomes of that process. In many cases the factors or variables we discuss do not stand alone, since they in turn are influenced by other variables. For example, the *Vreemdelingenwet 2000* cannot be seen in isolation from the general administrative law framework; nor can the *Vreemdelingenwet 2000* remain unaffected by European harmonization of asylum policy since the Treaty of Amsterdam. It is clear that we have to limit ourselves in our exploration of potentially relevant factors.

In section 4 we will analyse recent developments on the basis of generalized figures relating to decision-making in asylum cases during the past few years. Using reports by the National ombudsman, annual reports from the *Immigratie- en Naturalisatiedienst* (IND) and the district courts, and the detailed evaluation study of the effects of the *Vreemdelingenwet 2000*, we will discuss the influence of factors which may be relevant to decision-making in practice. In section 5 we will focus on the evaluation of the *Vreemdelingenwet 2000*, which was completed in 2006. On the basis of these data we will attempt to analyse the relationship between legal and non-legal factors and the quality of decision-making in asylum cases. This contribution is mainly exploratory in nature; it leads to the formulation of a number of research questions and conjectures. Some of these conjectures may be found in the concluding section – section 6.

2 Legal factors: changes in the asylum system

2.1 Fast but good

In the early 1990s Dutch authorities responsible for dealing with asylum cases were swamped with huge numbers of asylum applications. The IND and the judiciary were unable to deal with these applications quickly enough. As a result, asylum seekers got caught up in procedures which often lasted for years. This led to situations of uncertainty, especially for the asylum seekers involved, but also for the community. On 1 January 1994 an amendment of the *Vreemdelingenwet* came into force; its goal was to speed up the procedures. In order to achieve this goal, the admissions policy was tightened. This did not help: the number of asylum applications continued to grow and the attempt to cut down processing times failed. The government, which from 1998 to 2002 consisted of a coalition of social democrats and liberals, decided to try again, announcing in its coalition agreement that the procedures regulated in the *Vreemdelingenwet* would be improved and curtailed.[4] Speed and austerity were supposed to be the key features of the adapted policy. Five changes aimed at achieving this result were listed in the agreement. The quality of the first decision regarding the asylum application was to be improved considerably. Secondly, a rejection would mean that by law the authorities were entitled

4 *TK* 1997/98, 26 024, no. 9, pp. 86-87.

to give notice that the asylum seeker had to leave, and housing and support services would be terminated.[5] Thirdly, the administrative review stage would be abolished. A fourth alteration was that in future asylum seekers would be allowed to remain in the Netherlands while waiting for decisions in appeals to the district court. Finally, the possibility of appeal to a higher court would be introduced. Whereas only appeal to the district court had been possible previously under aliens law, in future asylum seekers would be able to appeal to the *Afdeling bestuursrechtspraak van de Raad van State* (Administrative Jurisdiction Division of the Council of State; herinafter *Raad van State*) against the district court's decision.

These amendments were in fact implemented. Improvement in the primary decision-making process was expected to result from the introduction of the 'notification of intent' procedure which was to become part of that process, replacing the administrative review stage. The *Vreemdelingenwet 2000*, which was introduced in April 2001, also included other changes. One significant change was the introduction of the 'two-step system' for granting residence permits: an asylum seeker is first given a residence permit for a limited period and then after being in the Netherlands for five years may apply for a permit for an unlimited period. As well as amendments to the Act there were also important policy changes which were not based on the *Vreemdelingenwet 2000*. One of these was the introduction and later tightening up of a quick decision-making procedure in asylum cases; according to this procedure, a request for asylum could initially be processed within 24 hours and later within 48 hours.[6] This accelerated decision-making procedure has always come in for a great deal of criticism, precisely because it entails a high risk of carelessness.

2.2 Notification of intent as opposed to objection procedure

In the *Vreemdelingenwet 2000* many improvements were made to the procedural provisions which applied to granting residence permits. A strict distinction was made in the Act between residence permits for asylum seekers and standard residence permits – i.e. residence permits granted in connection with work or family reunification. The objection stage of the asylum procedure was abolished. It was replaced by the 'notification of intent': the asylum seeker was to be given an opportunity to respond to an intended decision by submitting his or her point of view, after which a final decision would be made.

What is the difference between the objection procedure in the old Act and the notification of intent procedure which now applies? Under the old *Vreemde-*

[5] In the past separate decisions had had to be made about both the termination of housing and support services and the deportation of an asylum seeker. These decisions could then be contested in separate legal proceedings.

[6] According to Art. 1.1(f) Aliens Decree 2000, processing hours are the hours available at the application centre for investigation of the request. The hours from 6 p.m. to 8 a.m. and – except at the Schiphol application centre – the hours during weekends and public holidays do not count.

lingenwet, after receiving notification of the decision, the asylum seeker had four weeks – in derogation from the time limit of six weeks pursuant to Article 6:7 *Algemene wet bestuursrecht* (General Administrative Law Act) – to lodge an objection. In some cases the IND was obliged to seek the advice of an external body – the Advisory Committee on Alien Affairs. By virtue of Article 7:2 *Algemene wet bestuursrecht*, the interested party had to be heard before a decision could be made with regard to the objection.

By virtue of Article 39 of the *Vreemdelingenwet 2000*, if the Minister intends to reject a request for a residence permit for asylum or for the extension of a residence permit, the asylum seeker in question must be notified in writing of this intention and the reasons must be given. The asylum seeker may respond in writing to this notification by submitting his or her point of view. The time limit for this response is four weeks in the case of the rejection of a permit for a limited period or six weeks in the case of an intention to reject an application for extension of a permit for a limited period, to refuse a permit for an unlimited period, or to withdraw a permit.[7] However, this time limit is considerably shorter if the application is dealt with in the framework of the application centre procedure,[8] in which case only three processing hours are available to submit a point of view.[9] In the final decision rejecting the request the minister must respond to the point of view submitted.

The abolition of the objection procedure was a remarkable step. While on the one hand it was a way of speeding up the procedure, on the other hand it is questionable whether the substantive quality of the decisions can be guaranteed without an objection stage. After all, in administrative procedural law in general the objection stage is held in high regard. This preliminary procedure provides the administrative body with a second chance in the event that mistakes have been made in an initial decision. The procedure works like a filter: many conflicts are subsequently not brought before the court. If a case is in fact referred to the administrative court, a preliminary procedure means that a solid file has been built up, which facilitates the work of the court. Admittedly, this filter function is not as effective in asylum law as in other administrative areas. In a relatively high percentage of adverse decisions in response to objections, appeals were lodged all the same. When the *Vreemdelingenwet 2000* was introduced, more importance was attached to accelerating the procedures than to the advantages offered by the objection procedure. There have even been suggestions that the objection stage might be abolished in other areas as well.[10]

7 Art. 3.115(2) Aliens Decree 2000.

8 See section 3.2 for a more detailed description of the application centre procedure.

9 Art. 3.117(1-2) Aliens Decree 2000.

10 *TK* 1998/99, 26 732, no. 3, p. 10: 'The abolition of the objection stage is acceptable only if the quality of decisions on applications can be assured by including sufficient safeguards in the procedure. On the basis of the results of quality improvement in the various aliens departments and further decision-making as to the transfer of authority concerning the issue of permits for temporary residence from the Minister of Foreign Affairs to the Minister of Justice, it will be considered later whether the objection

All in all it seems as though the objection stage – which had become something of a sacred cow in administrative procedural law – is being demolished piece by piece. According to the 'direct appeal' provision of Article 7:1a *Algemene wet bestuursrecht* the compulsory objection procedure can be dispensed with if the administrative body consents to a request from the party with the objection to appeal directly to the administrative court.[11] The reasoning is that an objection procedure may mean an unnecessary, time-wasting duplication of work if consultation between the administrative body and the objecting party proves unable to settle the dispute. It seems that when a potential substantive improvement of a decision on the one hand is weighed against the speed at which that decision is reached, the first aspect is not always the one that wins out.

2.3 'Decisions with multiple consequences' and 'two-step residence permits'

Other means used to accelerate the procedure were to simplify it and to attach various legal consequences to rejections. Simplification of the procedure was achieved by introducing a system of 'two-step residence permits'. According to this system, when a residence permit for asylum is granted it is initially always a temporary permit, which can only be converted to a permit for an unlimited period after five years.[12] There are various grounds on which a residence permit for asylum may be granted, but they all lead to the same permit. This prevents the asylum seeker continuing with proceedings, even after receiving a permit, to try to procure a 'stronger' permit, as was customary under the older *Vreemdelingenwet*. Another aim of the new Act was to accelerate asylum procedures by ensuring that the rejection of an application for admission had various legal consequences relating to housing and support services and deportation. The decision is therefore referred to as a 'decision with multiple consequences'. A rejection also means that the asylum seeker may no longer lawfully remain in the Netherlands, that he or she must leave the Netherlands, that housing and support services will no longer be provided and that the competent authority may remove individuals who fail to leave the Netherlands of their own accord. Here again there is tension between speed and quality. The 'decision with multiple consequences' means that the IND has fewer decisions to make, which promotes speed. Moreover, the asylum seeker is not compelled to seek separate legal remedies to challenge separate decisions. On the other hand, splitting the decisions means that each point can be assessed separately.

procedure should eventually also be abolished in the case of regular procedures'. Various comments were made in response to this; see for example Winter & Schuringa (2005).

[11] This regulation came into effect on 1 September 2004.

[12] Originally this period was three years, but it has now been extended to five years in the Act passed on 24 June 2004 to amend the *Vreemdelingenwet 2000*, which provided for extension of the period for which the temporary residence permit for asylum is valid, Stb. 2004, 299. This Act came into force as of 1 September 2004 (Stb. 2004, 430).

But under the old *Vreemdelingenwet* it was already difficult for people to stay in the Netherlands if they had been refused residence permits. The 'decision with multiple consequences' seems to save time while the loss of quality may be limited. An important point is that under the *Vreemdelingenwet 2000* lodging an appeal in the first instance has suspensive effect, so that the asylum seeker may remain in the Netherlands while awaiting the outcome.

2.4 Appeal to a higher court

An appeal to a higher court leads to prolongation of the procedure. But this may mean that across the board the quality of the decisions is increased, since the possibility of lodging an appeal to a higher court provides greater legal unity and legal certainty in legal protection. In spite of these advantages, appeal to a higher court was not introduced into the whole of administrative procedural law. Under the old *Vreemdelingenwet* of 1994 further appeal was not possible either. This was compensated by the institution of a three-judge court at the competent district court of The Hague – the so-called Legal Uniformity Division, which was charged with settling the most important cases. The decisions of the Legal Uniformity Division were then regarded as indicative. Judges from various branches of the district court of The Hague alternated as members of this three-judge court. In itself this was an appropriate solution, but there is something to be said for introducing appeal to a higher court so that a different, higher judicial body can monitor uniformity. It is difficult to judge what the best solution is in asylum law, where time plays such an important role. At any rate, the legislators opted to introduce appeal to a higher court. In practice this does not take much more time because the *Raad van State* works very quickly. Figures relating to this may be found in section 4.5.

3 Non-legal factors determining legal quality

3.1 Introduction

Factors which influence the legal quality of a decision in an asylum case are determined not only by legislation but also by administrative policy, management decisions or the number of requests. In this section we will discuss a number of these factors which are not – or not directly – determined by the *Vreemdelingenwet 2000*.

3.2 The structure of the decision-making process: accelerated procedures at the application centres

For quite some time – since 1994 to be exact – there has been a distinction in asylum cases between a 'normal' procedure and an accelerated procedure. The accelerated procedure takes place at an application centre, of which there are two at present: at Schiphol and in Ter Apel.[13] At these application centres the decision-making process is focused on making quick decisions. Initially the application centre procedure was intended for applications which were 'certain to fail' – 'foreign nationals who claim to be "asylum seekers", but actually have flimsy stories (asylum tourism)' and 'other asylum seekers whose applications can be disposed of as inadmissible or manifestly unfounded without time-consuming investigation'.[14] Reference was made to the 'application centre criterion'. In the late 1990s the member of the government responsible for Alien Affairs tried to stretch this criterion to cover all cases for which no time-consuming investigation would be necessary. However, legal aid workers raised strong objections to this. The compromise reached was basically that the interpretation of the application centre criterion in the case law of the mid-1990s would be taken as the point of departure in practice. Agreements were also reached about the eligibility of several categories of cases for the application centre procedure. These agreements were laid down in the Aliens Circular (old). The *Vreemdelingenwet 2000* did not aim to make any changes to the way things were done at the application centres; nothing was regulated in the Act with respect to the application centre procedure. However, the Aliens Decree did include a certain measure of time – 48 processing hours – to be allocated to dealing with an application at an application centre (Article 3.112(1)(b), Aliens Decree 2000).[15] According to *Raad van State* case law, this means that no content-related criterion can be set – as had previously been the case – to determine which cases can be dealt with at an application centre. Any asylum application can be 'dealt with' at an application centre provided a decision regarding that application can be produced within 48 processing hours. In the past a case 'dealt with' in an application centre would by definition lead to a negative decision. Since April 2005 positive decisions have also been made at application centres. If an application is rejected at an application centre the decision can be brought before a district court, which examines the case to assess whether the minister has taken due care in reaching the negative decision.[16]

Dealing with asylum applications at application centres leads to fast decisions, but as far as the quality of the decisions is concerned it is very controversial.[17]

---

13 Due to over-capacity the application centre in Zevenaar was closed in the autumn of 2003 and converted into a processing office. Then the application centre at Rijsbergen was closed in the spring of 2004. At present (early 2007) plans are under discussion for an adaptation of the application centre procedure which might lead to the application centre in Zevenaar being opened again.

14 Letter from the Secretary of State for Justice to the President of the Lower House of the States-General, 7 June 1994, *NAV* 1994/6, p. 2.

15 Processing hours are the hours between 8 a.m. and 10 p.m.; see Art. 1.1(f) Aliens Decree 2000.

16 *Raad van State* 20 December 2001, *RV* 2001, 20, with note by Olivier; *Raad van State* 27 August 2001, *RV* 2001, 19, with note by Terlouw.

17 See for example Terlouw (ed.) (2003).

3.3 Quality and size of implementation system

If the regulations are satisfactory and the decision-making process is structured adequately, then some of the prerequisites for taking high-quality decisions have been met, but not enough. The implementation system must also be adequately equipped, both qualitatively and quantitatively, to perform the tasks assigned to it. In other words, there must be sufficient public servants who meet high standards. Under the 'old' *Vreemdelingenwet* the system was deficient in both respects – as is now acknowledged. Within the judiciary there were also backlogs which have only been converted to reasonably normal workloads since 2006. Staff shortages at the IND were compensated by hiring agency staff or at least temporary employees, as a result of which the quality of the decisions declined. This gave rise to a self-reinforcing effect: because a significant number of decisions on asylum applications were reversed (see Table 2 *infra*), the number of appeals to the court increased, so that backlogs also built up, as did the pressure on various 'links in the chain'.

Of course, the quality and size of an administrative implementation organization can be influenced. Investments can be made both in the size of an organization and in its quality – for example by providing additional training. Moreover, if these investments are structural in character, an administrative organization can build up experience and hold on to it. Just as an administrative organization can be improved by 'management decisions', certain measures may also lead to changes for the worse in the implementation organization. As a rule the quality of decisions will rise if more resources are made available and those resources can in fact be used for careful preparation of decisions. But the reverse is also true: the quality of decision-making may also decline rapidly due to deliberate management choices. It may be assumed that neither politicians nor senior civil servants strive towards poorer decisions. Nevertheless, government organizations also aim for an optimal mix of costs and benefits – for cost-effectiveness. Is this a goal which does not allow for concessions, in other words does it also apply to the legal quality of decision-making? Seen from a normative, rule of law point of view, it might be expected that the lawfulness of a decision is regarded as a more or less absolute quantity. Lawyers like to stress that there is no such thing as 'a bit more lawful' or 'a bit less lawful'. Nonetheless, it remains a relevant question whether in the everyday practice of decision-making – including decisions on asylum cases – the investments required to guarantee the quality of a decision are weighed against other factors. Obviously the assessment of lawfulness made by the court should be taken as the point of reference in determining the boundaries of this balancing process. In this respect strange things have been observed in aliens law in recent years. Since the introduction of the *Vreemdelingenwet 2000* it seems as though the assessments of lawfulness made by the judiciary have changed. For further discussion of this topic see section 4.5.

3.4 Quality and the number of applications

Management decisions may influence the quality of the handling of applications. The number of applications is a factor which influences the capacity needed. This number is not stable: asylum seekers leave their countries of origin as a result of events that are taking place there, and undeniably there are peaks in these developments. For example, the number of asylum applications from former Yugoslavia has dropped off considerably since the end of the war there (to 3% of the total number of applications in 2003, from Serbia and Montenegro). Apart from changes in the countries of origin which affect the number of applications, there is also incontrovertible evidence of 'rivalry' between the various reception countries in Europe. While the total number of applications within Europe has been declining since 2004, the applications are distributed across the countries in a different way each year. In the Netherlands the number of applications has dropped sharply since 2001. If the number of applications drops while capacity remains the same, more time is available to deal with the applications, which might mean an improvement in the quality of the decisions. Of course, in itself the quality of a decision says nothing about the outcome of the decision-making process. The relative numbers of applications granted and rejected may remain constant even though the overall quality of the decisions rises.

3.5 Speed and the number of applications

The size and quality of the administrative organization affect the quality of the decisions made. They also determine the speed with which the applications are processed. There seems to be a curious relationship between the number of asylum applications and the processing speed.[18] It is thought that for many years the number of applications in the Netherlands was significantly higher because of the refusal to increase staff numbers in the late 1980s and early 1990s. The explanation of this relationship may be that for asylum seekers – and probably for their travel agents in particular – one of the attractions of the Netherlands was that the lengthy decision-making process at least guaranteed shelter for a substantial period. When staff was in fact later expanded, around 2000 the average processing times dropped as a result.[19] The number of asylum applications started to fall as of 2000/2001.

---

[18] Grütters 2003, p. 23-32.

[19] As of 1 May 2002 the IND's staff size was over 3,700 FTEs. Practically all of these positions were filled. As a result of the strongly declining influx of asylum seekers an external recruitment halt has been announced for the IND and a project has begun to allocate some staff appointed for asylum cases to standard cases or deploy them as legal representatives.

3.6 Quality policy

Administrative organizations may establish policy with regard to the quality of service delivery. They may formulate objectives which are focused on the desired quality level of the decisions made. As part of this quality policy, standards may be set for the decision-making process; for example, a maximum acceptable number of judicial reversals may be laid down. Administrative bodies sometimes also lay down decision-making time limits for themselves in citizens' charters. Within the IND and the Aliens Department, in recent years policy focused on improving the quality of decision-making has been pursued on the basis of a quality assurance programme. The quality of decision-making can be influenced at the management level by adopting quality policy.

4 Decision-making in practice

In this section we will provide some initial insights into the effects of the *Vreemdelingenwet 2000* as regards its two most important objectives: speed and quality. To this end we will present figures relating to developments in asylum law, including the number of applicants, the application centre procedure, the duration of the decision-making process and the appeal procedures.

4.1 Number of applications

When the *Vreemdelingenwet 2000* was being prepared, the annual number of asylum seekers was estimated at 50,000.[20] In reality, even in the first year the *Vreemdelingenwet 2000* came into effect – 2001 – the number of applications submitted was lower than had been expected and it declined further in the succeeding years (see Table 1 *infra*). The figures for 2003 show a clear drop (±30%) in the number of applications in comparison with 2002. In 2002 the drop was over 40% as compared with 2001 and in 2001 the drop was 25% as compared with 2000. The trend continued unabated in 2004 with a total of 9,780 applications. In 2005 and 2006 the numbers rose again. According to the figures this was mainly as a result of the rise in numbers of second and consecutive applications by over 50%.[21] The numbers of first applications were 4,550 and 5,850 in 2005 and 2006 respectively. The decline in the number of applications seems to be good news as far as the expected quality of the decisions is concerned, since it may be assumed that if capacity remains the same there is more time to deal with each application so that the quality of the decisions made will increase.

---

[20] For comprehensive numerical prognoses see the appendix 'kwantitatieve uitgangspunten' (quantitative points of departure) in the 'ex-ante uitvoeringstoets' (ex ante implementation test). To be found at www.justitie.nl.

[21] See www.cbs.nl.

Table 1: numerical overview of decision-making regarding asylum applications, 1999-2006[22]

year »»	1999	2000	2001	2002	2003	2004	2005	2006
number of applications	39,300	43,560	32,579	18,667	13,400	9,780	12,350	14,465
% RC settle-ments*	12%	16%	22%	45%	40%	42%	50%	42%
positive deci-sions	13,490	9,730	10,580	8,820	6,552	–	17,030	–

* Since April 2005 positive decisions have also been made at the application centres. According to the IND annual report for 2005, that year 13% of the applications dealt with at the application centres were granted and 37% rejected. In 2006 these percentages were 13% and 29% respectively.

4.2 The percentage of application centre (AC) procedures

The percentage of applications dealt with according to the AC procedure fluctuates between 40% and 50%. The fluctuation in the figures can be attributed to asylum applications – including repeated applications – to which a moratorium on decisions applied.[23] Under the old *Vreemdelingenwet* a lower percentage of applications were dealt with according to the AC procedure. In 1999, 12% were dealt with at the application centres, in 2000 16%.[24] It cannot be denied that the decision-making procedure followed at the application centres has led to a considerable acceleration of decision-making in asylum cases. Within 48 processing hours (a maximum of five days) the asylum seeker receives a decision regarding his or her application. The outcome is not always the desired one, but at least there is a maximum of clarity and this promotes speed, which is a component of the quality concept. It is also interesting to note that the rest of the applications – the great majority – are dealt with according to the 'normal' procedure, which has not been accelerated. In the framework of the evaluation of the *Vreemdelingenwet 2000* research was done on the processing times of the asylum procedure.[25] The results showed that the median processing time of decisions on asylum cases which are not affected by any moratorium on decisions and which have not been investigated in further detail was 137 days. However, within the population the times vary widely: one quarter of the

22 These data are from Statistics Netherlands; see www.cbs.nl (from the StatLine database). The percentages of application centre settlements come from IND annual reports and from www.ind.nl. The figures relating to applications and accepted applications in 2003 come from the Aliens Chain Report (*TK* 2003/04, 19 637, no. 805, p. 39). It should be noted that this report gives a lower number of positive decisions than that given by Statistics Netherlands. According to the Aliens Chain Report 3,748 residence permits were granted in 2002.

23 A moratorium on decisions is an order by the Minister of Alien Affairs and Integration that no decision is to be made regarding an asylum seeker's application in view of the situation – expected to be temporary – in the asylum seeker's country of origin.

24 The 1999 percentage cannot be properly compared with the other figures because in 1999 the time available in the application centre procedure was raised from 24 to 48 processing hours.

25 Commissie Evaluatie Vreemdelingenwet (2006); Wilkinson et al. (2006), p. 349.

decisions are made within 35 days, while one quarter requires a processing time of 206 days or more. These figures correspond with those in the Aliens Chain Report, which show that in 2002 and 2003 in 20% to 40% of the applications no decision was made within the legal time limit of six months. In the meantime criticism has been expressed from all sides regarding the accelerated decision-making procedure at the application centres.[26] Legal aid workers say that due to the long opening hours (from 8 a.m. to 6 p.m.) they do not have a chance to build up relationships of trust with their clients. Quite often an asylum seeker has contact with as many as three legal aid workers during the 48 processing hours. An additional factor is the very short period of three processing hours available to a legal aid worker to submit a point of view. According to reports, in a large proportion of cases this pressure of time leads to legal aid workers deciding not to submit a point of view. In these cases the notification of intent procedure can hardly be seen as raising quality.

It was not the legislators who suggested that more asylum applications should be dealt with at application centres; this was in fact an administrative decision. Because the *Raad van State* determined that no content-related criterion applied for settlement at an application centre, administrative efforts were concentrated on the accelerated asylum procedure. The Minister even formulated a target figure – although it never made it into the parliamentary documents – of 80%. As a result the persistent tension between speed and due care was intensified. There is no doubt that the AC procedure is fast; but whether the decisions are made with due care is disputed. In response to this criticism the minister pointed out that the court upheld nine out of ten of the RC decisions. However, it must be borne in mind that a considerable number of cases do not culminate in substantive assessments because by that time the asylum seeker in question has left for an unknown destination and in many cases contact with the legal aid worker has also been broken.[27] Previously the number of reversals was significantly higher. This undoubtedly also has to do with the *Raad van State* case law (see section 4.5).

4.3 The number of positive decisions

Table 1 shows that the numbers of applications granted have fluctuated throughout the years. In the years prior to 1999 the number of positive decisions was higher (in 1998 15,100, in 1997 17,000 and in 1996 23,590). This is not surprising in itself in view of the larger number of applications submitted in the 1990s. In absolute figures, the number of permits granted has fallen. But if the number of positive decisions is compared with the number of

[26] See various contributions to Terlouw's volume, Terlouw (2003). See also the recommendation of the Adviescommissie voor Vreemdelingenzaken (2004); Human Rights Watch (2003); and the report issued by the Nederlands Juristen Comité voor de Mensenrechten (2003).

[27] In the accelerated procedure appeal against a rejection does not have suspending effect. The asylum seeker loses his or her rights to housing and support services and has to turn to emergency provisions.

applications submitted in the same year, we see that a relatively high number of applications were granted. However, this does not mean anything, because in most cases positive decisions apply to asylum requests submitted in a previous year. Moreover, the positive decisions also include residence permits granted for a limited period by virtue of Article 29(1)(d), *Vreemdelingenwet 2000* – the protection policy applying to all applications submitted by people from certain countries. In recent years, during certain periods this kind of policy has applied to asylum seekers from Somalia, Afghanistan and Iraq among other countries. Nevertheless, it will be interesting to keep track of future developments. It would be revealing if it turns out that there is an increase in the number of positive decisions in the future. Should this be the case, various hypotheses could be formulated to explain the phenomenon.

A first hypothesis might be that the acceleration of procedures leads to the availability of more capacity for the applications dealt with outside the application centres. As a result greater care can be devoted to investigation, which leads to more positive decisions. A competing hypothesis is that the drop in the number of asylum requests has led to a rise in the more serious requests as a proportion of the total number. Specifically, asylum seekers who do not have a serious story to back up their claim for asylum relocate to other countries because they want to avoid the accelerated procedure in the Netherlands. It is precisely a slow decision-making procedure that appeals to an asylum seeker without a strong case, because then at least he or she is guaranteed accommodation and other facilities for a certain period. This period in an asylum seekers' centre provides an opportunity to find out if it might be possible to remain in the Netherlands on other grounds or to stay in some other country in Europe or elsewhere. This hypothesis draws attention to a number of striking potential connections. If a larger proportion of asylum applications are 'dealt with' according to the accelerated procedure, the number of applications drops. If speed is seen as a component of quality in decision-making, then increased quality has been realized by the acceleration itself. If this leads to a drop in the number of applications, the rise in quality may be further enhanced by the fact that there is then more time left for a thorough investigation of the motives for seeking asylum.

4.4 Complaints and the duration of the decision-making process

It can be deduced from the complaints submitted to the IND that in general the length of processing is perceived as a major problem. In 2003 a total of 8,198 complaints were submitted, of which 1,200 had to do with asylum procedures. The vast majority of the complaints (81%) were about processing times.[28] In 2003 the National ombudsman observed that the asylum procedure was doing better and better on this score: 'Since the introduction of

[28] www.ind.nl.

the new *Vreemdelingenwet* 2000 the number of petitions about the processing time of asylum applications has dropped off considerably. Reference was already made to this in the annual report 2002. This trend has continued in 2003. However the National ombudsman has observed bottlenecks with respect to the duration of asylum procedures in which advice was requested or a closer investigation was set up'.[29] In 2004 8,496 complaints were submitted to the IND. According to the IND's figures, three-quarters of these complaints were about the processing time of applications or letters of objection. In 2005 this number rose to 13,205, but in 2006 the number of complaints dropped again, to 9,842. According to the IND, this drop was caused by the reduction in the number of applications and the fact that backlogs had been cleared, so that in recent years the processing times have been shortened.

In response to a report issued by the Netherlands Court of Audit about compliance with the legal time limits for making decisions and about possible explanations for and solutions to existing violations of time limits, the Cabinet observed that 'keeping to decision-making time limits must even be seen as one of the quality aspects of a soundly operating public administration'.[30]

4.5 Appeals

The *ex ante* implementation test carried out during the preparation of the *Vreemdelingenwet 2000* assumed that only 10% of the IND decisions against which an appeal was lodged in the first instance would be reversed. This is a considerably lower percentage than had previously been the case. However, it was assumed that a significant number of cases were dismissed on technicalities, for example because they were not eligible for the objections stage. It was expected that under the *Vreemdelingenwet 2000* this would occur less frequently, especially in view of the concentrated efforts made to improve the IND decision-making process.[31] Surprisingly enough, this very optimistic prognosis seems to be proving more and more correct, as can be seen in Table 2. One might conclude that the quality of the decisions has risen. A rival hypothesis might explain the drop in the percentage of appeals upheld by suggesting that the District Courts, under the influence of case law from the *Raad van State*, is more reserved – more 'marginal' – in its review.[32] In the opinion of the *Raad van State*, the credibility granted by the minister to the asylum seeker's story may only be marginally reviewed by a District Court. This means that the administrative body's position is now more easily defensible than previously, when there was a much more compelling judicial review; and this must have direct consequences for the number of judicial reversals.

---

29 Nationale ombudsman (2003), p. 398.

30 *TK* 2003/04, 29 495 (Beslistermijnen: waar blijft de tijd?), nos. 1-2, appendix, p. 52.

31 See the *ex ante uitvoeringstoets* EAUT (*ex ante* administration check), p. 7 (to be found at www.justitie.nl).

32 The standard judgment is *Raad van State* 27 January 2003, *RV* 1974-2003, 57 with note by Spijkerboer.

As has already been pointed out, the introduction of further appeal prolongs the procedure. The figures show that the *Raad van State* deals with aliens cases quickly: average processing times well under two months are excellent.[33] Not a single decision overstepped the 23-week standard referred to in Article 89(2), *Vreemdelingenwet 2000*. In 2001 few cases were presented because the *Vreemdelingenwet 2000* only came into force as of 1 April that year. In 2002 and 2003 a distinct rise in the number of cases could be observed. The *Raad van State,* in its capacity as an advisory body for the Dutch government, expected that 80% of the principal actions would be able to be settled out of court.[34] As Table 2 shows, this expectation was far exceeded.

Table 2: numerical overview of appeals, 2000-2003

year »»	2000	2001	2002	2003	2004	2005	2006
% upheld in first instance*	32%	39%	20%	13%	21%	20%	15%
asylum cases appealed	n/a	494	1,855	3,838	5,120	5,199	4,559
processing time in days	n/a	–	41	58	91	98	63
% out of court	n/a	92%	87%	85%	94%	95%	96%

* See the *Raad van State*'s annual reports 2000, 2001, 2002 and 2003.

5 Evaluation of the *Vreemdelingenwet 2000*

In 2006 the *Vreemdelingenwet 2000* was evaluated by an independent committee. The committee concluded – on the basis of an external study – that there were significant differences between the processing times of applications initially dealt with at application centres on the one hand and the processing times of applications decided according to the 'normal' procedure at the processing offices on the other. This is hardly surprising in view of the fast procedure at the application centres, but the committee argues that the difference is so great that it is better to refer to the short procedure – which takes a very short time – and the long procedure – which takes a very long time.[35] There are all sorts of reasons for the big differences in the processing times. The number of applications is certainly not one of these reasons, since that number has only dropped during recent years. The committee draws attention to the composition of the influx from certain countries of origin, which was thought to contribute to the delays in processing. In addition, the committee observes that in recent years capacity at the IND has declined considerably. There are also

33 See the *Raad van State*'s annual report 2003. Unfortunately the *Raad van State* does not refer to the number of cases upheld, classified according to the sort of case.

34 *TK* 1998/99, 26 732, no. 3, p. 99.

35 Commissie Evaluatie Vreemdelingenwet 2000 (2006), p. 21.

numerous disruptions which have undermined effective progress in implementation. The committee refers to the time spent answering the so-called 14/1 letters, which are actually applications for admission on the grounds of leniency,[36] the assumption of the standard admission tasks of the aliens police and efforts to get rid of backlogs such as large quantities of detention cases and old objection files. The committee calls for the backlogs to be cleared so that normal workloads can be realized, which would eventually considerably curtail processing times. The committee also suggests that measures should be taken to merge the fast AC procedure and the slow 'normal' procedure to some extent.

The committee also made a few comments about the quality of the asylum decisions. The findings of the study show that at present – in accordance with the objective of the Act – decisions on asylum cases are of better quality than the decisions in the first instance under the old Act. This is also true of decisions in the 'normal' procedure in comparison with the old decisions regarding objections. However, it was impossible to compare the quality of the present AC decisions with those made prior to the *Vreemdelingenwet 2000*. With some reservations, the committee concludes that as far as due care is concerned present decisions are comparable with the old decisions regarding objections. In other words, the abolition of the objection stage does not seem to have led to a deterioration in the quality of the decisions brought before the court. Whether this is relevant to other sections of migration law or of administrative law, as was suggested during parliamentary proceedings, is questionable. Discussions relating to asylum cases tend to include a lot of to-ing and fro-ing. It may well be easier to objectify disputes in other areas, so that an objection stage is less of a ritual and can really contribute something to the considerations which have to be made.

According to the committee, less care is taken over the decisions made according to the AC procedure than over those made according to the normal procedure. The committee therefore suggests that the minister should consider adapting the time limits in the AC procedure in such a way that the gains in quality which seem to have been realized in the normal procedure can also be achieved in the application centre procedure.

6 Concluding remarks

The *Vreemdelingenwet 2000* aimed to speed up and improve decision-making in asylum cases. To what extent were these objectives attained and what can be said on the basis of the available data about the factors which determine the quality of asylum decisions? Acceleration of the asylum procedure has certainly been partly realized. However, this is not so much due to the Act as to shifts in emphasis in the decision-making process which are a result

[36] These 14/1 letters were submitted to the IND between 14 January 2003 and 18 March 2005, appealing for residence permits in view of the special circumstances of the foreign national in question.

of the policy adopted by the Minister of Alien Affairs and Integration. These shifts were made possible partly by case law from the *Raad van State* concerning the 'AC criterion'. At the same time, the evaluation study of the operation of the *Vreemdelingenwet 2000* showed that in a significant proportion of cases the processing time of asylum applications dealt with according to the normal procedure exceeds the legal time limit. In a large number of cases – up to almost 50% for the cohorts submitting asylum applications in the last quarter of 2003 – the legal time limits are exceeded by six months.

On the basis of the evaluation study conclusions can also be drawn about the quality of the decisions involved in asylum cases. It seems that initial decisions are of higher quality than they were under the previous Act and comparable in quality to the old decisions regarding objections. The percentage of judicial reversals is sometimes referred to as a measure for the quality of asylum decisions. While this percentage has been dropping in recent years, it should be borne in mind that this may be partly attributable to changes in the judicial review of asylum decisions. According to the *Raad van State*, the District Court should only marginally review the administrative body's assessment of the facts in asylum cases, which is a radically different approach in comparison with the way the District Court in the first instance used to see its task. The *Raad van State* is in fact less critical of the quality of the IND's work than the old Legal Uniformity Division. The result is that fewer asylum decisions are reversed and lawfulness has thus increased, although this does not necessarily mean that the legal quality of decision-making in asylum cases has risen. Doubts about this are borne out by the criticism of legal aid workers, human rights organizations, the Advisory Committee on Alien Affairs and the Evaluation Committee on the *Vreemdelingenwet 2000* with regard to the settlement of asylum applications.

It has become clear that sufficient information is available about the speed of decision-making in asylum cases. Reports are issued regularly about the percentages of applications dealt with at the application centres. Information is also available about the processing times of primary decisions and decisions concerning objections. It is therefore all the more disappointing that the information available about how cases are actually handled is so fragmentary. While statistics do show how many residence permits are issued per year – also per category –, strictly speaking no relationship can be ascertained between these figures and the number of applications submitted, because of the relatively long processing times of decisions taken outside the application centres. The IND should collect cohort figures on decision-making and legal protection procedures in relation to the applications submitted during a certain period.

It is also remarkable that so little information is available about the quality of the decisions. The committee which evaluated the *Vreemdelingenwet 2000* could only comment – with reservations – on the quality of asylum decisions on the basis of file review. Unfortunately, file review did not provide clarity as to the quality of application centre decisions – and it is the degree of care taken with these decisions that is so controversial. As we have seen, the assessments of lawfulness made by the District Courts certainly do not provide conclusive answers as to the quality of the decisions. It is not even certain whether the reserved review currently carried out by the District Courts keeps the implementation of the *Vreemdelingenwet 2000* on the right track. The Minister of Alien Affairs and Integration should keep the Lower House informed not only about statistical trends in this area but also about the progress of the quality improvement programme initiated at the IND. Along the way, investigation of the legal quality aspects relevant to asylum decisions should shed more light on the development of the decision-making process in asylum cases.

In the policy area of immigration law speed is an important aspect of high quality in regard to decision-making – possibly more important than in other special sections of administrative law. Prompt action is particularly crucial when deciding whether or not protection should be given in the form of a residence permit. It is important for the community as a whole, but also for the asylum seeker in question. It is not implausible that when asylum seekers are thinking about which country to apply to for asylum, one of the factors that determines their choice is the processing time of applications, in the sense that a fast decision-making procedure has a certain deterrent effect. A question which is still to be examined is whether this may also lead to changes in the nature of the requests. One factor not previously referred to in this article is the return of rejected asylum seekers to their countries of origin. The sooner an application is dealt with, the sooner a return can be arranged. At that point no ties with the Dutch community have been built up and the asylum seeker has not become demotivated as a result of years of living in refugee centres. Discussions about the 'one-off amnesty', particularly distressing cases and the 'return policy' show how difficult it is to ensure that failed asylum seekers return to their countries of origin after spending years in the Netherlands. At the same time, the accelerated asylum procedure has its drawbacks; but we should take care not to throw out the baby with the bathwater. Research is needed to find ways of overcoming the present drawbacks within the context of a fast procedure.

CHAPTER 10

Public administration: 'At your service!'

L.J.A. Damen

1 Introduction

When do public administration decisions and decision-making have sufficient legal quality? In this essay I will take the idea of a service-oriented public administration – at the service of the 'ordinary' citizen – as a basic standard. Without such a basic standard – and of course other basic standards might also be chosen – it is impossible to assess whether decisions and decision-making have sufficient legal quality. Later on I will explain what I mean a service-oriented public administration. First I will introduce the discussion with a true story.

2 The burgomaster without a permit

2.1 The story

On 16 December 2006 the Dutch national newspaper NRC Handelsblad reported that Mrs Annemarie Jorritsma-Lebbink, burgomaster of Almere – a town of 181000 inhabitants in the centre of the Netherlands – and her husband[1] had installed a geothermal heating system in their new house. This system required 2 bores of up to 30 metres, two water pumps and a water circulation of up to 9.5 m3 per hour. Their house was built by the construction company Jorritsma Bouw for themselves and their married children's families. However, they had not obtained the necessary permits from the Provincial Executive of the province of Flevoland. This meant they were acting in violation of the *Grondwaterwet* (Groundwater Act), the provincial environmental order and the Provincial (spatial en environmental) Plan for Flevoland 2000.

After a tip from a local farmer the violation was verified. The burgomaster was then notified by the Queen's Commissioner and talks took place between the Queen's Commissioner, the town clerk and the burgomaster. In September 2006 it was decided that a geophysical investigation should be conducted to see if it was possible to legalize these installations and a few others which had by then been discovered. In the meantime the possibility of a non-enforcement permit or an exemption was suggested. The burgomaster failed to inform the aldermen and the municipal council of Almere, which – as she admits in December 2006 – was a political mistake. The Jorritsma's did not apply for the permit and exemption. While awaiting the outcome of the investigation into possible legalization they simply carried on with their illegal activities.

On 15 January 2007 the Provincial Executive decided – on the basis of the geophysical investigation – not to grant the Jorritsmas a permit or exemption because of the risk of groundwater pollution. They also decided that since legalization was now impossible enforcement measures should be taken against the

[1] Mr Jorritsma works for the construction company Jorritsma Bouw B.V. and is – like his wife – a minority shareholder in the company.

Jorritsmas' installation.[2] Moreover, all the neighbours were asked if they were pumping up groundwater, in which case enforcement measures could be taken against them as well, if necessary. On 27 February 2007 the Provincial Executive made a final decision not to grant the Jorritsmas a permit.[3]

2.2 The legal context

As we have seen, the Jorritsmas' actions must be regarded as violating the *Grondwaterwet*, the provincial environmental order and the Provincial (spatial and environmental) Plan for Flevoland 2000. In this Provincial Plan the Provincial Council had designated the area where the burgomaster lives as a 'strategic reserve' for water supply. In principle no new permits or exemptions for bores and water abstraction were to be granted, and even existing permits were to be withdrawn. About 45 farmers were forced to close their groundwater wells after the Provincial Executive had decided in the course of 2003 to withdraw the groundwater abstraction permits they had been given in 1997. The supreme administrative court in the Netherlands in these matters, the *Raad van State* (Council of State), deemed this policy to be 'not unreasonable'.[4] In the view of the *Raad van State* a very important factor was that restricting the number of abstraction wells and their installation and use by specialized water supply companies would reduce the chance of pollution, thus enhancing 'sustainable protection' of the groundwater. For compensation claims in respect of the withdrawals of permits the *Raad van State* refers to the special procedure laid out in the *Grondwaterwet*.

One farmer appealed against a coercive administrative action of which he had been notified. In his appeal he asked to be granted a transition period of 16 months to find an alternative – as other farmers had been – instead of 6 months. He claimed that there had been a non-enforcement policy. He lost the appeal.[5] At present there is no longer any question of a non-enforcement policy. In fact, the Provincial Executive is even conducting a lawsuit against the Dutch Ministry of Agriculture, Nature and Food Quality pursuant to the *Wet openbaarheid van bestuur* (Government Information Public Access Act) about data concerning famers' water abstraction in order to obtain the names of farmers conducting illegal water abstraction.[6]

---

2 *Een geval van grondboring in Overgooi*, www.almere.nl, February 2007, Bijlagen (Annexes) Part 2, Document 23. Previously the water supply company Vitens had made a negative recommendation and the local authority of Almere a positive recommendation (Annexes 21 and 22). The Provincial Executive expressed surprise at the fact that after years of passivity the Municipal Executive was now suddenly instigating a policy discussion about energy. Bijlagen (Annexes) Part 1, p. 41.

3 Press release 28 February 2007, www.provincie.flevoland.nl.

4 *Raad van State* 22 December 2004, LJN: AR7984-7989.

5 Chair *Raad van State* 18 November 2003, LJN: AN8861.

6 *Rechtbank* (District Court) Zwolle 21 February 2006, LJN: AV3139.

2.3 The problem

The problem in the case outlined above is illustrated by the arguments brought forward by the Provincial Executive and the burgomaster when the case came into the public eye in December 2006.

The burgomaster made the same excuses as most people usually do in similar circumstances: 'We didn't know and nobody told us'. In her first statement Mrs Jorritsma said that she and her husband had not known that they needed a permit and an exemption. In a later statement she said: 'We should have known better'. The burgomaster said that when her husband first talked with town officials about the options for the property they had bought he had mentioned his plan for installing geothermal heating and that 'the municipality had been very enthusiastic about it'.[7] According to the burgomaster, the installation was mentioned in their application for a building permit:[8] 'neither the municipality, nor the installer, nor the supplier of the system pointed out to my partner that a permit might be required'. Apparently the architect who submitted the application for the building permit did not tell them either. The burgomaster also said: 'Precisely because we kept that whole process at a distance we became particularly vulnerable'.[9] Mr Jorritsma expressed his willingness to apply for the required permits at this point. In anticipation of receiving the desired result, Mrs Jorritsma invoked the principle of equality: 'the local hospital was granted a permit, and they use much more water'.[10]

At the political level, in December 2006 the burgomaster asked the municipal council for an independent investigation 'into the relevant facts and events, and an overview of the responsibilities and powers of the various government authorities', because her integrity might be questioned. Her request was granted. After the report was published, on 8 February 2007 the municipal council rejected a motion of no-confidence with votes split along the lines of coalition versus opposition. The motion was based on the view that the burgomaster had not acted in accordance with the administrative integrity which might be expected, as laid down in the municipal bye-law Administrative Integrity Code of Conduct.[11]

---

7 Confirmed in *Een geval van grondboring in Overgooi*, p. 22.

8 Confirmed in *Een geval van grondboring in Overgooi*, p. 31.

9 This is an example of the universal problem of the responsibility of the client for the activities of his or her contractor, advisor, representative ad litem, etc., if things go wrong. *Centrale Raad van Beroep* (Central Appeals Tribunal) 2 November 2004, *USZ* 2005/11, states that 'in principle the action or omission of a representative is attributed to the party who has appointed this individual to act on his behalf'. However, in the case of a fine for a tax violation, the intention or gross negligence of a tax consultant cannot be attributed to the taxpayer: *Hoge Raad* (Supreme Court) 1 December 2006, 40369, *NJB* 2007, p. 241, no. 226.

10 *Een geval van grondboring in Overgooi*, Bijlagen (Annexes) Part 1, p. 51. Mrs Jorritsma evidently had a copy of this exemption at her disposal.

11 See *Een geval van grondboring in Overgooi*, Verslag (Report), p. 13-14.

The provincial authority's objections to Mrs Jorritsma's lines of defence are just as classic as her reactions. First of all, every citizen is assumed to know the law. To a high degree this is – inevitably – a legal fiction, but in this case it should be noted that Mr Jorritsma himself works for and is part-owner of a construction firm and must therefore be aware of the many different permits and exemptions needed for building projects. Moreover, prior to 2002 Mrs Jorritsma was a minister of Transport and Communications and also of Economic Affairs, and must also have known that permits were required and been familiar with the *Grondwaterwet*. According to a spokesman for the provincial authority, the province's enforcement measures against the 45 farmers attracted a great deal of publicity, which in his opinion could not have escaped the Jorritsmas' notice. In addition, every citizen who starts a building project is responsible for finding out what permits are needed and if necessary to seek expert advice. The outcome of possible proceedings at the administrative court remains to be seen.

2.4 The citizen's own responsibility or a government that serves the public?

An administrative authority which serves and assists the public must do its best to ensure that citizens get what they are entitled to; it must provide information, ask questions, help to find solutions.[12] The service-oriented administrative authority helps citizens to realize their freedom. In 1989 Scheltema defined one of the four main characteristics of the democratic state under the rule of law as the principle of a service-oriented public administration.[13] at the service of society, the community, the public interest, and also at the service of individual citizens. Citizens are increasingly regarded as customers of the government who must be served as well as possible by the government's products. Customer-friendliness at the counter, customer-friendly decision periods, a 'one-counter policy', etc., are all in line with this view. This policy of customer-friendliness applies mainly to citizens who apply for something the administrative authority is willing to go along with – a benefit or a permit which does not do the administrative authority any harm – or even better, something which will reflect well on the administrative authority. In cases of this kind the administrative authority adopts a neutral, sympathetic and/or customer-friendly attitude. Just fifteen years later, it seems as though the opposite principle has been adopted: 'the citizen at the service of the public administration', under the motto 'long live the citizen's own responsibility'![14] In cases in which a citizen wants something the administrative authority is not keen on, or at least which does not interest it, the citizen rapidly acquires the image of an enemy, an opponent. Rather than a service-oriented administration which aims to redress the inequality between the government and the 'ordinary' citizen, we frequently

[12] Damen et al. (2005), nos. 150-153.

[13] Scheltema (2002), p. 24; Schlössels (2004), p. 29.

[14] Cf. L.J.A. Damen (2004), p. 161-162; Ortlep (2004).

see an administrative authority (and its 'public servants') which assumes a more formal attitude and refers to the citizen's 'own responsibility'. Consultations, decisions and proceedings are conducted aggressively; the citizen is perceived as a calculating adversary. Under the motto of the 'citizen's own responsibility', the slightest legal quibble is picked on to impede citizens. This situation led the Vice President of the Council of State H.D. Tjeenk Willink to ask: 'How legitimate is a public administration in which only the most competent citizens, and then only with difficulty, can find their way, and not those for whom the democratic state under rule of law was also intended'?[15]

What degree of legal quality may we expect from the provision of information and the decision-making process? Can municipal services and public servants who deal with applications for permits be expected to point out to the applicant that other permits and exemptions are also required? Where is the borderline between the citizen's responsibility and the service provided by the municipality?

3 Points of departure for a service-oriented administration

3.1 Introduction

A service-oriented government administration and a high degree of legal quality go further than the problem outlined above. The administration must 'provide information, ask questions, empathize, help to find solutions'. Within the boundaries of legislation and case law that is sometimes flawed and of the public interest of the community which is to be served, service-oriented administrative body or public servants must adopt a *benevolent attitude* and consider how they can help citizens to get what they are entitled to. What exactly is a *benevolent attitude*?

By a benevolent attitude I mean that an administrative body and its public servants should regard themselves in every respect as servants of the citizens and should meet their explicit or implicit wishes as well and to as great an extent as they possibly can. This benevolent attitude is quite different from *leniency*.

> It is a common occurrence for administrative bodies to think that they are meeting a citizen's wishes out of *leniency* and not because they have an obligation to do so. Their view is that the citizen is actually not entitled to a benefit with retroactive effect, or to the withdrawal of a dismissal, or to compensation of medical expenses incurred abroad but that these things are granted out of leniency. In cases like this sometimes the administrative body thinks it is unreasonable that it also has to pay the legal costs which have been incurred.[16]

---

[15] Http://www.raadvanstate.nl/speeches/speech_show.asp?speech_id=44; *de Volkskrant* 9 January 2007.

[16] *Centrale Raad van Beroep* 12 January 1999, *AB* 1999, 141 with note by Bröring, *JABW* 1999, 27; *Central Raad van Beroep* 7 July 2005, *TAR* 2005, 155, *USZ* 2005/344; *Centrale Raad van Beroep* 16 May 2006, *AB* 2006, 283 with note by Bröring, *JB* 2006/236 with note by Keinemans, *RSV* 2006/280.

The idea that a public authority may make a decision on the grounds of leniency – as a kind of favour – is based on a misunderstanding. It assumes – especially in the case of a discretionary power in which interests can be weighed up against each other – that an administrative body has several options which are all equally lawful. Then, out of leniency, the administrative body opts for the decision which is the most favourable for the citizen, although it could also just as lawfully opt for a decision which was much less favourable for the citizen. But in actual fact the administrative body is always bound by law – not by leniency – to make the decision which is most favourable for the citizen, or at least the decision the citizen wants; it is very rare that there are several decisions which are all equally lawful.[17] On the other hand, an administrative body may never give a citizen more than he or she is entitled to, even out of leniency.[18] Generosity is not appropriate in the relationship between citizen and administration, governed as it is by the law.[19]

The misunderstanding arises because in a case involving a discretionary power the administrative court cannot review the decision thoroughly but must review it marginally and therefore must sometimes respect a choice which is not optimally reasonable. This does not alter the fact that the administrative body has an obligation to make the most reasonable choice. As Professor Konijnenbelt, a member of the *Raad van State* – partly on the grounds of his judicial experience – wrote concerning Article 3:4(2) of the *Algemene wet bestuursrecht* (General Administrative Law Act):[20] 'the standard should be: the highest degree of reasonableness!'[21]

Administrative authorities should adopt a benevolent attitude. They can do this by:

a) *active and adequate information provision*, dovetailed as much as possible to the situation of the individual citizen;
b) giving a *helping hand* to citizens submitting applications so as to avoid people missing out on benefits, etc.;
c) *fair play and giving citizens a voice* rather than impeding their chances (including their procedural chances);
d) *meticulous preparation*, asking questions about the citizen's wishes and examining the feasibility of those wishes with appropriate administrative and technical accuracy (best technical advice, state-of-the-art solutions);
e) choosing the *most favourable alternative* when considering possible solutions and by choosing the decision which is the *least painful* for the citizen

---

[17] National ombudsman 12 January 2006, *AB* 2007, 36 with note by Stolk, assumes that a decision made by the Public Prosecutor is lawful but inappropriate because it contravenes the requirement of proportionality. In my opinion the decision is therefore also unlawful.

[18] For the role of the principle of legality see also *Raad van State* 4 December 2006, *AB* 2006, 158 with note by Sewandono, *JB* 2006/151 with note by Peters, *Ars Aequi* 2006, p. 635 with note by Damen.

[19] See Damen (2006), p. 779-781.

[20] 'The adverse consequences of an order for one or more interested parties may not be disproportionate in relation to the purposes served by the order'.

[21] Konijnenbelt (2005), p. 256.

when an onerous but not punitive decision is made;

f) *punctual decision-making*, at least always within the legal time limit.

The requirements listed above should apply without any concessions in two-party relationships – those involving only one citizen and one administrative body. If several citizens are involved in the decision-making process – usually with conflicting interests – the administrative body must serve several citizens and the public interest as well, and then it is more difficult to meet all these requirements without making any concessions, especially requirement E. In such cases the administrative body has to choose between a wide variety of – often contradictory – interests, and it may not always be possible to please everyone. Nevertheless, all of the requirements are still relevant in these cases, precisely to prevent certain interests being overlooked. For example, if economically interesting activities are involved a prejudice can easily develop in favour of the entrepreneur. The builder tends to be the winner. The third party whose interests are affected can easily be seen as a troublemaker. Or as Professor Van Buuren, a member of the *Raad van State* – partly on the grounds of his judicial experience – wrote: 'the situation as regards the legal protection of citizens against injustice in spatial planning is not at all rosy. For people living in the neighbourhood the road to success is strewn with so many pitfalls and spikes that they seldom reach the finishing line. People living in the neighbourhood can strike a blow against the public administration, but they hardly ever win the war. The administration can hold out the longest, has alternative paths at its disposal, there are no fatal time limits for the administration and the administration can always come back on the rebound. For citizens who want to stop a development or a project it is an unequal struggle'.[22]

3.2 Active and adequate information provision

How far does the obligation to actively provide information, dovetailed as much as possible to the situation of the individual citizens, extend? A very long way, I would say, especially if we assume for the moment that we are talking about an obligation to make an effort, not an obligation to obtain a result. An obligation to obtain a result would probably involve excessive liability risks, especially in view of the legal quality of the body of public servants as it now stands. This highlights the need for better and in particular more timely information to be provided by administrative bodies, complaints committees and administrative courts.[23]

Various officials of the municipality of Almere now have the best intentions to provide 'customer-oriented information', but the alderman in charge warns us that they have no legal duty to do so.[24]

---

[22] Van Buuren (2004).

[23] Commissie Evaluatie Awb III (2007), p. 62.

[24] *Een geval van grondboring in Overgooi*, Bijlagen (Annexes) Part 1, pp. 6, 9, 81.

Adequate information provision implies that the citizen should also be able to rely on the correctness of the information given about his or her individual situation. According to the case law this is not very likely to be the case. An administrative body is not easily bound by information given by public servants. Suppose a public servant, working under the auspices of the burgomaster and aldermen of Almere, had told the Jorritsmas that they did not need any further permits or exemptions; judging by the case law, the Jorritsmas would not have been justified in relying on this information being correct and therefore believing that no enforcement measures could be taken against them.

An argument in favour of this situation is the need for flexibility; if it were changed administrative bodies could only let their public servants give very basic information. Of course, the solution to this problem is – first and foremost – better training for these officials. Otherwise competent citizens will resort en masse to asking for written information in 'have-I-understood-this-correctly?' letters. But the problem then is that in many cases written information provided by government bodies is accompanied by a disclaimer.[25]

What role does the citizen's own expertise play? Here too the guiding principle is the compensation of inequality. In the case law it is assumed that an expert property developer should be more aware of the need to ask further questions, possibly in writing, than an 'ordinary' citizen.[26] Apparently the Jorritsmas are regarded as having more expertise than 'ordinary' citizens.

In the case of the Jorritsmas, the municipal officials in charge of granting the building permit should have warned them that another permit or exemption might be necessary. This obligation is not laid down in current law, but it is in accordance with the idea of a service-oriented public administration. If this case had involved an 'ordinary' citizen, the failure to warn should have constituted grounds for compensation, by virtue of the principle of compensation of inequality. But the Jorritsmas, with their experience and knowledge, should have known better. At the very least they should have made a greater effort to obtain information.

However, the best system would be one in which a citizen can submit his or her entire plan and file at the front office, and is then entitled to specific and reliable information from the administrative body's public servants as to what is needed to obtain all the required permits and exemptions.

3.3 A helping hand

It occurs frequently that citizens miss out on benefits to which they are entitled. They fail to apply for a grant or a benefit to which they are in

---

[25] Cf. Scheltema (1997), p. 6-7; cf. my note under *Hoge Raad* (Supreme Court) 27 November 1992, in: Van Buuren, Polak & Widdershoven (eds) (2003), p. 258-271; Pront-van Bommel (2006).

[26] *Raad van State* 2 September 1999, *BR* 2000, p. 321, *Gst.* (2000) 7122.7 with note by Teunissen, *RAwb* 2000, 125 with note by Peters.

fact entitled, for example because they cannot face the red tape involved, lack the bureaucratic skills required or because they are ashamed.[27]

A good solution to this is the 'forms brigade' – proposed by a member of the municipal council of Almere – which would help citizens to fill out application forms for benefits for which they have not applied previously because the forms and procedures are so complicated.[28] The municipal administration of Groningen has set up an extensive campaign to make sure that citizens who are entitled to special support, rent allowances or care allowances but have not applied for them do in fact receive them.[29] This is *pro-active service* – helping citizens to obtain what they are entitled to, but which otherwise they might not have obtained. Probably many more initiatives of this kind are being undertaken throughout the Netherlands.

Sometimes an administrative authority does not have the information required for an initiative of this kind at its disposal. For example, many people over 65, especially ethnic minorities, are entitled to supplementary benefits because they do not receive full old-age pensions by virtue of the *Algemene Ouderdomswet* (National Old Age Pension Act). In principle, to receive a full pension a person has to have lived in the Netherlands from the age of 15 to 65. Many people from ethnic minorities do not meet this requirement and therefore receive an old-age pension which is below the minimum income. A government body called the *Sociale Verzekeringsbank* (Social Insurance Bank), which is in charge of paying old-age pensions, knows about everyone over 65 who does not receive a full old-age pension. A possible solution would be for the *Sociale Verzekeringsbank* to pass on these data to the municipalities where the people in question live so that they can take action. However, some municipal administrations have decided to mandate the *Sociale Verzekeringsbank* to be responsible for giving supplementary benefits to people over 65 so that there is 'one counter' for both old-age pensions and for supplementary benefits.[30] In this way concentration of powers may lead to higher legal quality, and better service of the public.

3.4 Fair play and giving citizens a voice

According to the National ombudsman, 'for administrative bodies the requirement of fair play means that they must give citizens an opportunity to make use of their procedural chances. This requirement means that an administrative body should interpret a citizen's letter of complaint sympatheti-

---

[27] Raad van Economisch Adviseurs (2007), p. 9: 'het beleid is niet toegesneden op de beperkt rationele en slecht geïnformeerde burger die in alle lagen van de bevolking voorkomt' ('the policy is not geared to the limitedly rational and poorly informed citizens who are to be found in all layers of the population'); Cf. Laemers et al (2007), p. 83.

[28] *Almere Vandaag*, Local newspaper 9 December 2006.

[29] 'Minima laten miljoenen Euro's liggen' ('Minimum income groups miss out on millions of euros'), *Gezinsbode* (local newspaper) 31 January 2007.

[30] Van Everdingen (2006).

cally in the light of the regulation laid down in the law for dealing with complaints, without raising unnecessary formalities for the citizen'.[31] The right of complaint is based on the principle of a service-oriented public administration.[32]

It is not only in regard to complaint procedures that administrative bodies can be expected not to procedurally wrong-foot citizens. Nevertheless, many administrative bodies do not regard certain 'I-do-not-agree-with-this' letters as notices of objection.[33] A more sympathetic interpretation of citizens' letters is required.

It is important to give citizens a voice in more general terms – possibly in informal procedures[34] – by taking them seriously, and by dealing with their complaints[35] and letters punctually and satisfactorily. Lack of response or late responses are a cause of considerable annoyance to many citizens.[36]

The right to hear and to be heard is also relevant in this framework, especially in relation to 'onerous decisions'. This principle, which was developed in Community law, means that a citizen can bring forward his or her point of view before the onerous decision in question is made final, and that the citizen is entitled to sufficient preparation time and an opportunity to inspect the relevant documents.[37] In proceedings at the administrative court an administrative authority does not have party autonomy; it must be completely open about all legal and factual issues. If the administrative authority is unable to do so, the administrative court may amplify the facts on its own initiative and shall amplify the legal basis on its own initiative (Article 8:69 of the *Algemene wet bestuursrecht*).

The Jorritsmas can hardly claim a lack of fair play or that they were not heard, since lengthy consultations were held with them before the Provincial Executive decided to deny the permit and proceed to enforcement. Apparently they had a special position.

3.5 Meticulous preparation

It is also very important to investigate carefully, to listen attentively to citizens, to ask further questions about their wishes and to examine the feasibility of those wishes with the appropriate administrative and technical accuracy (best technical advice, state-of-the-art solutions). When an onerous

31 Nationale ombudsman (2006) (complaint in English rather than Dutch).

32 Winter et al. (2007), p. 21.

33 Cf. *Raad van State* 19 January 2005, *AB* 2005, 130; *Centrale Raad van Beroep* 18 August 2005, *AB* 2006, 28; *Raad van State* 29 March 2006, *AB* 352; *Raad van State* 25 October 2006, *AB* 2007, 28, all with notes by Damen.

34 Commissie Evaluatie Awb III (2007), p. 15.

35 Commissie Evaluatie Awb III (2007), p. 7-8.

36 Cf. Nationale ombudsman (2007).

37 Commissie Evaluatie Awb III (2007), p. 52-53.

decision is involved, an administrative body's investigation and the grounds given for the decision must meet even higher demands.

If an administrative body cannot meet a citizen's wishes itself, it should refer the citizen elsewhere, preferably within the time limit. An application for grant A may have to be converted into an application for subsidy B, because grant B will actually be approved.[38]

In dubio pro inquisitione (if in doubt, find out). Why not check to see what the citizen in question actually wants, for instance in relation to an unclear notice of objection? This requirement was sufficiently met in the case of the Jorritsmas.

3.6 Most favourable alternative, least painful solution

Once an administrative body – and its public servants – has started to help the citizen to find possible solutions, then of course it must choose the *most favourable* alternative for the citizen. Within the boundaries of what is legally possible, the citizen's wish has priority.[39]

A *punitive administrative sanction* is intended to hurt the offender. The principle of the least painful solution does not apply in such cases. However, the penalty must be in reasonable proportion to the severity of the offence. Things are different with regard to *onerous decisions* which are *not punitive*. This includes orders requiring a citizen to partially or wholly restore something to its original condition or to stop doing something which is unlawful, as in the case of the Jorritsmas. It also includes other onerous decisions which are not related to any preceding offence, such as denying a benefit or subsidy, imposing a tax assessment or withdrawing a permit on the grounds of a policy change. With respect to these non-punitive but onerous decisions an administrative body must choose the decision which is least painful for the citizen. This depends partly on the public interests involved. Sometimes compensation for loss resulting from a government decision will be appropriate. For example, the question arises whether it is sufficient for the Jorritsmas to seal off their installation. Or should they also fill in the bores drilled through the strata of clay? If a provincial authority withdraws the permits of 45 farmers on the grounds of altered policy insights, are these farmers not entitled to compensation on the grounds of the principle of equal distribution of public burdens?

In short, what sacrifices can an individual citizen be expected to make to serve the public interest? A universal requirement under administrative law is that impairment of citizens' interests should be minimized; this criterion should always be taken into account.

---

[38] *Centrale Raad van Beroep* 5 August 1996, *AB* 1997, 27, *RSV* 1997/30. Also *Raad van State* 29 July 1996, *JB* 1996/190 with note by Heldeweg. For more about the 'helping hand' see Nicolaï (1997), p. 160-161.

[39] Damen et al. (2005), nos. 806-807.

3.7 Punctual decision-making

Over the past ten years the topic of promptness and drive on the part of administrative authorities has attracted more interest.[40] Many administrative bodies have now taken measures to ensure a less time-consuming decision-making process. However, there are still some administrative bodies which come nowhere near taking their decisions within the legal time limits, let alone tighter ones.

However, the attention paid to promptness over the past decade also means that speed may become so dominant that it has an adverse effect on quality. Promptness may then lead to unnecessary objection and appeal proceedings or to frustration on the part of citizens who cannot face filing a lawsuit, or if they do file a lawsuit run a high risk of not obtaining a substantive judgment from the court due to various procedural booby traps.[41]

Occasionally thinking in terms of speed has also become so dominant at the administrative courts that it has put pressure on legal quality. The court makes insufficient use of its discretionary powers of investigation and takes too little time for sufficiently meticulous substantiation of its judgments.

4 Legal quality assurance

There are certain important prerequisites for a service-oriented public administration. First and foremost, quality assurance systems should be developed. The administrative court monitors the legal quality of decision-making, but only partially and selectively. For all sorts of reasons, many citizens decide not to protest against unlawful, 'wrongly negative' decisions. Numerous 'wrongly positive' decisions never make it to the court – especially in two-party relationships – because the citizen who has benefited from the decision is satisfied, pockets the (undeserved) gains and keeps his or her mouth shut. If the citizen does take the matter to the court, he or she determines the extent of the proceedings (Article 8:69(1) *Algemene wet bestuursrecht*),[42] and can therefore keep certain components of the decision-making process out of the proceedings. Thus except for political and administrative supervision an administrative body can often just do as it pleases, even if it makes decisions which contravene the law and public interest. However, quality checks are stimulated by administrative supervision. Some 'decision factories' hold internal checks, whereby an error margin of 1% is regarded as acceptable. Visitations and other forms of benchmarking are also becoming more and more common. Quality on a small scale is unquestionably improved by the fact that the Queens' Commissioners

---

40 Cf. Scheltema (1996). Cf. the recent reports brought out: Vos, Saris & Van der Vlugt (2007).

41 Cf. Damen (2006A).

42 'The district court shall give judgment on the basis of the notice of appeal, the documents lodged, the proceedings during the preliminary examination and the examination in court'.

and burgomasters have an obligation to publish 'residents' annual reports' for which they ask their executive officials for various data, for example concerning the promptness of decision-making or the handling of telephone calls and complaints.

At present various quality-assurance systems are being developed, with internal and external checks. A continuous learning process makes it possible to make further improvements.[43] The element which requires the most development is the learning process – systematically learning from complaint, objection and appeal procedures.[44]

4.1 What will it cost, this service-oriented public administration?

Service-oriented public administration is both inexpensive and expensive. The costs are low if public servants consider citizens' wishes sympathetically in the same amount of time. The costs are high if they then have to spend time thinking up better solutions, providing useful, reliable, individualized information, etc. The costs are also high if better lawyers have to be appointed and the current lawyers given better training. Research has shown that citizens attach a great deal of importance to the reliability and expertise of the public servants they speak to, but are often disappointed.[45] However, cutbacks could be made by reducing the amount spent on general managers and consultants, who are valued far too highly.

It would not necessarily cost more money if the political administrators were to concern themselves with the quality of implementation instead of constantly making new policy.[46] Less 'government by remote control' would not have to lead to higher costs either. It would simply mean that the politicians were doing something different for the same amount of money.

After the explosion of a fireworks factory in the middle of the city of Enschede on 13 May 2000 (13 casualties, many people injured, many millions of euros in damage) it turned out that draft environmental permits were very rarely examined even by the alderman responsible for environmental affairs in Enschede, let alone by the whole board of burgomaster and aldermen as the competent administrative authority.[47] Most of the decision-making had been mandated to the public servants. The political administrators were only consulted in serious problem situations.[48] The politicians were 'governing by remote control'.

Perhaps the fireworks disaster would not have been prevented if the alderman had been more closely involved, but a political administrator with a bit

---

[43] Cf. Scheltema (2006).

[44] Commissie Evaluatie Awb III (2007), p. 9-10.

[45] Laemers et al. (2007), p. xiii.

[46] Raad van Economisch Adviseurs (2007), p. 10-11.

[47] Commissie Onderzoek Vuurwerkramp (2001), p. 39, 230.

[48] Commissie Onderzoek Vuurwerkramp (2001), p. 99, 206.

of common sense might have asked if it was really such a good idea to allow a fireworks factory in the middle of a residential area get bigger and bigger, on the principle of toleration and legalization.[49] When an objection against a draft environmental permit which asked 'how it was even conceivable in this day and age that an enterprise of this kind was housed in a residential area like this' was laid aside because the objection referred to spatial planning and the business was not located in a residential area but in an industrial zone, perhaps an alderman who was actively involved would not have remained silent.[50] Read with a little more sympathy, this objection could have been regarded as relevant to environmental affairs. One thing is certain – the explosion paid no heed to the boundaries of the industrial zone.

Clearly in this case the administration was serving someone – but apparently only the owners of the fireworks factory. The municipal authorities were systematically tolerant and systematically failed to take enforcement measures, to the detriment of the public interest and in the long run at the cost of many lives.

If it is not possible to create a service-oriented administration with the amount of tax money that politicians are prepared to ask their voters to pay, choices should be made: which basic tasks are to be performed, which other tasks are not? For example, a municipal authority ought to choose public safety as one of its core tasks, and not only because Article 2 of the European Convention on Human Rights compels it to do so.[51]

4.2 Efficiency

It is important for political administrators to understand that the government is a very specific organization which must be managed in a completely different way than a business.[52] A minister who sees him or herself as a board member of 'The Netherlands Ltd.' is definitely barking up the wrong tree. Management thinking in terms of 'Zwolle Ltd.' or 'The Netherlands Ltd.' can have disastrous effects, leading to a more stringent attitude towards the public and a greater lack of sympathy. In implementing policy it is then easy to forget that the focus should be on helping citizens to get what they are entitled to.

---

49 The judgment passed by the *Rechtbank* of Almelo on 2 April 2002, LJN: AE0935, in the criminal law proceedings against the owners of the fireworks factory included some critical remarks, apparently giving voice to the anger among the local population; it states that the city of Enschede and its public servants had performed their tasks in a 'completely incomprehensible fashion'; that 'the city set the wrong priorities by using far too much of its limited manpower on new prestige projects', and that the administration's conduct had been 'inconceivably careless'.

50 Commissie Onderzoek Vuurwerkramp (2001), p. 47; Commissie Onderzoek Vuurwerkramp (2001), p. 238-239, 256.

51 ECHR 31 November 2004, 48939/99 (Öneryildiz), *AB* 2005, 43 with note by Woltjer, *NJ* 2005, 250 with note by Alkema.

52 Raad van Economisch Adviseurs (2007).

This does not alter the fact that administration must also be efficient. However, if aiming for efficiency results in a failure to appreciate that public administration is a completely different sort of organization from a business, it may result in stimulating the wrong responses. For example, if the dispensation of administrative justice is financed according to the number of judgments passed, this acts as a stimulus for the court not to spend much time on extensive preliminary investigations but to arrange court hearings as soon as possible and to ensure that cases cannot easily be reopened. If each separate judgment is financed, this acts as a stimulus to pass a separate judgment for each case number instead of passing a single judgment for a number of parallel cases. The same applies to various other so-called performance contracts with public authorities.

5 Conclusion

It would be worthwhile considering the idea of a service-oriented public administration in greater depth and analysing what it might mean, especially in cases involving several parties. The presence of third-party interests complicates the implementation of service-oriented administration considerably because it entails choosing between a wide variety of often conflicting interests, and in such cases it is not always possible to please everyone. Third parties whose interests are affected are often perceived as troublemakers and the opportunities provided for them to comment as lightning rods. An additional complication is that when – as in the case of the Enschede fireworks factory – town planning and the environment are involved, the public interest may play a very important role. On the other hand, it is perfectly feasible for two-party relationships to be dealt with according to the methods outlined above – administrative authorities are welcome to try them!

CHAPTER II

What about the quality of decision-making?

G.H.M. Tromp

"When Atticus looked down at me I saw the expression on his face that always made me expect something. 'Do you know what a compromise is?' he asked.
'Bending the law?'
'No, an agreement reached by mutual concessions....' "
Harper Lee, To kill a mockingbird

1 Quality and confidence

Societies can only exist if people keep their promises, even when those promises play out over a longer period of time. Basically, it all comes down to the confidence that exists among people, confidence based on deep-rooted patterns of socially accepted standards, of social rules. When promises are not kept, social sanctions are often the price paid for that deviant behaviour.[1]

Apart from a few isolated patches in our private lives, our large-scale bureaucratic and complex society is, for the greater part, overshadowed by organic solidarity:[2] relationships between people are almost entirely dominated by impersonal rules, in many cases enshrined in law. Viewed from a social science perspective, the rules of law are agreements between individuals formalized by the 'powers that be' which can be enforced by the state. For that reason, first and foremost, rules of law have a different character to other social rules that govern people's behaviour.

In theory, rules of law strengthen the confidence among people in modern society: it has become the lubricating oil of the state. Max Weber wrote almost a century ago that people in modern society can count on the rule of law because the system of modern, rational law is aimed at reliability and predictability, with the exclusion of arbitrariness.[3] He was right. If conflicts arise, which they do from time to time, rules of law help to settle the matter, not with force but, equally, not without the threat of sanctions from on high. Society at large feels protected against such sanctions because the government, which takes decisions on the basis of the law, is bound by the same rules. If people are law-abiding, the government cannot harm them. This principle of legality is one of the essential prerequisites for a state becoming a constitutional state, a state ruled by law.

Also in theory, rules of administrative law in particular strengthen the confidence among members of the public and members of government. As a consequence the quality of governmental decision-making could be measured against the extent to which that decision-making conforms to the requirements of predictability and reliability.

1 For a short explanation, see De Swaan (2001).

2 A term coined by sociologist Emile Durkheim, contrasted against the mechanical, automatic solidarity of simple societies.

3 Weber (1922), particularly p. 468-493.

So, if one were to generalize about the governmental decision-making process, it is of crucial importance to examine the confidence of society at large in the observance to the letter and in the spirit of the law by the authorities. Can we say that such confidence exists between members of the public and government? Is the fulfilment of prevailing expectations, created by legislation, a two-way street? Or is application of the rule of law actually more about *'Begriffsjurisprudenz'*, legal chicanery, which is more likely to breach confidence and predictability?

In the context of this article, I shall make a cautious, exploratory attempt to answer these questions. Illustrating my argument with a case in point, I shall describe an example of modern decision-making practice, and the relevant legislation it was faced with.

Although it is not a case that can stand up as an empirical model for everyday decision-making, it is a case which, in Weber's terminology, can be viewed as a ideal-type: aspects of a social phenomenon are highlighted allowing us to trace the essential characteristics of the phenomenon, even if not all of these aspects are present in all concrete occurrences of that social phenomenon. In the Schaphalsterzijl case, many elements come together in one way or another which do not come together in that form or connection in other, more ordinary cases. But all these elements are always part of the process of decision-making in which public and government have different opinions about what to do.

This article[4] concentrates on the various decisions taken by various authorities that were necessary to obtain planning permission for a pumping station with a lock at Schaphalsterzijl, in the local authority of Winsum, in the province of Groningen. The decisions at issue are the formal decisions which had to be taken according to different kinds of law: the *Waterschapswet* (Water Board Act) the *Wet op de Ruimtelijke Ordening* (Planning Act)[5], the *Algemene wet bestuursrecht* (General Administrative Law Act), *Gemeentewet* (Municipalities Act), *Monumentenwet* (Protected Buildings Act):

- the decision about the choice of the site (water board, 19 December 1995);
- the decision to start preparations for a new development plan (local council, 17 September 1996);
- the decision whether or not to follow the exemption procedure of the development plan (local council, 17 June 1997);
- the decision to apply for permission to depart from the development plan (local council, 11 June 1998);
- the decision to grant that permission (provincial council executive committee, 23 September 1998);

[4] In the context of this article, it is hard to do justice to the interesting cultural, historical, hydrological, constructional and landscape-related aspects of the case. It is equally hard to do justice to the widespread, thorough knowledge displayed by the pressure group in question.

[5] *Wet op de Ruimtelijke Ordening* (Planning Act), which plays an important role in this case, is now obsolete. The 'Article 19' procedure described in this case bears a more than passing resemblance to the same project procedure in the revised act. See also note 21.

- the decision to depart from the development plan (local council, 17 November 1998);
- the decision to grant planning permission (local council executive committee, 3 August 2000).

2 The *Schaphalsterzijl* case: the background

In late 1993 in Groningen, the most northern province of the Netherlands, the provincial council held a memorable meeting. The subject for consideration was the subsidence of the Groningen earth floor and how to deal with the consequences. The subsidence, caused by natural gas extraction from the Slochteren gas field in the province of Groningen, appeared to be much more serious than expected. Thus the provincial council executive committee had had a study carried out on how to tackle the implications.[6] They proposed a package of measures to follow, referred to as 'variant 5a'.

The minutes of the meeting show that none of the various parliamentary parties was comfortable with the package of measures.[7] The assembled delegates believed variant 5a to be inferior to another package of measures, 'variant 5a*'. Nonetheless, the provincial council executive committee got its way. The argument that variant 5a* was not only more expensive, but also very time-consuming – the procedure for obtaining planning permission would apparently take between five and eight years – was enough to convince everyone. That decision was the prelude to the Schaphalsterzijl issue, an issue that, what with one thing and another, would drag on for a decade.

3 The prelude to demolition

The decision about the choice of a site by the water board, 19 December 1995

On the basis of this decision by the provincial council, the local water board decided to build a pumping station with lock in the Mensingeweersterloopdiep, close to the town of Winsum. However, the Winsum local authority had other ideas: in its view, the openness of the landscape would be irretrievably damaged; it would be much better to site the pumping station at Schaphalsterzijl, where there had been a sluice of that name since 1459. 'From a social and historical point of view' wrote the local council executive commit-

---

6 The damage may be considerable: excessively wet fields for agriculture, flooded cellars, damp, and subsidence and cracks in buildings in urban areas. In addition, there may be subsidence of revetment walls and other constructions on the banks of waterways, coupled with reduction in the clearance under non-moveable bridges. Such damage can, in part, be tackled by altering the water level.

7 Minutes of the meeting of the Groningen provincial council, 15 December 1993.

tee to the councillors, 'it would make sense to keep it at that site.'[8] The water board would later state that they had a sympathetic ear for Winsum's arguments concerning the implications for the landscape in the valuable Reitdiepgebied. A choice for the site of Schaphalsterzijl would, according to the board, indeed represent a confirmation of its heritage.[9]

As the Subsidence Committee[10] had no complaints about the Schaphalsterzijl site, there was nothing to stop the water board taking such a preliminary decision. In accordance with the public consultation by-law (inspraakverordening),[11] the preliminary decision was deposited for public inspection. Shortly thereafter, the water board asked the local authority to approve Schaphalsterzijl as the site for the construction of a pumping station with lock. From the appended construction plans, it was clear that the existing sluice system would have to be dismantled. A great number of indignant responses from the public was the result of the plans of the water board. A bit surprised at the number of responses, the board organized a special information evening, inviting two heavyweight 'interested parties' to discuss the matter. Then the water board weighed up the pros and cons and decided, on 19 December 1995, to build the pumping station with lock at Schaphalsterzijl. One of the concessions under which the decision was taken was that the pumping station was to be built while *modifying* (my italics) the existing structure.

The preliminary decision set out for public inspection had clearly let the genie out of the bottle. More than 480 opinions were received, most opposing the choice of site. Some of the opinions confirm a passionate affection for the landscape, combined with considerable knowledge thereof. The objections against the choice of site were primarily cultural, historical[12] and landscape-related.[13] The opinion of a group set up in August 1995, the *Behoud en Restauratie Schaphalsterzijl* working group, is particularly striking. Its trademark was not only passion but above all a great bureaucratic competence.[14]

---

8 Letter from the local council executive committee to the councillors, 19 September 1994.

9 Decision of the Noorderzijlvest water board, 19 December 1995.

10 The Nederlandse Aardolie Maatschappij (NAM) agreed to meet the cost of all measures aimed at countering damage (including that to property in public ownership) under the terms of the 'Overeenkomst Groningen-NAM inzake regeling vergoeding kosten bodemdaling aardgaswinning 1983' (contract between the Province of Groningen and NAM relating to the compensation scheme for subsidence as a result of natural gas extraction). The measures in question are to be taken by the Subsidence Committee.

11 From Art. 79 *Waterschapswet* (Water Board Act).

12 The reference is to two nearby sluices, Aduarderzijl and Schouwerzijl which, with their original lock-keeper's cottages, were restored and, together with Schaphalsterzijl and its lock-keeper's cottage, form a unique historical unit in the Reitdiepgebied area.

13 All opinions cite the fact that the area had been put forward for inclusion on UNESCO's World Heritage List.

14 That opinion closes with the words: 'In coming to your preliminary decision, you have almost certainly also taken into account geo-morphological, cultural, historical, aesthetic, policy-related, economic,

What the documentation makes clear is that the water board had no comprehension of what was driving the groundswell of opposition. In a meeting with *Stichting Industrieel Erfgoed Noord-Nederland* (SIEN, Trust for the Preservation of the Industrial Heritage of the Northern Netherlands), also opposed to the preliminary decision, the chair of the water board asked his interlocutors whether or not they knew how this sort of sentiment had actually been created; how come so many people had warmed to the issue?[15] In his opinion, the preliminary decision took into account both landscape issues and sociocultural issues. He found himself wondering whether those opposed to the proposal were actually aware that the decision would guarantee the future of Schaphalsterzijl. Later, in the explanatory notes to the water board's decision, in December 1995, this cryptic observation would become clear: 'the decision endorses the social and historic qualities of the site; these qualities even form a significant reason for choosing the Schaphalsterzijl site. In contrast to the many concerned parties, the cultural and historical value lies in the site rather than in the repeatedly rebuilt sluice, currently in a serious state of disrepair.'

The meeting, one week later, with members of the *Behoud en Restauratie Schaphalsterzijl* working group, was fraught. The members wanted answers to real questions: why were no alternative sites studied? Was it known that selection of the Schaphalsterzijl site would lead to demolition of the system of sluices? The water board managed to evade the first of these questions and confirmed the second: the intention was not to combine the building of a new pumping station with the renovation of the old system of sluices. What's more, the water board also maintained that the possibility of building an underground pumping station had been examined, but that there were no such pumping stations with comparable capacity in the Netherlands. Less than two years later, it would become apparent that this information was made up.

In the explanatory notes to the decision on the site, the Schaphalsterzijl site was deemed a good choice for water management reasons; the cultural and historical reasons for maintaining the original sluice complex were fended off with the claim that the place, not the sluices, had cultural and historical significance. Renovation was rejected. 'Modification in place of renovation does not, however, mean that none of the historic value is left over. The profile is important, as is maintaining the old line of the dyke, but choice of materials is also important.' That concludes the review by the water board of the landscape-related, cultural and historical opinions. The other arguments were commented on succinctly and formally. No attention was paid to the commitment and passion of the opponents.

---

recreational, environmental and architectural aspects. However, we have not yet seen evidence of this on your part. We would therefore like to take this opportunity to ask you to furnish us with a breakdown of the categories on which the preliminary decision is based, so that we may take these into consideration.' (Opinion of the working group, 15 September 1995)

15 Minutes of the meeting with SIEN, 23 November 1995.

Just before the end of 1995, *Stichting Behoud Schaphalsterzijl*[16] submitted a number of complaints to the water board concerning the way in which the consultation procedure had been followed. The complaints procedure was finished off two and a half years later, in April 1998, after the National ombudsman had declared the complaint[17] from the Schaphalsterzijl Preservation Trust well-founded in December 1997. The water board's complaints panel then went so far as to partially acknowledge some of the claims of the trust, though it rejected others. The water board's day-to-day management also came in for criticism: responses to the consultation procedure should have been dealt with on their merits. On the strength of that point, the water board appended an addendum to the decision of 19 December 1995 (on 24 July 1998), which belatedly discussed the submitted complaints. In July 1998, the water board solicited approval from the provincial authorities in the question of the decision on the site[18] and on 23 September 1998, approval was duly granted without any further comment.

The first cut is the deepest. The water board, locked away from the community it served behind the impenetrable veneer of civil-servanthood, appeared not to appreciate an 'active civil society' and the confidence of the people in 'efficient governance' has certainly not increased.[19] The water board's failure to take members of the public seriously did nothing to help the swiftness of the decision. Approval was not granted until two and a half years after the decision.

4 From demolition to renovation.

The decision to start preparations for a new development plan by the local council, 17 September 1996

Once the water board had taken the decision to build the pumping station at Schaphalsterzijl, it disappeared into the background of the decision-making process, to be replaced in the foreground by the Winsum local authority. The local authority had received an outline planning application from the water board which would eventually lead to an application for full planning permission. Such permission can only be granted if the application is in line with the development plan. This was not the case, hence the local authority's use

16 The Schaphalsterzijl Preservation Trust, the successor to the working group.

17 The complaint from the Schaphalsterzijl Preservation Trust was deemed inadmissible by the water board as they did not view the working group as an interested party in the sense of Art. 1:2 of the *Algemene wet bestuursrecht* and consequently failed to recognize the trust or its successor. The National ombudsman rejected the water board's claim by clarifying the article using legal precedent. For more on this point, see No 5 September 1998, *AB* 1998, 276.

18 Under Art. 148 *Waterschapswet* (Water Board Act).

19 An 'active *civil society' and 'efficient governance'* are two conditions for government efficiency according to Wetenschappelijke raad voor het regeringsbeleid (2002), p. 10.

of the 'get-out clause' (the 'anticipation' or exemption procedure) offered by Article 19 of the *Wet op de Ruimtelijke Ordening* (WRO; Planning Act).[20] Officially, this procedure takes 32 weeks, including all opportunities for consultation. In the case of Schaphalsterzijl, this decision-making process took more than four and a half years: in January 1996, the application for exemption was received and heard and in August 2000 the local council executive committee issued full planning permission.

> Of course, that is a symptom of the fact that while the 'Article 19' procedure was running, another procedure was running parallel to that one (relating to the recognition of Schaphalsterzijl as a monument for conservation). But there was more to it than just that. In a bid to mollify the commotion around the situation or, in terms of this article, to win back the confidence of the members of the public while, at the same time, acknowledging the fact that the locks had been presented as having potential listed-building status, it appears that the authorities in question, the local authority and the provincial authority, believed it more prudent to 'help' the water board in the process.

While the consultation procedure on the site decision was still ongoing, the day-to-day management of the water board had already made the decision to choose the site of Schaphalsterzijl. That can be seen from the reports of the provincial working group that was instigated at the initiative of the provincial council executive committee of Groningen, in which all officers involved were sitting: representatives of the local authority, the architectural consultants, the provincial authority, the Department for the Preservation of Historic Buildings and Sites (*Rijksdienst voor Monumentenzorg*) and the building-aesthetics committee for Groningen. The latter had proposed that the existing lock and accompanying lock-keeper's cottage, in combination with the Reitdiepdijk, be given listed-building status.[21] That meant that it would be difficult to demolish the old complex without a fight. Even the provincial council executive committee was aware of this and tried to find some middle ground[22] so that Schaphalster-

---

20 This procedure is followed in 'anticipation' of an intended wholesale or partial alteration of the development plan. Prior to the procedure, the local authority must have taken a decision on the alteration of the development plan and obtain permission to depart from the development plan from the provincial council. Only after that may the local authority, i.e. usually the local council executive committee (unless the local council as a whole wishes to exercise its power), permit departure from the prevailing development plan. Up to that point, the application for planning permission must be deferred under the *Woningwet* (Housing Act).

21 Not long after, SIEN and the Schaphalsterzijl Preservation Trust also put forward the sluice for listed-building status.

22 As reform of the provincial authority and the strengthening thereof was being debated at the time, provincial councils made sure that they were the authority pulling the strings. The initiative for creating this working group must be seen in that context.

zijl's listed-building status would not be compromised and the pumping station would be built, nonetheless.

This working group, meeting behind closed doors,[23] prepared an alternative design for the pumping station. The first meeting was held in November 1995, before the water board had formally taken the site decision. The course that was plotted at that point can be summarized as follows:

- the choice of site, Schaphalsterzijl, was written in stone;
- the idea of an underground pumping station was not on the table;
- the new design was to combine the old (the existing sluice) with the new (the pumping station);
- the local authority was to instigate the 'Article 19' procedure due to the pressure of time;[24]
- members of the public and pressure groups were to be consulted prior to any decision, and their ideas/concerns were to be taken seriously.[25]

In the January 1996 Local Planning Authority (LPA) meeting (Raadscommissie Ruimte), councillors appeared to be less than overjoyed with the working group's position. They recommended that the local council executive committee also study other sites. However, in the meantime the preliminary decision for building at Schaphalsterzijl was published, subject to a four-week period for hearing opposing views.[26] Assessment of such opposing views was left to the working group. There was little further input from the local authority. All that was left to wait for was the final report from the provincial working group.

That report appeared in March 1996. The provincial working group had done it! A design, alternative 4c, put forward by the in-house architect had been deemed worthy of further development.[27] This design stated that the old sluice buildings could be renovated in so far as this was appropriate from the perspective of water management. Further renovation was beyond the scope of that report.

With that, the ball was back in the local authority's court. When, in March 1996, the local council executive committee informed the members of the LPA of the latest state of play, a commotion ensued because the executive had not

---

[23] With much difficulty and, eventually, by invoking the *Wet openbaarheid van bestuur* (Government Information Public Access Act), the Schaphalsterzijl Preservation Trust was able to gain access to the minutes of meetings of this working group and make them public.

[24] This criterion, developed through case law, became redundant with the revision of the Dutch *Wet op de Ruimtelijke Ordening* (Planning Act) in 2000. In its place, the current requirement is for justification of the choices made in the development plan.

[25] It is remarkable, given the state of prevailing legislation, that this is listed as a separate item.

[26] The consultation procedure was a stipulation of the Dutch *Wet op de Ruimtelijke Ordening* and legislated for in the 1994 Winsum consultation by-law. The public preparatory procedure under the Dutch *Algemene wet bestuursrecht* is factored in to that.

[27] Of the alternative designs submitted by the general public, more than twenty in total, just one was discussed in a provincial council working group.

followed up on the recommendation (from January) to study other sites as well. But the commotion was short-lived and the local executive took the following step in the procedure: organizing a hearing for oral treatment of objections received. The hearing was on 24 April 1996.[28] The local executive then scheduled an information evening[29] for 19 June 1996 on the design chosen by the working group for the building work at Schaphalsterzijl.

Debate was heated at the hearing in April. Members of the public felt that the wool had been pulled over their eyes because the de facto decision to go ahead with building at Schaphalsterzijl had already been taken, although it was precisely the site that most objections pertained to. The Schaphalsterzijl Preservation Trust weighed in with a new approach: use of an impartial specialist who rejected Schaphalsterzijl as a site based on strong arguments.[30] During this hearing, other sites were explicitly highlighted by the trust.

At the information evening in June the local council executive committee, assisted by the water board, architectural consultants and the Department for the Preservation of Historic Buildings and Sites,[31] presented alternative 4c for the construction of a pumping station with lock at Schaphalsterzijl. The evening was punctuated with trenchant comments from informed sources. Thereafter, the local council executive committee continued the formal procedure leading to a decision to start preparations for a new development plan: first of all the preliminary decision was referred to by the Local Planning Authority in August 1996 for their advice, and then the actual decision-making would take place in the plenary session of the local council in September 1996.

The councilors in the LPA were split, probably not least because of the incessant action on the merits of the case[32] of the Schaphalsterzijl Preservation Trust. Their objections were, of course, in the order of the lack of alternative sites,

---

[28] Together with the submitted opinions and alternatives, the minutes of the hearing ultimately formed part of the decision-making process on the preliminary decision, i.e. at this point still in line with the *Wet op de Ruimtelijke Ordening* and the consultation by-law.

[29] The local authority was under no legal obligation to do so.

[30] The recommendation in question is from E.R.M. Taverne, lecturer in the history of architecture and urban design at the RUG in Groningen, also cited is the location study performed by the Delta Vorm group, a firm of landscape architects in Utrecht.

[31] When the application for listed-building status was submitted by the Building Aesthetics Committee in Groningen (November 1995), no less, the representative of the Department for the Preservation of Historic Buildings and Sites made it clear that he supported building at Schaphalsterzijl: '...supposes that at various times in the past there have been alterations made to the Schaphalsterzijl site and finds that, if there is now a need to do so due to subsidence, we have reached another significant point in the history of Schaphalsterzijl.' (Minutes of the provincial council's Schaphalsterzijl Consultation Group, 24 November 1996).

[32] Although the consultation process had no legal basis, the local authority, in common with many other local authorities, had enshrined the public's right to speak at local council meetings in the rules for procedure. The Schaphalsterzijl Preservation Trust used this on each occasion and continued to plague council members with written information and points of view.

though they also touched on the lack of adequate consideration of the objections submitted, the design, the fact that there was no fish ladder, the scant renovation of the old sluice, the lack of a bascule bridge, the necessity of advice from independent experts, etc. At the local council meeting in September 1996 it was close. The CDA faction tabled a motion for the withdrawal of the preliminary decision pending a study into alternative sites. The motion was rejected with a vote of eight to seven. The proposal for preparing revision of the development plan was adopted with the same voting pattern. The Council thereupon set up a confidential committee with the task of advising on the aesthetic aspects[33] of the complex.

> Even though it was executed at the eleventh hour, operation 'Renovation rather than Demolition' appeared to have been a success: the preliminary decision for preparing revision of the development plan was adopted. Perhaps out of a sense of disquiet about the role of the water board that felt first and foremost responsible for the water level and had little or no cultural or historical sentiment, the local authority and the provincial authority sought solace in informal consultations by setting up the provincial working group. They did all they could to come to a solution which could bank on widespread support. There had to be a trade-off in the form of renovation of the historical complex, as they were already committed to the site of Schaphalsterzijl. No further discussion was possible on that point. The advantage of this 'appeasement' of the public and councillors, by proposing renovation, appeared not to counterbalance the disadvantage of sticking to that one site, come what may. In view of the atmosphere at both the hearing and the information evening, not forgetting the voting patterns within the local authority, attempts by the authorities to build bridges with the public had not yet borne fruit. However, the setting up of the provincial working group had again slowed down the decision-making process.

5 Insufficient information on underground pumping stations

The decision whether or not to follow the exemption procedure of the development plan, taken by the local council, 17 June 1997 and 17 March 1998

The next step in the decision-making procedure was the decision whether or not to follow the exemption procedure.[34] This would appear to be a reasonably easy step that can be taken without further ado. However, in the Schaphalsterzijl affair, this is not the case. First of all, the confidential commit-

---

[33] According to the minutes of the meeting, building-aesthetics aspects relate to 'the outward appearance of the structure and the nature of the situation and environs.' (Schaphalsterzijl meeting, 25 November 1996).

[34] See Art. 19a (3-11) of the old-style *Wet op de Ruimtelijke Ordening* (Planning Act).

tee would have to issue its recommendations on the appearance of the pumping station. That process was to take the committee, which did not comprise councillors alone,[35] four months.

Almost immediately, the water board came up with a final design. The members of the committee had the feeling that they had been taken unawares and the chair made it clear to the water board that the procedure was not about presenting a fait accompli. Criticism was *also* directed at the design in particular: the height, the glass walls, the lack of a bascule bridge, the sluice gates and the fudging of the restoration. Although the water board representatives agreed to 'consider' the comments, the chair could foresee problems. He duly summoned the architect and water board to an extraordinary meeting. And not without some success: by the following meeting an amended design had been prepared, in which the glass walls had partially been replaced with stone and the height had been altered. Inclusion of revolving doors in the design was impossible, according to the water board, and use of a bascule bridge had been discouraged by the Department for the Preservation of Historic Buildings and Sites. Most party factions could accept the design, although questions remained.

Once the way had been prepared for a successful exemption procedure in this manner, the water board submitted the application for planning permission in March 1997; this was an implicit request for departure from the development plan.[36] The local council as a whole wanted free rein on the exemption procedure rather than leave it to the local council executive committee. Thus the preliminary decision regarding the start of the exemption procedure, in April 1997, was discussed with the LPA. Not everything went as could have been expected from the minutes of the confidential committee. In the consultation procedure, the Schaphalsterzijl Preservation Trust was unequivocal in its opinion that a bascule bridge would be a better solution for a conservation area than a fixed one and that such a construction should not have iron sluice gates, but wooden mitre doors[37] instead. External experts supported the written representations. The trust's representative also pointed out that an underground pumping station was indeed an option, despite the water board's statements to the contrary. She pointed out that the underground pumping station (Gorzeman) at Hellevoetsluis which has a larger pumping capacity than was needed at Winsum was functioning perfectly well. That statement was also supported by authorized documentation. The members of the LPA felt uncomfortable about the incorrect and incomplete information in this respect from the water board. However, most of the irritation directed towards the water board resulted from a letter from the water

35 During the first meeting, the chair, the mayor, put forward a proposal to the officers of the water board, the architects and the engineers with whom the water board worked, the building-aesthetics committee and the Department for the Preservation of Historic Sites and Buildings, to the effect that they join the LPA. It was carried without objection.

36 At the same time, the water board applied for consent to alter the listed building. This was a question for the local council executive committee.

37 In this case, mitre doors are actually 'revolving' doors.

board to the local council executive committee[38] which denied that the restored construction would fulfil a water-management function. As most party factions had been fighting the building of a pumping station at Schaphalsterzijl to the bitter end, because the old construction would be given a new function, this was asking for trouble. The mistrust towards the water board was increasing.

After the LPA meeting, the question remained whether the local council would indeed decide in favour of an exemption procedure. The local council executive committee was afraid that that would not be the case, so it went to talk with the water board once more. Its members managed to gain the concession of having mitre doors at the eastern end instead of sluice gates, but that was as far as it went. For that reason, it was no surprise when, at the decisive meeting of the local council on 17 June 1997, a motion tabled by the CDA and GPV party factions was passed, once more with the smallest possible majority, eight votes to seven. The motion demanded that the executive committee should reconsider the decision because the councillors had been misinformed, and should look into the feasibility of an underground pumping station.

> All efforts on the part of the local council executive committee, the creation of a confidential committee and the extraordinary meeting with the water board achieved nothing: the exemption procedure was not instituted.[39]The capacity of the action group in the question of trusting and believing information provided by the authorities, studying every angle by using independent experts and publishing the results obtained, was spectacular and successful. There was no question of trust; rather the scepticism seemed well placed.

How were the parties to break out of the impasse? It was of course obvious what they were going to do: eschewing formal procedures and holding negotiations behind closed doors.[40] On this occasion, the initiative came from the water board. Councillors were invited to an informal gathering with officers from the architectural consultants, the engineering consultants and, for the first time, a representative from the Subsidence Committee. An underground pumping station now appeared to be one of the options after all, although the site was still non-negotiable. Reason enough for some of the party factions to cease co-operation with this sort of negotiating tactic. They did not relish the prospect of being trapped in a snare set by the local council executive committee and the water board. The result is that the councillors' original joint irritation towards the water board slowly evolved into a schism between those true to the executive committee and the rest.[41]

---

[38] The letter was dated 17 April 1997.

[39] The implication was that the executive committee could no longer deal with the application for consent to alter the listed building.

[40] The minutes of the meetings are matters of public record.

[41] See the exchange of correspondence in that period.

After three further behind-closed-doors meetings,[42] and after most councillors had reiterated their belief in Schaphalsterzijl as the best site under an amended design, variant 5a with a sluice 'inside' the dyke,[43] the schism was clear. The first signs became apparent on 15 December 1997 in the LPA meeting and then on 17 March 1998 in the council meeting.[44] The local council executive committee's proposal to start the exemption procedure was adopted with a majority of 11 to 4.

All the informal negotiating had, eventually, led to amendment of the construction work and to a widely backed decision to start the exemption procedure. That, though, was internal discussion between councillors. Members of the public, in this instance the Schaphalsterzijl Preservation Trust in particular, were out of the picture, although they provided all the relevant, de facto information. Their next chance came with the formal procedure. The exemption procedure allowed for the presentation of written submissions. Five people took the opportunity to criticize the plans. Most unrest appeared to have ebbed away, thanks to the concessions made in the building plans.

6 Ensnared in conflicting interests?

The decision to apply for permission to depart from the development plan (verklaring van geen bezwaar) by the local council, 11 June 1998, and the decision to grant that permission by the provincial council executive committee, 23 September 1998

1998 was a busy and important year in the Schaphalsterzijl issue. Following the water board and local authority's lead, the executive committee of the provincial council now had its turn in the decision-making process, prompted by preliminary steps taken by the local authority. The next step in the exemption procedure could now be taken: the application for permission to depart from the development plan to the executive committee of the provincial council of Groningen. On 11 June 1998 the local council would decide whether or not to apply for that permission.[45]

---

[42] Alternative building plans were mooted at those meetings by the water board, including one for an underground pumping station, a viable alternative after all.

[43] In variant 4c, (first design), the sluice was still 'outside' the dyke, meaning that the building work would impinge more on the landscape of the Reitdiep. Both the mitre doors to the east and the sluice 'inside' the dyke can be viewed as a concession to the objections to the initial design.

[44] On 10 February 1998, there had already been a council meeting in which the preliminary decision in amended form (variant 5a) was re-stated. At that meeting, motions on a number of issues, an independent study into an alternative location, an underground pumping station, a sluice 'outside' the dyke and the use of materials from the region were rejected by a substantial majority. The executive committee's proposal to re-state the preliminary decision was adopted by eleven votes to four.

[45] Once the exemption procedure had been started, the executive committee could deal with the water board's application for consent to alter the listed building. Moreover, the Cabinet Minister for Education,

That decision would have to been made by a new council, as there had been local elections in the intervening period. A new councillor had been sworn in for the VVD faction, one who earned his 'daily bread' as a legal assistant with the water board. In that position, he had been the formal contact with the local authority in the Schaphalsterzijl case. When, on 11 June, the application for permission to depart from the development plan came up for debate, the first question was whether the position of the new councillor was an example of gerrymandering. Legal arguments[46] were traded from councillors[47] who felt that the new councillor should not have a vote in the matter. The local council executive committee invoked Article 28 of the *Gemeentewet* (Municipalities Act) to explain that the councillor in question was at liberty to decide whether or not to vote on the matter. That was an end to that particular discussion.

In accordance with the local authority procedure for public consultation by-law (de gemeentelijke inspraakverordening), the preliminary decision of the local council executive committee, to apply for permission to depart from the development plan, was accompanied by the views and concerns of members of the public and a response to the4se by the executive committee. The Schaphalsterzijl Preservation Trust had collated a comprehensive, well-ordered dossier outlining its position. It included previous written and oral evidence for the debate. The concerns addressed the procedure followed, the lack of cultural and historical insight, the location, the incorporation of the design into the landscape, the type of restoration work, the building plans, the water-management arguments, etc; the dossier was supported by a counter-appraisal from a range of independent experts.[48] This counter-appraisal, and its almost wholesale snubbing by the local council executive committee, was a significant reason for the controversy in the local council. Another reason for political in-fighting was a clause in the local authority's proposal in which the executive committee warned the councillors not to re-open discussion on prior decisions. Taking all aspects into consideration, the result of the vote was not astounding. The proposal for applying for permission to depart from the development plan was passed with the smallest possible majority: eight votes to seven; the contentious councillor voting in favour. Straight after the vote, the spokesman of the GPV party

---

Culture and Science put Schaphalsterzijl on the list of protected buildings in May 1998.

46 Art. 28 of the *Gemeentewet* (Municipalities Act), sub-section 1(a), specifies that a councillor may not vote on a motion 'that affects him personally, whether directly or indirectly, or as the agent of another'. Art. 2:4 of the *Algemene wet bestuursrecht* specifies that a government body must perform its duties without prejudice, and that the body must guard against anyone either within the body itself (directly or indirectly), or with a personal interest in a decision able to influence the decision-making process.

47 They were notified of the sections of the Act in question by the Schaphalsterzijl Preservation Trust.

48 Including Messrs. Kerkstra, lecturer in Landscape Architecture at the University of Wageningen, Borger, lecturer in Historic Geography at the University of Amsterdam, Lintsen, lecturer in History of Technology at the Technical Universities of Delft and Eindhoven, Van Beek, of the Amsterdam Academy of Architecture, Pilon, former chief engineer at the Directorate General of Public Works and Water Management, and Dr Ligtendag, author of *De wolden en het water.*

announced that he would petition the crown to quash the decision on grounds of conflict of interest. Fellow councillors were quick to condemn him. Words were exchanged such as 'disruptive' and 'lamentable'; he was accused of 'playing fast and loose with the interests of the local authority.'[49]

However, the decision had been taken and, on 16 July 1998, the local council executive committee duly applied for permission to depart from the development plan from the provincial council executive committee. Almost simultaneously, the water board petitioned the provincial council executive committee for approval for the site decision of 19 December 1995[50] with the addendum enforced by the National ombudsman and the complaints panel of the water board.[51]

In the meantime, the Ministry of the Interior had investigated the possibility of a conflict of interest.[52] But, in the Ministry's view, although the local authority's decision posed serious questions, it could not be quashed because it first had to be ratified by the provincial council executive committee.[53] In relation to the provincial authority, the Ministry stated that the provincial authority could refuse permission to depart from the development plan on one of two grounds: either if it was in violation of the law or in violation of an adequate county planning.[54] The Ministry expressed its expectations that the provincial council executive committee would 'cover the aspects addressed by me in their deliberations'.

That did not happen. The provincial council executive committee stood fast on the point that assessing the legality of this local authority decision was not their task and that all they had to do was assess whether the legal provisions of the *Wet op de Ruimtelijke Ordening* had been observed from a procedural point of view.[55] Leaving this issue to one side, they did want to voice their opinion that the fundamental right of councillors to vote should not be breached. They had no theoretical objections to building a pumping station with lock on the Schaphalsterzijl site by modifying the existing complex. On 23 September 1998,

---

49 See the minutes of the public meeting of the Winsum local authority, 11 June 1998.

50 Art. 148 of the *Waterschapswet* obliges them to do so.

51 See Section 3.

52 '... even a "functional" interest can, under certain circumstances, result in a conflict of interest. In the case at hand, it is also important to note that the councillor in question worked not only for the other body involved, but, over and above that, he was the civil servant dealing with this case and took part in the process for the Noorderzijlvest water board, at the same time taking part in consultations with relation to the pumping station.'

53 The Articles of the Act relating to approval of decisions are 16 and 19a of the old-style Planning Act, and Art. 10:25 and 10:32 of the *Algemene wet bestuursrecht*. The fact that a decision which has not been approved cannot be quashed is covered by Art. 10:38.

54 Art. 10:27 of the *Algemene wet bestuursrecht* and Art. 19(2) of the old-style Planning Act.

55 This refers to aspects covered by Art. 19a: that the documents are open to public scrutiny, that there is provision for submissions, etc.

the Groningen provincial council granted the Winsum Local Authority the requested permission.

Four years later, the *Raad van State* (Council of State) was to adjudge (in appeal proceedings) that under the circumstances, it had been easy to make the situation look like a conflict of interest. 'For the local authority, this should have been a reason to prevent a decision on exemption being taken by the slenderest margin possible, each councillor's vote thus ... decisively influencing the decision-making process'.[56] Anyone who thinks that the local authority's decision could be substantially reconsidered as a result of this has hold of the wrong end of the stick. An procedure for reparation was started and, in November 2002, the local authority reiterated its decision. The question had led to serious delay. More importantly, the decision-making process had damaged the general public's sense of justice; all the more because the local complaints commission and the court had already decided that nothing was the matter in terms of the legal shenanigans.

Another aspect, somewhat snowed under in the heat of the discussion on the question of a conflict of interest, was whether or not decisions, once made, should once more be debated. Of course, this has everything to do with the reliability of the authorities, but on the other hand it is seldom possible to lay a finger on the actual point of no return. 'Tunnel vision' is an appropriate term here.[57]It makes the decision-making process for the general public (and often for the councillors representing the public too) decidedly foggy, which is hardly beneficial to mutual trust and predictability.

7 The courts loom

Decision to depart from the development plan, by the local authority, 17 November 1998, and planning permission, by the local council executive committee, 3 August 2000

The ball was now firmly back in the local authority's court and things started to move apace. On 17 November 1998, the local council decided to grant permission to depart from the development plan. That happened (again) by the slenderest of margins. The formalities over, all that remained was a ritual dance. The local council executive committee then granted the water board consent to alter the buildings in the Schaphalsterzijl conservation area. As expected, the Schaphalsterzijl Preservation Trust lodged an administrative appeal against this, on the grounds that the *Monumentenwet* (Protected Buildings Act) has suspensory effect. Reports were appended to the administrative appeal which shed a different light on water management in the area. The water board immediately

---

[56] *Raad van State* 7 August 2002, 200200897/1.

[57] The Infrastructure Projects Select Committee of the Lower House of the Dutch parliament (the Duivesteijn Committee) was to come up against such tunnel vision again and again in its inquest into the spiralling costs associated with the construction of the Betuwe goods line.

asked the court to lift the suspension due to the pressing interest. On 26 February 1999, the court ruled that it was not convinced of the urgency of the petition of the water board. The court held that the administrative appeal should run its normal course in the local complaints committee, where the new information on water management could play a role. The suspensory effect was not lifted.

Not until nine months later, in December 1999, did the water board *ask* the local authority to continue the administrative appeal. That happened in March 2000, and on 11 May 2000, the local council executive committee held that the administrative appeal against the granting of the listed building consent was unfounded. Not long afterwards, the Schaphalsterzijl Preservation Trust lodged an appeal with the court, whereupon the water board again requested that the court lift the suspensory effect. On 28 July 2000, the court found in favour of the water board. Thereafter, the local council executive committee could grant planning permission in the form that had been solicited on 23 February 1998: with exemption from the development plan, the reason for a stay of planning permission was off the table; the court award also meant that the stay of listed building consent was over.

These decisions taken by the local council executive committee signal the end of primary decision-making in this case. Administrative and formal appeals will not be discussed further. Suffice to say that in the appeals procedure, the courts twice found in favour of the Schaphalsterzijl Preservation Trust on procedural grounds. Accordingly, the procedures in question were carried out again, correctly this time, though the result remained the same. In 2003 building work at Schaphalsterzijl began, and it ended in 2004.

> The local authority and water board were like two peas in a pod. Only at the water board's request did the local authority eventually deal with the administrative appeal, more than twelve months after it had been submitted. Quite how this state of affairs came about is not recorded in the files.

8 Final words

The formal decision-making structure for a 'Article 19' procedure of the *Wet op de Ruimtelijke Ordening* for permission to depart from the development plan is in no way simple.[58] 'Outsiders' will necessarily have difficulty with the complex procedure, and the term 'outsiders' need not be limited to the public at large: it may also include their official representatives. That level of complexity often obfuscates the transparency of the procedure. The intertwining of this formal procedure with various informal procedures makes the decision-making process that much more opaque. This has implications for the general public and their representatives alike. The general public, who are not

[58] Although the 'Article 19' procedure was overhauled in the 2000 Planning Act, the current 'independent project procedure' remains complex.

au fait with the small print of legislation, do not know the difference between consultation, information, views, concerns and objections or at what moment they should present their concerns, objections or views. The Schaphalsterzijl Preservation Trust is a good example of this. It lost sight of what would happen as a result of its actions. When, where and how can fundamental objections to a preliminary design play a role in the formal decision-making process? The decision to cry wolf at every stage of the process appears to have been fuelled by such uncertainty. As a result, with the passing of time the trust was viewed (and sometimes even treated) as a troublemaker. The quality of decision-making, where confidence between public and government is still a measure of that quality, could be improved by making the whys and wherefores of the consultation process more transparent. But this not only applies to the general public: even public representatives can hardly see the wood for the trees any more. The complexity of the legal procedure makes it difficult to assess which of the decisions in the decision-making chain is the 'one that can make a difference'. While having the air of a reliable administrative body, tunnel vision may be the result.

Much attention has been paid to informal decision-making thanks to the local council executive committee's foresight, and in particular that of the burgomaster. From the start, it was clear that the Schaphalsterzijl issue was controversial. Hence it was understandable that a forward-looking local authority would attempt to create widespread support. But was that merely the thin end of the wedge? When will it be time to sum up the situation and make concessions? The unswerving focus on the Schaphalsterzijl site and the continual refusal to study other locations led to significant delays in the process, but the real legacy is the chasm between the public and the authorities. That single-minded focus on the selected goal was one of the reasons for what in social science is called the unintentional result of social action: precisely by insisting on a specific goal, that goal, speedy construction of a pumping station, became impossible to achieve.[59] An alternative explanation can be found in Janis's 'groupthink' theory.[60] From that, we can deduce that civil servants and their officials and consultants form close-knit groups, which resist outsiders and, above all, outsider's ideas. These groups strive for self-assurance and unanimity. The low opinion and treatment of the many pre-eminent experts introduced by the trust could be explained by that. Could this be called arbitrariness? The role played by recommendations from consultants, even mandatory recommendations, in relation to independent decision-making by the authority in question should be further investigated.

Last but not least, let us turn to the consultation procedure. As we have seen, the lengthy decision-making process surrounding Schaphalsterzijl cannot be blamed on the law and drawn-out mandatory consultation procedures. A diffe-

59 Selznick discussed this issue in his classic work *Tennessee Valley Authority and the grass roots* (1949): 'A commitment in social action is an enforced line of action; it refers to decision dictated by the force of circumstance with the result that the free or scientific adjustment of means and ends is effectively limited.' Selznick (1949), p. 255.

60 For a brief overview, see Janis (2002).

rent course of events in the consultation procedures might have led to fewer objections and appeals. A study[61] by students of the Administrative Law and Public Administration section of the Faculty of Law at the University of Groningen shows that the local authority had met its legal requirements to provide a consultation process. The concerns of the public at large and suchlike were also taken into account in the formal decision-making process. However, in the conclusion to the study we read: 'Nonetheless, we find it hard to avoid the impression that the local council executive committee had pre-ordained the choosing of Schaphalsterzijl and was therefore reluctant to waver from that choice. The submissions entered and arguments raised were more or less all dealt with, although this could well have been just to undermine them, creating greater legitimacy for the choice of the Schaphalsterzijl site.' This has grave implications for the predictability of action by the authorities: the authorities always have the upper hand. The organs of hearing work perfectly well, but are they listening?

What does this summary mean in relation to the hypothesis? In the introduction, I suggested that the quality of decision-making determines whether or not the public at large will have faith in the authorities. The previously cited study into the constitutional state[62] lists a number of conditions for its proper functioning. In this case, what is important is that public authorities work properly, the existence of an active civil society and that the general public has sufficient faith in the rule of law. In the Schaphalsterzijl case, both the first and last criterion is open to question. Whether and how one influences the other is a question for another study. The hypothesis that the quality of decision-making and the degree of confidence among public and government are closely intertwined has in any event not been refuted. The second criterion, an active civil society, was within our grasp but is clearly not valued enough. For years in the Netherlands, there has been much discussion about the so-called 'gap' between the people and government. The prevailing sentiment is that such a gap should be closed by structural reforms, for instance a different electoral system. If nothing else, this study clearly shows that it is not the structure of government action that needs reform but the culture.

---

61 *De casus Schaphalsterzijl* (The Schaphalsterzijl Case), Administrative Law Studies Department, August 2004.

62 Wetenschappelijk raad voor het regeringsbeleid (2002).

Bibliography

ACHTERBERG (1984)
Norbert Achterberg, 'Algemeines Verwaltungsrecht', in: A. von Mutius, K.H. Friauf & H.P. Westermann (eds.), *Handbuch für die öffentliche Verwaltung, Band 1, Grundlagen*, Neuwied 1984.

ADVIESCOMMISSIE VOOR VREEMDELINGENZAKEN (2004)
Adviescommissie voor Vreemdelingenzaken (Advisory Committee on Alien Affairs), *Naar één snelle en zorgvuldige procedure*, The Hague 2004.

ALGEMENE REKENKAMER (2000)
Algemene Rekenkamer (Court of Audit), *Verantwoording en toezicht bij rechtspersonen met een wettelijke taak (several volumes)*, The Hague 2000.

AYRES & BRAITHWAITE (1992)
Ian Ayres & John Braithwaite, *Responsive Regulation: Transcending the Deregulation Debate*, New York [etc] 1992.

BEETHAM (1974)
D. Beetham, *Weber and the Theory of Modern Politics*, London 1974.

BENVENISTE (1987)
G. Benveniste, *Professionalizing the Organization: Reducing Bureaucracy to Enhance Effectiveness*, San Francisco 1987.

BERENSCHOT (1995)
Berenschot, *Onderzoek beleid en uitvoering asielzoekers*, Utrecht 1995.

BICKERS (2001)
K.N. Bickers, *Public Policy Analysis: A Political Economy Approach*, Boston 2001.

BLACK (1976)
D.J. Black, *The Behavior of Law*, New York 1976.

BORGER, WINTER & SCHELTEMA (1996)
S. Borger, H.B. Winter & M. Scheltema, *Beschikken over kwaliteit. Advies over de beschikkingverlening in vreemdelingenzaken door de IND*, Groningen 1996.

BOVENS & ZOURIDIS (2002)
M.A.P. Bovens & S. Zouridis, 'Van street-level bureaucracy naar screen-level bureaucracy', *NJB* 2002, p. 65-74.

BRAITHWAITE (2002)
John Braithwaite, *Restorative Justice & Responsive Regulation*, New York [etc] 2002.

BRENNINKMEIJER ET AL. (2003)
A.F.M. Brenninkmeijer et al., *Handboek mediation*, The Hague 2003.

BRENNINKMEIJER ET AL. (EDS.)(2003)
A.F.M. Brenninkmeijer et al. (eds.), *De taakopvatting van de rechter*, The Hague 2003.

BRÖRING (1993)
H.E. Bröring, *Richtlijnen: over de juridische betekenis van circulaires*,

leidraden, aanbevelingen, brochures, plannen (dissertation University of Groningen), Deventer 1993.

BRÖRING (1993)

H.E. Bröring, 'Beleidsregels. Een beknopte biografie', in: J.L. Boxum et al. (eds.), *Aantrekkelijke gedachten*, Deventer 1993, p. 387-400.

BRÖRING & WINTER (1996)

H.E. Bröring & H.B. Winter, 'Massale beschikkingverlening en het bestuursrechtelijke trechtermodel', in: R.L. Vucsán (ed.), *De Awb-mens: boeman of underdog? Opstellen aangeboden aan Leo Damen*, Nijmegen 1996., p. 11-29.

BRÖRING & MARSEILLE (2002)

H.E. Bröring & A.T. Marseille, 'De ongekende vrijheden en beperkingen van artikel 4:6 Awb', *JBplus* 2002, p. 54-71.

BRÖRING (2005)

H.E. Bröring, *Rationele "willekeur". Enkele opmerkingen over discretionaire boetebevoegdheden (inaugural lecture Groningen)*, Groningen 2005.

BROWN & MARRIOT (1999)

H.J. Brown & A.L. Marriot, *ADR: Principles and Practice*, London 1999.

VAN BUUREN, POLAK & WIDDERSHOVEN (2003)

P.J.J. van Buuren, J.E.M. Polak & R.J.GM. Widdershoven (eds.), *AB Klassiek: standaarduitspraken bestuursrecht, opnieuw geannoteerd*, Deventer 2003.

VAN BUUREN (2004)

P.J.J. van Buuren, 'De burgeronvriendelijke kant van het ruimtelijk bestuursrecht', *Gst.* (2004) 7214.156.

CENTRAAL BUREAU VOOR DE STATISTIEK (2006)

Centraal Bureau voor de Statistiek (Statistics Netherlands), *Rechtspraak in Nederland 2004*, Voorburg/Heerlen 2006.

COLLEGE VAN TOEZICHT SOCIALE VERZEKERINGEN (1997)

College van toezicht sociale verzekeringen (Social Insurance Supervisory Board), *De Algemene wet bestuursrecht en de Werkloosheidswet*, Zoetermeer 1997.

COLLEGE VAN TOEZICHT SOCIALE VERZEKERINGEN (1999)

College van toezicht sociale verzekeringen (Social Insurance Supervisory Board), *Straffen met beleid*, Zoetermeer 1999.

COMMISSIE EVALUATIE AWB II (2002)

Commissie evaluatie Awb (General Administrative Law Act Evaluation Committee) II, *Toepassing en effecten van de Algemene wet bestuursrecht 1997-2001*, The Hague 2002.

COMMISSIE EVALUATIE AWB III (2007)

Commissie Evaluatie Awb (General Administrative Law Act Evaluation Committee) III, *Toepassing en effecten van de Algemene wet bestuursrecht 2002-2006*, The Hague 2007.

COMMISSIE EVALUATIE VREEMDELINGENWET (2006)
Commissie Evaluatie Vreemdelingenwet (Aliens Act 2000 Evaluation Committee), *Evaluatie Vreemdelingenwet 2000, De asielprocedure (vol. 2)*, The Hague 2006.

COMMISSIE ONDERZOEK VUURWERKRAMP (2001)
Commissie onderzoek vuurwerkramp (Fireworks Disaster Investigation Committee), *A. De vuurwerkramp, Eindrapport*, Enschede/The Hague 2001.

COMMISSIE RECHTSBESCHERMING VAR (2004)
Commissie Rechtsbescherming VAR (Judicial Review Committee of the Administrative Law Association), *De toekomst van de rechtsbescherming: van toetsing naar geschilbeslechting*, The Hague 2004.

COUWENBERG (2003)
O. Couwenberg, *Incomplete contracten, een rechtseconomische benadering (inaugural address University of Groningen)*, Groningen 2003.

DAALDER (1985)
H. Daalder, 'Sturing, het primaat van de politiek en de bureaucratische cultuur in Nederland', in: M.A.P. Bovens & W.J. Witteveen (eds.), *Het schip van staat. Beschouwingen over recht, staat, en sturing*, Zwolle 1985, p. 197-206.

DAMEN (1993)
L.J.A. Damen, 'Bestaat de Awb-mens', in: J.L. Boxum et al. (eds.), *Aantrekkelijke gedachten*, Deventer 1993, p. 109-129.

DAMEN (2004)
L.J.A. Damen, 'Is de burger beter af onder het bestuursrecht van 2004 dan onder dat van 1993'?, *NTB* 2004, p. 155-162.

DAMEN ET AL. (2005)
L.J.A. Damen et al., *Bestuursrecht 1*, The Hague 2005.

DAMEN (2006)
L.J.A. Damen, 'Heeft een minister een hart?', *Ars Aequi* 2006, p. 779-781.

DAMEN (2006A)
L.J.A. Damen, 'The long and winding road', in: A.W. Heringa et al. (eds.), *Het bestuursrecht beschermd*, The Hague 2006, p. 85-97.

DIEPERINK (2002)
M.A.M. Dieperink, 'Omtrekken van een algemene regeling voor intrekken', in: C.H. Bangma, M.A.M. Dieperink & C.N.J. Kortmann, *De vijfde tranche (Jonge VAR-reeks 1)*, The Hague 2002, p. 49-84.

DIENST SOCIALE ZAKEN EN WERK GEMEENTE GRONINGEN (2003)
Dienst Sociale Zaken en Werk gemeente Groningen (Department of Social Affairs and Employment, Municipality of Groningen), *Jaarplan 2004*, Groningen 2003.

DIESING (1962)
P. Diesing, *Reason and Society*, Urbana 1962.

DONNER (1984)
A.M. Donner, *Werkt de rechtsstaatidee bureaucratie in de hand?*, Amsterdam 1984.

DONNER (1987)
A.M. Donner, *Nederlands bestuursrecht: algemeen deel*, 5th impression, Alphen aan de Rijn 1987.

DONNER (2004)
J.P.H. Donner, 'Naar een slagvaardige bestuursrechtspraak', *NTB* 2004, p. 143-145.

DOORNBOS & SELLIES (1997)
N. Doornbos & J.P.P. Sellies, *Het overlegmodel in de asielprocedure*, Nijmegen 1997.

DUNN (2004)
W.N. Dunn, *Public Policy Analysis: An Introduction*, New Jersey 2004.

ENQUÊTECOMMISSIE UITVOERINGSORGANEN SOCIALE VERZEKERINGEN (1993)
Enquêtecommissie uitvoeringsorganen sociale verzekeringen (Committee of inquiry into social security administrative bodies), *Rapport*, The Hague 1993.

VAN EVERDINGEN (2006)
M. van Everdingen, 'Bijstand voor 65-plussers met een onvolledige AOW-uitkering: de juridische aspecten van een samenwerking tussen acht gemeenten en de SVB', *PS Documenta* 2006, p. 1072-1082.

FALUDI & VAN DER VALK (1994)
A. Faludi & A. van der Valk, *Rule and Order: Dutch Planning Doctrine in the Twentieth Century*, Dordrecht 1994.

FORTIN & VAN HASSEL (2000)
Y. Fortin & H. van Hassel, *Contracting in the New Public Management: from Economics to Law and Citizenship*, Amsterdam 2000.

GEMEENTELIJKE OMBUDSMAN AMSTERDAM (2006)
Gemeentelijke ombudsman Amsterdam (Municipal ombudsman, Amsterdam), *Onverwacht huisbezoek*, Gemeente Amsterdam, Dienst Werk en Inkomen, 3 juli 2006, RA0612157 (see www.gemeentelijkeombudsman.nl).

GRIFFITHS (1978)
J. Griffiths, *Is Law Important?* Deventer 1978.

GRIFFITHS (2003)
J. Griffiths, 'The Social Working of Legal Rules', *Journal of Legal Pluralism* 2003 (48) p. 1-84.

GRÜTTERS (2003)
C. Grütters, 'Asielcijfers in perspectief', in: A.B. Terlouw (ed.), *Binnen 48 uur, zorgvuldige behandeling van asielverzoeken?*, Centrum voor Migratierecht, Nijmegen 2003, p. 23-32.

GUBA & LINCOLN (1994)
E.G. Guba & Y.S. Lincoln, *Fourth Generation Evaluation*, Beverly Hills 1994.

DE HAAN, DRUPSTEEN & FERNHOUT (1978)
P. de Haan, Th.G. Drupsteen & R. Fernhout, *Bestuursrecht in de sociale rechtsstaat: instrument en waarborg*, Deventer 1978.

DE HAAN, DRUPSTEEN & FERNHOUT (1998)
P. De Haan, Th.G.Drupsteen & R. Fernhout, *Bestuursrecht in de sociale rechtsstaat, bestuurshandelingen en waarborgen*, Deventer 1998.

HÄRTEL (2005)
I. Härtel, 'Mediation im Verwaltungsrecht', *JZ* 2005, p. 753-763.

HARTS (1981)
H.L.A. Hart, *The Concept of Law*, Oxford 1981.

HENRY (1986)
N.L. Henry, *Public Administration and Public Affairs*, New Jersey 1986.

HERTOGH (2005)
M.L.M. Hertogh, 'The social making and social working of legislation', in: N.E.H.M. Zeegers, W.J. Witteveen, & B.M.J. van Klink (eds.), *Social and Symbolic Effects of Legislation under the Rule of Law*, New York 2005, p. 163-181.

HERWEIJER & WINTER (1995)
M. Herweijer & H.B. Winter, 'Evaluation of Legislation: Change or Improvement?', in: W.J.M. Kickert & F.A. van Vught, *Public Policy and Public Administration in the Netherlands*, London 1995, p. 149-163.

HERWEIJER, DE JONG & DE RIDDER (2005)
M. Herweijer, P.O. de Jong & J. de Ridder, *Oordelen over effecten van bestuursrecht: een verkenning van het debat en de bevindingen van sociaal-wetenschappelijk onderzoek*, Groningen 2005.

HOEKSTRA (2004)
J. Hoekstra, 'De in het wetsvoorstel voor de nieuwe Wet ruimtelijke ordening opgenomen en voorgestelde mogelijkheden om ten onrechte verleende aanleg-, sloop- en bouwvergunningen in te trekken', *BR* 2004, p. 1-12.

HUMAN RIGHTS WATCH (2003)
Human Rights Watch, *Fleeting Refuge: The Triumph of Efficiency over Protection in Dutch Asylum Policy*, April 2003.

VAN DER HOEVEN (1989)
J. van der Hoeven, *De drie dimensies van het bestuursrecht*, Deventer 1989.

HOOGVLIET, (2001)
G.M.H. Hoogvliet, De *Awb* en het *vreemdelingenrecht*, Deventer 2001.

HOUWELING (2006)
P. Houweling, *Van vergunning naar algemene regel. Een onderzoek naar de wenselijkheid van de vergunningvervangende amvb's op het terrein van het milieurecht (dissertation University of Tilburg)*, The Hague 2006.

INGRAM & MANN (1980)
H.M. Ingram & D.E. Mann, *Why Policies Succeed or Fail*, Beverly Hills 1980.

INSPECTIE WERK EN INKOMEN (2003)
Inspectie Werk en Inkomen (Inspection Service for Work and Income), *De uitvoering van de Algemene bijstandswet in Amsterdam: stand van zaken eerste kwartaal 2003*, Zoetermeer 2003.

INSPECTIE WERK EN INKOMEN (2003A)
Inspectie Werk en Inkomen (Inspection Service for Work and Income), *De inschakeling van een private partij bij de uitvoering van de Algemene bijstandswet door de gemeente Maarssen*, Zoetermeer 2003.

INSPECTIE WERK EN INKOMEN (2006)
Inspectie werk en inkomen (Inspection Service for Work and Income), *Beoordeeld en bejegend. Onderzoek naar de wijze waarop UWV een zorgvuldige bejegening voor WAO- en Wia-gerechtigden nastreeft*, Zoetermeer 2006.

JANIS (2002)
I.L. Janis, 'Groupthink: the desperate drive for consensus at any cost' (1971) in: J.M. Shafritz and J.S. Ott, *Classics of organization theory*, Orlando 2002.

JANS (1998)
J.H. Jans, 'National Legislative Autonomy? The Procedural Constraints of European Law', *LIEI* 1998, p. 25-58.

JANS ET AL. (2002)
J.H. Jans et al., *Inleiding tot het Europees bestuursrecht* (2nd ed.), Nijmegen 2002.

JANS & DE GRAAF (2004)
J.H. Jans & K.J. de Graaf, 'Bevoegdheid = verplichting? Enkele opmerkingen over de uitspraak van het Hof van Justitie in de zaak Kühne & Heitz', *NTER* 2004, p. 98-102.

JANS & VEDDER (2007)
J.H. Jans & H.H.B. Vedder, *European Environmental Law* (3rd ed.), Groningen 2007.

JANS ET AL. (2007)
J.H. Jans et al., *Europeanisation of Public Law*, Groningen 2007.

DE JONG (2003)
G.T. de Jong et al. (eds.), *Algemeen-Bijzonder: de wisselwerking tussen algemene en bijzondere regelingen in het privaatrecht*, The Hague 2003.

KAGAN (1978)
R.A. Kagan, *Regulatory Justice: Implementing a Wage-Price Freeze*, New York 1978.

KAGAN (1991)
R.A. Kagan, 'Adversarial Legalism and American Government', *Journal of Policy Analysis & Management* 1991, p. 369-406.

KAGAN (2001))

R.A. Kagan, *Adversarial Legalism: The American Way of Law*, Cambridge 2001.

VAN KEMENADE (1997)

J.A. van Kemenade, *Bestuur in geding*, Haarlem 1997.

KLOOSTERMAN ET AL. (2002)

D.R. Kloosterman et al., *In zelfstandigheid geregeld*, Groningen 2002.

KONIJNENBELT (1975)

W. Konijnenbelt, 'Rechtsverwerking door het bestuur: het vertrouwensbeginsel in het administratieve recht', in: M. Scheltema & W. Konijnenbelt, *De rechtsverwerking in het administratief recht* (VAR-reeks LXXIV), Groningen 1975, p. 59-117.

KONIJNENBELT (2005)

W. Konijnenbelt, 'Alles in één keer goed', *Gst.*(2005) 7228.72.

LANE (1993)

J. Lane, *The Public Sector: Concepts, Models and Approaches*, London 1993.

LAEMERS ET AL. (2007)

M.T.A.B. Laemers et al., *Awb-procedures vanuit het gezichtspunt van de burger*, The Hague 2007.

LOTZ (2005)

K.W. Lotz, 'Buchbesprechungen', *Die Verwaltung* 2005, p. 422-424.

MACAULAY (1963)

S. Macaulay, 'Non-contractual relationships in business: a preliminary study', *American Sociological Review* 1963, p. 55-67.

MACAULAY (1966)

S. Macaulay, *Law and the Balance of Power: Automobile Manufacturers and their Dealers*, New York 1966.

MAJONE (1989)

G. Majone, *Evidence, Argument and Persuasion in the Policy Process*, Yale University Press 1989.

MARSEILLE (1993)

A.T. Marseille, *Voorspelbaarheid van bestuurshandelen: een onderzoek naar de rechtsregels en beslissingen over het volgen van scholing met behoud van uitkering (dissertation University of Groningen)*, Deventer 1993.

MAURER (2006)

H. Maurer, *Algemeines verwaltungsrecht*, Munich 2006.

VAN MEEGEN (2001)

H.J.H. van Meegen, 'Het vertrouwensbeginsel; Ontwikkelingen in de jurisprudentie', *JBplus* 2001, p.19-32.

MINTZBERG (1979)

H. Mintzberg, *The Structuring of Organizations*, Englewood Cliffs 1979.

NATHAN (1995)

R.P. Nathan, 'Reinventing Government: what does it mean?', *Public Administration Review* 1995, p. 213-215.

NATIONALE OMBUDSMAN (2002)

Nationale ombudsman (National ombudsman), 'Jaarverslag 2002', *TK* (Parliamentary Documents of the Dutch Lower House) 2002/03, 28 825, nos. 1-2.

NATIONALE OMBUDSMAN (2003)

Nationale ombudsman (National ombudsman), 'Jaarverslag 2003', *TK* (Parliamentary Documents of the Dutch Lower House) 2003/04, 29 460, nos. 1-2.

NATIONALE OMBUDSMAN (2005)

Nationale ombudsman (National ombudsman), 'Jaarverslag 2005', *TK* (Parliamentary Documents of the Dutch Lower House) 2005/06, 30 530, nos. 1-2.

NATIONALE OMBUDSMAN (2007)

Nationale ombudsman (National ombudsman), *Burgerbrieven gemeenten*, Report 2007/015, The Hague 2007.

NEDERLANDS JURISTEN COMITÉ VOOR DE MENSENRECHTEN 2003

Nederlands Juristen Comité voor de Mensenrechten (Dutch Section of the International Commission of Jurists), *De AC-procedure: De achilleshiel van het asielbeleid*, Leiden 2003.

NICOLAÏ (1990)

P. Nicolaï, *Beginselen van behoorlijk bestuur (dissertation University of Amsterdam)*, Deventer 1990.

NICOLAÏ (1997)

P. Nicolaï, 'Algemene beginselen van behoorlijk bestuur', *NTB* 1997, p. 159-167.

NOORDAM (2004)

F.M. Noordam, 'De loonsanctie, beslist niet het mooiste kind van de Poortwachter', *Sociaal Maandblad Arbeid* 2004, p. 439-450.

NOORDAM (2006)

F.M. Noordam, *Socialezekerheidsrecht*, Deventer 2006.

ONDERZOEKSCOMMISSIE TOEPASSING ABW (1993)

Onderzoekscommissie toepassing ABW (Committee of inquiry into the application of the Social Assistance Act), *Het recht op bijstand. Naar een beheerst proces bij de toekenning van de bijstand*, The Hague 1993.

ORTLEP (2004)

R. Ortlep, 'De Afdeling en de dienende burger', *JBplus* 2004, p. 259-266.

OSBORNE & GAEBLER (1997)

D. Osborne & T. Gaebler, 'Reinventing Government: How the Entrepreneurial Spirit is Transforming the Public Sector', *Political studies* 1997, p. 127.

OTTO (2004)
W. Otto, 'NEN-normen', *NJB* 2004, p. 1750-1751.
DEN OUDEN, JACOBS & VERHEIJ (2004)
W. den Ouden, M.J. Jacobs & N. Verheij, *Subsidierecht*, Deventer 2004.
PARSONS (2001)
W. Parsons, *Public Policy: An Introduction to the Theory and Practice of Policy Analysis*, Cheltenham 2001.
PEL & SPLIET (2003)
M. Pel & M.A. Spliet, 'Implementatie van mediation naast rechtsspraak. Court-annexed mediation in Engeland...een lichtend voorbeeld?', *NJB* 2003, p. 1897-1902.
PERROW (1972)
C. Perrow, *Complex Organizations*, Glenview IL 1972.
PITSCHAS (2004)
R. Pitschas, 'Mediation als Methode und Instrument der Konfliktmittlung im öffentlichen Sektor', *NVwZ* 2004, p. 396-403.
DE POORTER (2004)
J.C.A. de Poorter, 'Het belangvereiste in bestuursrechtelijke procedures', in: E.C. Pietermaat & J.C.A. de Poorter, *Toegang tot de rechter: processuele openbaarheid en belang* (Jonge VAR-reeks 2), The Hague 2004, p. 51-93.
PRONT-VAN BOMMEL (2002)
S. Pront-van Bommel, *Bestuursrechtspraak (dissertation University of Amsterdam)*, The Hague 2002.
PRONT-VAN BOMMEL (2006)
S. Pront-van Bommel, 'Rechtszekerheid in concreto. Aanspraak op gerichte informatie van het bestuursorgaan', *NTB* 2006, p. 146-152.
PROTTAS (1979)
J.M. Prottas, *People-Processing: the Street-Level Bureaucrat in Public Service Bureaucracies*, Lexington MA 1979.
RAAD VAN ECONOMISCH ADVISEURS (2007)
Raad van Economisch adviseurs (Council of Economic Advisors to the Dutch Lower House), *Lof der eenvoud*, Advice 2007/1, The Hague 2007.
DE RIDDER (1994)
J. de Ridder, 'Ministeriële verantwoordelijkheid en politiek-ambtelijke verhoudingen', in: D.J. Elzinga (ed.), *Ministeriële Verantwoordelijkheid in Nederland*, Zwolle 1994, p. 279-291.
DE RIDDER, DIJKSTRA & KEMKERS (2002)
J. de Ridder, G.A. Dijkstra & R.H.C. Kemkers, *Artikel 19 in de praktijk. De eerste effecten van een wetswijziging*, Deventer 2002.
DE RIDDER & KEMKERS (2002)
J. de Ridder & R.H.C. Kemkers, 'Inertie en aanpassing, de implementatie van artikel 19 lid 2 WRO', *Beleidswetenschap* 2002, p. 236-258.

DE RIDDER (2004)
J. de Ridder, *Een goede raad voor toezicht (inaugural lecture University of Groningen)*, The Hague 2004.
RAAD VOOR MAATSCHAPPELIJKE ONTWIKKELING (2002)
Raad voor Maatschappelijke Ontwikkeling (Council for Social Development), *Bevrijdende kaders*, The Hague 2002.
DE ROO & JAGTENBERG (2003)
A. de Roo & R. Jagtenberg, *De praktijk van mediation in ons omringende landen: een vergelijkend onderzoek verricht in opdracht van het Ministerie van Justitie*, Rotterdam 2003.
ROSSI & FREEMAN (1989)
P.H. Rossi & H.E. Freeman, *Evaluation: A Systematic Approach*, London 1989.
RUITER (1986)
D.W.P. Ruiter, 'Beleidsregels zijn algemeen verbindende voorschriften', *Bestuurswetenschappen* 1986, p. 65-70.
SCHELTEMA (1984)
M. Scheltema, 'Enkele gedachten over het vertrouwensbeginsel in het publiekrecht', *RM Themis* 1984, p. 538-549.
SCHELTEMA (1989)
M. Scheltema, 'De rechtsstaat', in: J.W.M. Engels et al. (eds.), *De rechtsstaat herdacht*, Zwolle 1989.
SCHELTEMA (1996)
M. Scheltema, 'Het tijdigheidsbeginsel', in: R.L. Vucsán (ed.), *De Awb-mens: boeman of underdog?*, Nijmegen 1996, p. 241-253.
SCHELTEMA (1996A)
M. Scheltema, 'Van rechtsbescherming naar een volwaardig bestuursrecht', *NJB* 1996, p. 1355-1361.
SCHELTEMA (1997)
M. Scheltema, *De wondere wereld van het bestuursrecht, (valedictory speech University of Groningen)*, Deventer 1997.
SCHELTEMA (2006)
M. Scheltema, 'Leve de Awb-mens!', in: K.J. de Graaf, A.T. Marseille & H.B. Winter (eds.), *Op tegenspraak*, The Hague 2006, p. 99-109.
SCHLÖSSELS (1998)
R.J.N. Schlössels, *Het specialiteitsbeginsel: over de structuur van bestuursbevoegdheden, wetmatigheid van bestuur en beleidsvrijheid (dissertation University of Maastricht)*, The Hague 1998.
SCHLÖSSELS (2003)
R.J.N. Schlössels, *Het besluitbegrip en de draad van Ariadne (inaugural lecture University of Nijmegen)*, The Hague 2003.
SCHLÖSSELS ET AL. (EDS.) (2004)
R.J.N. Schlössels, 'Dimensies van rechtsbeginselen', in: R.J.N. Schlössels et al. (eds.), *In beginsel*, Deventer 2004, p. 13-43.

SCHREUDER-VLASBLOM (2006)
M. Schreuder-Vlasblom, *Rechtsbescherming en bestuurlijke voorprocedure*, Deventer 2006.

SCHUELER (2003)
B.J. Schueler, *Zand in de machine (inaugural lecture University of Amsterdam)*, Amsterdam 2003.

SCHUURMANS (2005)
Y.E. Schuurmans, *Bewijslastverdeling in het bestuursrecht (disseration Free University in Amsterdam)*, Alphen aan den Rijn 2005.

SIEGEL (2005)
T. Siegel 'Buchbesprechungen, Mediation und Verfahren (book review of: S. Vetter)', *Die öffentliche Verwaltung: Zeitschrift für Verwaltungsrecht und Verwaltungspolitik* 2005, p. 573.

SIMON (1976)
H.A. Simon, *Administrative Behavior: a Study of Decision-Making Processes in Administrative Organizations* (3rd ed.), New York 1976.

SNELLEN (1987)
I.Th.M. Snellen, *Boeiend en geboeid (inaugural address University of Tilburg)*, Alphen aan de Rijn 1987.

SNELLEN (1991)
I.Th.M. Snellen, 'Autopoiesis and steering: the rule of identity', in: R.J. in 't Veld, et al., *Autopoiesis and Configuration Theory: New Approaches to Societal Steering*, Dordrecht 1991, p. 151-160.

SOCIAAL CULTUREEL PLANBUREAU (2002)
Sociaal en Cultureel Planbureau (Social and Cultural Planning Office), *Sociaal en Cultureel Rapport 2002. De kwaliteit van de quartaire sector*, The Hague 2002.

SOCIALE VERZEKERINGSBANK (2004)
Sociale Verzekeringsbank (Social Insurance Bank), *Jaarverslag 2003*, Amstelveen 2004.

SOCIALE VERZEKERINGSBANK (2006)
Sociale Verzekeringsbank (Social Insurance Bank), *Jaarverslag 2005*, Amstelveen 2006.

SORGDRAGER (2004)
W. Sorgdrager, *De last van bezwaar. Een onderzoek naar de mogelijkheden voor vermindering van de instroom van bezwaren en beroepen en verhoging van de efficiency van de afhandeling* (internal report, Employees' Insurance and Benefits Office), 2004.

SPARROW (2000)
M.K. Sparrow, *The Regulatory Craft, Controlling Risks, Solving Problems, and Managing Compliance*, Washington, D.C. 2000.

STERKE (1989)
M.E. de Sterke, 'Opgewekte verwachtingen', *Gst.* (1989) 6880, p. 261-267.

STONE (2002)
D. Stone, *Policy Paradox: The Art of Political Decision Making*, New York 2002.

STRUYCKEN (1910)
A.A.H. Struycken, *Administratie of Rechter. Beschouwingen over de moderne rechtsstaatsgedachte naar aanleiding van de aanhangige ontwerpen tot regeling der administratieve rechtspraak*, Arnhem 1910.

DE SWAAN (2001)
A. de Swaan, *Human societies, an introduction*, Malden 2001.

SELZNICK (1949)
P. Selznick, *Tennessee Valley Authority and the grass roots*, New York 1949.

TERLOUW (ED.) (2003)
A.B. Terlouw (ed.), *Binnen 48 uur, zorgvuldige behandeling van asielverzoeken?*, Centrum voor Migratierecht, Nijmegen 2003.

TEUNISSEN (2004)
J.M.H.F. Teunissen, 'De herziening van de Woningwet op het punt van de handhaafbaarheid en de handhaving', *NJB* 2004, p. 418-424.

VAN THIEL (2000)
S. van Thiel, *Quangocratization: Trends, Causes and Consequences (dissertation University of Utrecht)*, Utrecht 2000.

TIROLE (1999)
J. Tirole, 'Incomplete contracts: where do we stand?', *Econometrica* 67 1999, p. 741-781.

TOLLENAAR (2004)
A. Tollenaar, 'Het problematische gelijkheidsbeginsel', *Bestuurswetenschappen* 2004, p. 428-438.

TOLLENAAR (2006)
A. Tollenaar, 'Over vrijstellingsbeleid en flitsvergunning', *Openbaar Bestuur* 2006, p. 32-36.

UITVOERINGSINSTITUUT WERKNEMERSVERZEKERINGEN (2003)
Uitvoeringsinstituut werknemersverzekeringen (Employees' Insurance and Benefits Office), *Jaarplan 2004*, Amsterdam 2003.

UITVOERINGSINSTITUUT WERKNEMERSVERZEKERINGEN (2004)
Uitvoeringsinstituut werknemersverzekeringen (Employees' Insurance and Benefits Office), *Jaarverslag (*Annual Report) *2003*, Amsterdam 2004.

UITVOERINGSINSTITUUT WERKNEMERSVERZEKERINGEN (2006)
Uitvoeringsinstituut werknemersverzekeringen (Employees' Insurance and Benefits Office), *Jaarverslag* (Annual report) *2005*, Amsterdam 2006.

IN 'T VELD (1995)
R.J. in 't Veld, *Spelen met vuur: over hybride organisaties*, The Hague 1995.

VERHEIJ (1997)

N. Verheij, 'Vertrouwen op de overheid', in: J.B.M. Vranken, N. Verheij & J. de Hullu, *Vertrouwensbeginsel en rechtszekerheid in Nederland* (report for the Vereniging voor de Vergelijkende Studie van het recht van België en Nederland (Association for Comparative Studies of Dutch and Belgian Law), Deventer 1997, p. 39-90.

VERHEIJ (2006)

N. Verheij, 'Uit zuinigheid naar relativiteit. Naar een Schutznormvereiste in het bestuursrecht', in: A.W. Heringa et al. (eds.), *Het bestuursrecht beschermd*, The Hague 2006, p. 99-112.

VETTER (2004)

S. Vetter, *Mediation und Verfahren*, Berlin 2004.

VISITATIECOMMISSIE WETGEVING (2000)

Visitatiecommissie wetgeving (Legislation Review Committee), *Regels en Risico's*, The Hague 2000.

VISITATIECOMMISSIE WETGEVING (2002)

Visitatiecommissie wetgeving (Legislation Review Committee), *Van Wetten Weten*, The Hague 2002.

VISITATIECOMMISSIE JURIDISCHE FUNCTIE EN WETGEVING (2007)

Visitatiecommissie juridische functie en wetgeving (Legal Remit and Legislation Review Committee), *Met recht verbonden*, The Hague 2007.

VISSER & HOMBURG (1995)

T. Visser & G. Homburg (Regioplan Onderzoek), *Evaluatie herziene Vreemdelingenwet*, Amsterdam 1995.

VOS, SARIS & VAN DER VLUGHT (2007)

M. Vos, 'Tijdig beslissen, een mission (im)possible?', C.M. Saris, 'Tijdig beslissen, het doel dichterbij?', Y.M. van der Vlugt, 'Leren van klachten', in: *Niet tijdig beslissen*, The Hague 2007.

DE VRIES (1999)

M.S. de Vries, 'Developments in Europe: The idea of policy generations', *International Review of Administrative Sciences* 65 (4) 1999, p. 485-504.

DE VRIES (2002)

M.S. de Vries, 'The changing functions of law and its implications for government and governance', *International Review of Administrative Sciences* 68 (4) 2002, p. 599-618.

DE VRIES (2005)

M.S. de Vries, 'Generations of interactive policy-making in the Netherlands', *International Review of Administrative Sciences* 71 (4) 2005, p. 577-591.

DE WAARD (ED.) (2000)

B. de Waard (ed.), *Negotiated Decision-Making*, The Hague 2000.

WEBER (1922)

Max Weber, *Wirtschaft und Gesellschaft*, Tübingen 1922.

WETENSCHAPPELIJKE RAAD VOOR HET REGERINGSBELEID (2002)
Wetenschappelijke raad voor het regeringsbeleid (Scientific Council for Government Policy), *De toekomst van de nationale rechtsstaat* (WRR-rapport 63), The Hague 2002.

WIGGERS-RUST ET AL. (ED.) (2000)
L.F. Wiggers-Rust et al., *Toepassing van mediation bij conflicten in het leefomgevingsbeleid*, The Hague 2000.

WILDAVSKY (1984)
A. Wildavsky, *The Politics of the Budgetary Process*, Boston 1984.

WILSON (1941)
Woodrow Wilson, 'The study of administration: an essay', *Political Science Quarterly* 1887, p. 197-222. (1941: 481-506).

VAN WIJK, KONIJNENBELT & VAN MALE (2002)
H.D. van Wijk, W. Konijnenbelt & R.M. van Male, *Hoofdstukken van bestuursrecht* (12th ed.), The Hague 2002.

VAN WIJK, KONIJNENBELT & VAN MALE (2005)
H.D. van Wijk, W. Konijnenbelt & R.M. van Male, *Hoofdstukken van bestuursrecht* (13th ed.),The Hague 2005.

DE WIJKERSLOOTH (1999)
J.L. de Wijkerslooth, 'Geschreven privaatrecht of ongeschreven publiekrecht, Preadvies VAR', in: A.J.C. de Moor-van Vught, J.L. de Wijkerslooth & N. Verheij, *Verschuiving van de magische lijn* (VAR-reeks 122), Alphen aan den Rijn 1999, p. 75-105.

WILKINSON ET AL. (2006)
Wilkinson et al. (Significant), *Doorlooptijden asielprocedures Vreemdelingenwet 2000*, The Hague 2006.

WINTER & SCHURINGA (2005)
H.B. Winter & T.H.G. Schuringa, 'Afschaffen bezwaar in reguliere zaken: bezint eer ge begint!', *Migrantenrecht* 2005/9, p. 303-305.

WINTER ET AL. (2007)
H.B. Winter et al., *Klagen bij bestuursorganen*, The Hague 2007.

ZOURIDIS (2000)
S. Zouridis, *Digitale disciplinering: over ICT, organisatie, wetgeving en het automatiseren van beschikkingen*, Delft 2000.

ZUURMOND (1994)
A. Zuurmond, *De infocratie: een theoretische en empirische heroriëntatie op Weber's ideaaltype in het informatietijdperk*, The Hague 1994.

ZIJLSTRA & VAN OMMEREN (EDS.) (2003)
S.E. Zijlstra & F.J. Van Ommeren, 'Slotbeschouwing: de rechtsstaat als toetsingskader', in: F.J. van Ommeren & S.E. Zijlstra (eds.), *De rechtsstaat als toetsingskader*, The Hague 2003, p. 301-320.

ZWART (1999)
T. Zwart, 'De republiek der rechters?', in: H.R.B.M. Kummeling (ed.), *Het bestuursrecht als agenda voor het staatsrecht*, Deventer 1999, p. 87-121.

Authors

Dr. K.F. Bolt

Korine Bolt (1974) is Assistant Professor of Administrative Law at Tilburg University. Until 2006 she worked at the Department of Administrative Law and Public Administration at the University of Groningen.

Prof. H.E. Bröring

Herman Bröring (1959) is Professor of Law at the University of Groningen.

Prof. L.J.A. Damen

Leo Damen (1945) is Professor of Administrative Law in the Department of Administrative Law and Public Administration at the University of Groningen, a Deputy Justice of the Central Appeals Court for the Public Service and Social Security Matters, and a Deputy Judge of the District Court of Groningen.

Dr. K.J. de Graaf

Kars de Graaf (1976) is Assistant Professor of Administrative Law in the Department of Administrative Law and Public Administration at the University of Groningen.

Prof. J.H. Jans

Jan Jans (1956) is head of the Department of Administrative Law and Public Administration at the University of Groningen and a professor of administrative law. His publications relate mainly to European law, European environmental law, European public law and Dutch public law. His publications include *European Environmental Law* (Groningen 2007) and, as co-author, *Europeanisation of Public Law* (Groningen 2007).

Prof. M. Herweijer

Michiel Herweijer (1955) has been Professor of Public Administration in the Department of Administrative Law and Public Administration at the University of Groningen since 1989. He has published on the effects of legislation and methods of policy analysis.

Dr. A.T. Marseille

Bert Marseille (1961) is Associate Professor of Administrative Law in the Department of Administrative Law and Public Administration at the University of Groningen.

Prof. F.M. Noordam

Frits Noordam (1942) was Professor of Social Security Law from 1986 to 2006 in the Department of Administrative Law and Public Administration at the University of Groningen. He has served as a member of the boards of several government agencies in the Dutch social security system. Noordam has published on a wide variety of aspects of social security law.

Prof. J. de Ridder

Jacobus de Ridder (1949) is Professor of Administrative Supervision in the Department of Administrative Law and Public Administration at the University of Groningen.

A. Tollenaar, LL.M.

Albertjan Tollenaar (1978) is a postdoc working on social security law and Assistant Professor of Administrative Law in the Department of Administrative Law and Public Administration at the University of Groningen.

H.D. Tolsma, LL.M.

Hanna Tolsma (1980) is a PhD student at the Department of Administrative Law and Public Administration at the University of Groningen. Her research project will address questions raised by the implementation of consensual decision-making methods in the current administrative decision-making process.

Dr. G.H.M. Tromp

Greetje Tromp (1946) is Assistant Professor of Public Administration in the Department of Administrative Law and Public Administration at the University of Groningen.

Dr. H.B. Winter

Heinrich Winter (1962) is Associate Professor of Administrative Law in the Department of Administrative Law and Public Administration at the University of Groningen.